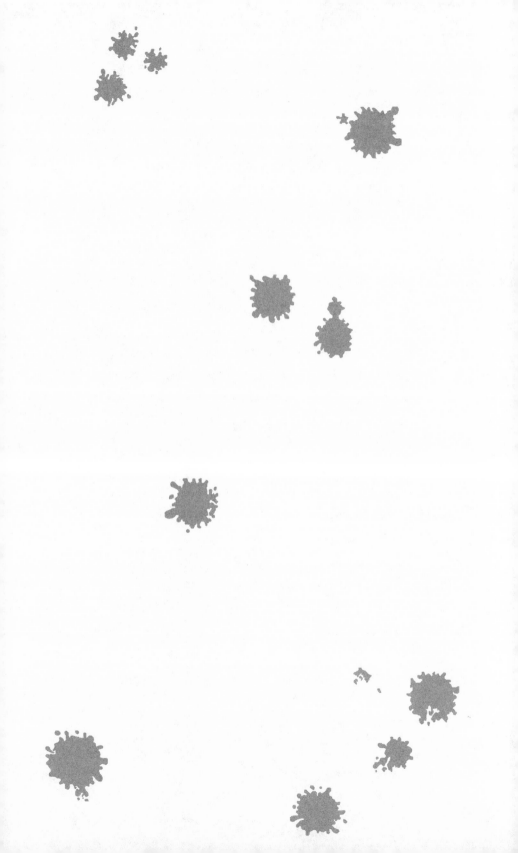

*Killer Books*

*Writing,*

*Violence,*

*and Ethics*

*in Modern*

*Spanish*

*American*

*Narrative*

# KILLER BOOKS

BY ANÍBAL GONZÁLEZ

University of Texas Press ⟵⟶ Austin

Requests for permission to reproduce material
from this work should be sent to Permissions,
University of Texas Press, P.O. Box 7819, Austin,
TX 78713-7819.

∞ The paper used in this book meets the minimum
requirements of ANSI/NISO Z39.48-1992 (R1997)
(Permanence of Paper).

*Library of Congress Cataloging-in-Publication Data*

González, Aníbal.
    Killer books : writing, violence, and ethics in
modern Spanish American narrative / by Aníbal
González. — 1st ed.
        p.        cm.
Includes bibliographical references and index.
ISBN 0-292-72839-5 (cloth : alk. paper)
    1. Spanish American fiction—20th century—
History and criticism.  2. Spanish American
fiction—19th century—History and criticism.
3. Ethics in literature.  4. Violence in literature.
5. Authorship—social aspects.  6. Literature and
society—Latin America.  I. Title.
PQ7082.N7 G663  2002
863'.609358—dc21              2001027917

*To my son Andrés Emil*
*To my wife Priscilla*

# CONTENTS

## PREFACE AND ACKNOWLEDGMENTS

A study of this sort must necessarily be inconclusive, because such is the nature of the dilemmas raised by the encounter between ethics and writing: When is it right to write? Are writers demonic or angelic, abject or sublime, or both? Is writing always ultimately allied to violence and repression? It may seem foolish to pose these questions, and in such absolute terms, but this is the way ethical discourse functions, and these are the very same sorts of queries posed by Spanish American writers in their narratives.

I have endeavored to be careful, in the sense of "responsible," in my own writing of this book. In this regard, I have tried (with the copyeditor's welcome aid) to be faithful to the grammar and the nuances of a language, English, that belongs to me even less than my own mother tongue, Spanish. I have also tried to interpret and represent fairly the views of the Spanish American writers I have studied—from Nájera to Cortázar—as well as of the critical and theoretical sources from which I have benefited, which are mainly deconstructionist and philosophical thinkers. If I have learned anything from this study, it is that there is always in writing a demonic residue of error, although the responsibility for it must still be mine for having dared to interact with writing in the first place. Responsibility also implies a sense of gratitude, which I gladly assume: all of my concrete debts appear in the notes and the bibliography to this book. More generally, special thanks must go to John W. Kronik, who read this book in its initial stages and gave me wise counsel on its structure. I am also indebted to Charles E. Scott, Sparks Professor of Philosophy at Pennsylvania State University, for his generous reading of an early version of chapter 2. Needless to say, they are blameless for the errors and omissions in this book. I am also grateful to the Spanish American writers who have honored me with their friendship over the years and, without necessarily endorsing my theories, have shared with me some of their insights: Alfredo Bryce Echenique, Antonio Benítez Rojo, Tomás Eloy Martínez, Luis Rafael Sánchez, and Ana Lydia Vega. My gratitude goes as well to a group of dear friends and colleagues in the profession: Carlos J. Alonso, Roberto González Echevarría, Arturo Echavarría, Luce López-Baralt, Mercedes López-Baralt, Sylvia Molloy, and Enrique Pupo-Walker. As always, I seek to follow their example of how to write with commitment and with care.

*Killer Books*

# *Killer Books*

## *Writers,*
## *Writing,*
## *and Ethics*
## *in Spanish*
## *America*

La letra con sangre entra.
Las letras no embotan la lanza.
—TRADITIONAL SPANISH SAYINGS[1]

The letter kills, but the spirit gives life.
—SAINT PAUL, 2 CORINTHIANS 3:6

In a well-known passage of the *Divine Comedy* that may be a gloss of the Pauline verse, Dante Alighieri recounts the heartbreaking story of Paolo and Francesca, who fell in love and kissed while reading a book together, at which moment they were found and killed in a vengeful rage by Francesca's husband. As Francesca's tormented ghost tells Dante, "Galeotto fu il libro e chi lo scrisse: / quel giorno più non vi leggemmo avante" (A Galleot was the book and he who wrote it; we read no further in the book that day; *Inferno* V, 137–138). The term *Galeotto*, as Charles Singleton notes in his commentary, referred to the knight Gallehault in the Arthurian tale of Lancelot of the Lake, a version of which Paolo and Francesca were reading. Knowing of Lancelot's love for Queen Guinevere, King Arthur's wife, Gallehault arranged for Lancelot and the queen to meet, and, in the course of that interview, urged Guinevere to kiss Lancelot, thus beginning the guilty love between the two. "From the part he played on this occasion," says Singleton, "the name of Gallehault ('galeotto'), like that of Pandarus ('pander'), became a synonym for 'go-between'" (94–95). However, the book Paolo and Francesca were reading was more than just the intermediary for their illicit love; it was also the cause of their deaths. To come upon a story by a man of letters about a "killer book" may seem strange at first. Precisely because he was a writer, however, Dante knew whereof he spoke. As the citation from Saint Paul reminds us, he was not the first writer, nor would he be the last, to view writing in such a sinister light.

More than six centuries later, a Spanish American author and critic who had of course read both Saint Paul and Dante wrote a book that voiced similar sentiments in a wholly different context. *La ciudad letrada* (The lettered city) was published posthumously in 1984 after Angel Rama's untimely death in an air disaster, and it soon became one of the most influential works of contemporary Spanish American literary criticism. In an article commenting on *La ciudad letrada*'s widespread influence, Carlos J. Alonso took particular note of Rama's pessimistic view of the written word's effect on Spanish American society and underscored how the Uruguayan critic "demonizes" writing:

Rama's achievement in *La ciudad letrada* was to put the continent's cultural history beyond Good and Evil, so to say, not by suspending the relevance of moral categories—as in Nietzsche—but rather by collapsing the two categories into one: that is, by subsuming all writers and intellectuals under the demonic rubric of "*letrado*." In Rama's *ciudad letrada* there are no heroes, only *letrados* who are irrevocably and irremediably tainted—although to a larger or a lesser extent, to be sure—by their contact with the written word. ("*Rama y sus retoños*" 286)

But Rama's gloomy view of the *letrado*, and of writing as a whole, is, as I have suggested, only a recent instance in a long tradition of distrust of the written word in Western culture, a distrust that often goes beyond mere logocentrism to become a virtual "graphophobia."

By this rather cacophonous term, I allude not so much to a fear of writing that might lead one to avoid it (which clearly does not happen with most authors), but to an attitude towards the written word that mixes respect, caution, and dread with revulsion and contempt. This attitude is displayed by literary critics (as one might expect) as well as by authors. Most evident in self-reflexive or metaliterary texts, it is, of course, profoundly conflict ridden. However, despite the name I have chosen to give it, it is not a pathological condition but a normal, indeed necessary, component of all thought about writing.

In some respects, graphophobia is analogous to the mixture of antipathy and fascination that Edward Said has posited on the part of some orientalists towards their subject matter (*Orientalism* 150–151ff.). A friend of the French poet Victor Hugo once remarked about Hugo's attitude towards books from and about the Orient that "he doesn't like them, but he makes use of them" (Schwab 363). Raymond Schwab further observed that Hugo, "faced with the Asian immensities, . . . generally saw in them not images of liberating plains nor . . . of exalting summits, but rather images of a dark and vertiginous abyss" (Schwab 364).

Similarly, graphophobia is haunted by a sense of writing's vertiginous quality, its utter alienness. Writing's strangeness, however, unlike that of Asia for the orientalists, which was a by-product of Western racism and imperialism, can never be reduced to a comfortable familiarity. The more writers learn about the origins and mechanisms of writing, the less they seem to like what they discover, and the more they recoil from what they have learned. It is as though, in order to write, one need be blind not only to the precise mechanisms of signification and their paradoxes, but also to the ethical implications of the act of writing itself.[2]

We are so used to hearing about the virtues of literacy, or about the benefits of the written word, that at first the idea that writing might be viewed otherwise seems odd or eccentric. As Jacques Derrida has shown, however, praise of writing is usually praise of a certain kind of writing, that which obeys the dictates of grammar and thought, becoming merely a vehicle for the expression of ideas and modeling itself on speech.[3] Alongside the paeans to literacy in Western culture, there have always been the paeans to orality, viewed as a "superior" form of language because of its associations with thought and self-presence, which are in turn linked to metaphysical notions such as truth, beauty, and good. Within this hierarchical system, speech is the father, the source of truth and goodness, the lord and master of writing, and the written word is always under suspicion as a potentially subversive, malevolent, and rebellious form

of language. From the outset, then, graphophobia is implicit in Western culture.

Graphophobia, however, also arises from the experience of writing, not merely from the ideological exaltation of speech. This experience is generally characterized by a sense of resistance, even of struggle, as writers grapple with the system of material signs that is writing and try to bend it to their will. The modern locus classicus of the experience of writing as hard work (which is shared by most mortals) is the letters of Gustave Flaubert, collected in his *Correspondance*. But, as Ernst Robert Curtius reminds us, the hard labor—indeed, the suffering—implicit in the act of writing was already noted by Roman and medieval Latin writers. In the Middle Ages, says Curtius,

Many a man wrote poetry groaning and sweating. . . . That composing poetry, especially Latin poetry, which was still regarded by many of Dante's contemporaries as the only genteel variety, was to many a matter of great labor can be seen from the highly popular phrase, the poet will now end the poem or section of it because the Muse has grown weary. What torture writing poetry could be is shown by the epistle of an unknown poet to a young man who is extolled for his cleverness and advised to submit to "the whip of poetry" if he wishes to develop his gifts to the utmost. . . . The author of the *Ecbasis captivi* admits at the beginning of his work that he had unfortunately spent his youth thoughtlessly, but now, even though it be late, he wishes to improve himself by assiduous work. Hence he writes verses. This banishes sleep and constrains him to a scanty diet. Very often he finds himself scratching his head and biting his nails over his composition; he upon whom lies such a task has renounced sloth. (468–469)

Similar confessions did not abound in Spanish American literature until the twentieth century. Perhaps one of the most heartfelt contemporary declarations of writing as a struggle is César Vallejo's sonnet "Intensidad y altura" (Intensity and height), whose first quatrain reads:

I want to write, but it comes out foam,
I want to say a great deal, but I get stuck;
There's no spoken cipher that's not a sum,
No written pyramid without a core.

Quiero escribir, pero me sale espuma,
quiero decir muchísimo y me atollo;
no hay cifra hablada que no sea suma,
no hay pirámide escrita, sin cogollo.                    (50)

Suspicion of writing dates from as far back as Plato and resurfaces during periods of cultural and artistic crisis, such as the baroque, romanticism, modernism and high modernism, and—even as it was being exposed and undermined in the work of Derrida and others—postmodernism.[4] Feelings of dread and outright fear associated with the letter go back even further, to the very dawn of writing. They are implicit, for instance, in the cuneiform inscriptions of the warrior kings of Assur and Nineveh, or the later hieroglyphs of the Egyptian pharaohs, which were meant to impress readers with the might and near divinity of the rulers (Martin 44, 102–103). The connection made by these early militaristic cultures between writing and warfare evokes notions not only of discipline and regimentation, but also of writing's links with the body, and particularly with bodily injury and death.

In turn, the fear of writing, because of its association with the disciplinary power of the state, derives from an even more ancient tradition linking writing with magic and with otherworldly powers. As Henri-Jean Martin reminds us, the ancient Egyptians "believed in the creative virtue of words and in their dangerous power," which was why their god of writing, Thot, was also "reputed to be a dangerous magician" (18–19, 103). Martin further marvels at the persistence of similar beliefs even into our age, as evidenced in the destruction of statues and defacement of inscriptions carried out in the name of reform or revolution. "And who among us [he asks rhetorically] has not paused before pronouncing or writing a definitive word?" (19).

In Spanish America after the conquest, as elsewhere around the world, civilization has been persistently linked to writing and letters. Spanish American culture is in fact not an oral culture, although some of its members may not know how to read. Its profoundly literate character, as Angel Rama's *La ciudad letrada* demonstrates, has paradoxically little to do with literacy rates and more with the fact that this is a society founded on a pervasive utilization of writing and a deep respect for it.[5] In spite of this foundation, or perhaps even because of it, writing was from the very beginning regarded in Spanish America with a mixture of mistrust and awe. This reaction was also largely due to writing's oppressive role during the traumatic events of the conquest, when the predominantly oral indigenous peoples were forced at swordpoint to accept the European invaders' system of graphic representation.[6] At the same time, the Europeans, in a move familiar to colonizers and colonized around the globe, condemned the ideographic or pictographic sign-systems of the Indians as works of the Devil and proceeded to eradicate them through massive book burnings.

Indeed, the Americas experienced the "violence of the letter" in a drastic and overwhelming, utterly physical manner.[7] Not only were the sons of the Indian elites forcibly acculturated and made to learn Latin and Spanish along with the European alphabet, but they, along with their indigenous brethren and the enslaved Africans who were brought soon afterwards, experienced in their very bodies the intense sort of control made possible only through writing: the innumerable edicts, laws, permits, regulations, logbooks, and account books with which the Europeans attempted to keep their New World subjects, as well as their own people, in line.[8] As Roberto González Echevarría reminds us, during colonial times the (phallic) symbol of the letter of the law, and of the violence that was visited upon those who disobeyed it, was the *picota*, or pillory, where "the citizens of the domain were whipped, tortured, shamed, their severed organs put on public display" (*Myth and Archive* 49).

In this context in which letters and the law were presumed to be inextricably linked, in which writing served as a model for the quasi-military ordering of the world, writers who desired to contest or to resist the law, both in Spain and in its colonies, frequently took recourse to the "magic" or "demonic" tradition of writing, invoking writing's potential to dissemble, confuse, and undo. Although Juan Ruiz's medieval *Libro de buen amor* (Book of good love, 1330–1334) is an important precursor in this regard, the founding text in this oppositional graphophobic tradition is undoubtedly Fernando de Rojas's *La Celestina* (1499), written shortly after Columbus reached the New World and when the foundations for Spain's patrimonial and centralizing empire were being laid. The character of the old bawd and go-between Celestina, as González Echevarría convincingly argues, uncovers through the ideological mediation of magic and witchcraft, and by means of the literalization of other characters' rhetoric, the metaphors of physical, bodily violence that underlie language (*Celestina's Brood* 14–16ff.). The vision of writing and literature that emanates from Rojas's play is deeply pessimistic, based on a denial of language's effectiveness both as a vehicle of dialogue and exchange, and as a means to preserve and transmit moral values (*Celestina's Brood* 31ff.). The fact that this denial takes place in language, and specifically in writing, can be seen as a further indication of language's paradoxical unreliability.

A similarly profound sense of writing's association with base materiality, moral decay, and political oppression is evident in colonial Spanish American works of the seventeenth century and after: from the *Primer nueva corónica y buen gobierno* (1615) by the indigenous Andean chronicler Guamán Poma de Ayala, to *El Carnero* (c. 1638) by the chronicler of New Granada Juan Rodríguez Freyle, to the satiric poetry of *Diente del Parnaso* (written c. 1690, published 1873) by the Peruvian Juan del Valle y Caviedes, to *El Lazarillo de ciegos caminantes* (1776) by the Spanish *visitador* Alonso Carrió de la Vandera, to Spanish America's first self-proclaimed novel, *El Periquillo Sarniento* (1816) by the Mexican José Joaquín Fernández de Lizardi.[9] It must be stressed that the graphophobia displayed by these and other writers of the seventeenth and eighteenth centuries did not lead them to avoid writing but was instead made to serve a moralizing purpose in which one form of writing was used to condemn another. By reveling in the scatological and abject facets of writing,[10] these authors implicitly questioned the state-sanctioned equation between letters and the law, or between writing and justice. Ultimately, however, unlike the ever skeptical Fernando de Rojas, whose anarchic and violent view of language placed writing beyond good and evil, most of the writers I have mentioned displayed a Manichaean attitude towards the letter. In other words, writing, although tainted by mortality and malevolence, was for them a key weapon in the struggle between good and evil. These authors' pessimism about the nature of the written word was tempered by their appeal to logocentrism, embodied either in religious ideology or, during and after the eighteenth century, in a metaphysical appeal to Reason. Although they saw evil at work in writing and in language as a whole, it was a lesser, controllable evil, like the *diablo cojuelo* of the baroque Spanish satirist Vélez de Guevara,[11] a lame devil caught in a bottle, and no match for the greater forces of transcendent good to which most writers claimed allegiance in one form or another.

This dynamic continued in Spanish America during the so-called national period, or roughly the first two-thirds of the nineteenth century. By then, political ideology had replaced religion as the *logos* that kept writing's corrosiveness in check. A liberal and anticlerical writer such as Ricardo Palma in his delightful *Tradiciones peruanas* (Peruvian traditions, 1872–1883), for instance, would often ironically allude to the Devil in his texts in order to scandalize his more conservative and religious compatriots. Parodying the conservatives, in the introduction to "El alcalde de Paucarcolla" (The mayor of Paucarcolla), Palma grumbles:

One must agree that what they call civilization, enlightenment, and progress in our century has done us a disservice by suppressing the Devil. In colonial times, when His grace went around, feeling more self-important than Cardinal Camarlengo, and chatting with the progeny of Adam, there was barely a case of suicide or incestuous love every fifty years or so. Out of fear and respect for the hot coals and molten lead, sinners agonized in uncertainty before committing crimes that today are common occurrences. Today the Devil has nothing to do, for good or ill, with us miserable mortals; the Devil has already gone out of fashion, and not even the friars mention him in the pulpit; the Devil is dead and buried.

If, by one of God's miracles, I am again elected to Congress, I shall have to present a new law to resuscitate the Devil and return him to the full performance of his ancient duties. We need the Devil; give him back to us. When the Devil lived and there was a hell, there was less vice and roguery in our land.

In the name of *pyrotechnic* history and *phosphorescent* literature, I protest the suppression of the Evil One. To eliminate the Devil is to kill tradition. (*Tradiciones peruanas completas* 270–271)

Romantic writers in Spanish America, like their European peers, frequently identified with Satan in their works, seeing him as the archetypal rebel and antiauthoritarian figure par excellence. But this was all done mostly in a jocular, satirical spirit, intended to preempt the demonization to which these writers themselves were often subjected by their conservative adversaries. It was a game of masks, and all in good fun. Significantly, despite the attempts by the Argentine romantics to examine the nature of evil embodied in the figure of the dictator or the *caudillo* (in works such as Esteban Echeverría's "El matadero" [1838], Domingo Faustino Sarmiento's *Facundo* [1845], and José Mármol's *Amalia* [1855]), no Spanish American writer until the late nineteenth century ever came close to reflecting as deeply on the links between art and evil as did the Englishman Thomas De Quincey, in his darkly ironic essay *On Murder Considered as One of the Fine Arts* (1827).

Not until the rise of the Spanish American modernists during the 1880s did the ethical questioning of societal problems, which the sense of graphophobia had been made to serve, begin to be turned inwards, towards literature and writing themselves. Among the many twentieth-century concerns that the modernists inaugurated in Spanish America was precisely that of the ethical implications of art and literature. In their quest to define and justify literature in its own terms (and not according to the other dominant discourses of the age, such as those of law, science, or religion), the Spanish American modernists delved deeply into the mysteries of writing, and like their European symbolist peers, asked probing questions about the way literature was made, about its relation to the individual and to society, and about the power of words to change the world.

Nevertheless, through their contacts with nineteenth-century philology (as exemplified in the works of Ernest Renan, Hyppolite Taine, and Marcelino Menéndez Pelayo, among many others) and their experiences as journalists (which most of them were at one time or another), the modernists eventually arrived at a view of literature that contradicted their strongly held aestheticist beliefs. Already the modernists, emulating Flaubert and the French Parnassians, had accepted and loudly proclaimed the notion that writing (particularly in its "artistic" form, that is, as literature) was hard work, an experience often approximating agony.[12] Both philology and journalism reinforced this view of writing as labor and presented the modernists with an even more demystified view of language and writing. To begin with, both discourses viewed language as an object, as a human construct fraught with historical and social connections. But journalism went even further: it undermined the nineteenth-century notion of the author as privileged emitter of his work and, by turning texts into merchandise, subordinated aesthetic value to market value. While philology still saw writing as a transcendent vehicle that enabled readers to link up with the world of ideas, with the *logos*, journalism (like Rojas's *Celestina* centuries earlier) constantly displayed writing's gross materiality and its links with the worldly, the criminal, and the excremental. Thus, the modernists wavered, sometimes quite violently, between two extreme views of writing: in the words of Rubén Darío, writing revealed either "the rhythm of the immense mechanics of the heavens" (*el ritmo de la inmensa mecánica celeste*) or "the horror of literature" (*el horror de la literatura*; Jiménez, *Antología crítica* 196, 208).

This back-and-forth movement of the modernists, which was often manifested in a "positive" view of the written word for public consumption and a "negative," graphophobic one in intimate texts, nevertheless gave rise in Spanish America, I would argue, to a true ethics of writing, that is, to a propensity to ask not only how one can use writing as a critical tool or as an instrument of power, but more importantly, why one chooses to write in the first place. If writing is not a neutral, almost ethereal, docile and malleable vehicle, which can be used for either good or evil, but instead is a material entity, heavy and resistant, and "tainted" by its collusion with the state and its attendant violence, as the graphophobic tradition insisted, why on earth would any moral person have anything to do with it? The Platonic branch of the graphophobic tradition also insisted that writing, both as an entity and as an activity, was devoid of moral principles, or rather, that its guiding principles were anarchy and lawlessness. Whether one sees writing as the servant of an oppressive, militaristic state, or, as Plato put it, "dumb characters which have not a word to say for themselves and can not adequately express the truth" (*The Works of Plato* 445), the question remains: Can writing ever be fully justified?

This question may seem absurd in a practical, commonsense context, since one can immediately enumerate the utilitarian benefits of writing and note how impossible society as we know it would be without the visual representation of language. However, there are numberless writers for whom "*to write* is an intransitive verb," as Roland Barthes put it (*Critical Essays* 145). For these "writers-as-artists," who consider writing an end in itself, and who produce the bulk of what, despite all the attempts to avoid it, is still studied and revered as "literature," the question takes on a profound urgency. Is there not danger in placing one's life in the service of so fickle a phenomenon, so dubious an activity? Moreover, does all "literary" or "artistic" use of writing not entail a certain measure of abuse—abuse *of* writing itself, inasmuch as it should be handled carefully and wisely, like fire or some other potentially destructive force, and abuse *by* writing, inasmuch as making use of writing for purposes other than those of strict communication implies a culpable and irresponsible ignorance of writing's violent origins and negative powers?

The issue also arises of why the attraction some feel towards writing is so strong that it overpowers all the warnings of common sense and good judgment, as if it were some sort of compulsive or addictive behavior beyond the subject's conscious control. Of course, the notion of the artist (whether painter, musician, or writer) sacrificing everything for the sake of art was already a cliché at the end of the nineteenth century, but also, long before that, literature abounded in cautionary tales—of which *Don Quixote* is the most famous instance—about the power of writing to alienate both writers and readers, driving them into error and errancy. The Platonic metaphor of writing as both drug and poison is already sufficiently well known (see Derrida, *Dissemination* 117–128); perhaps it should be joined more explicitly, however, with another: that of writing as addiction.

Is there something addictive about writing that makes it a graphic analogue to "the demon rum," to gambling, or to the white lines of cocaine, and the writer akin to the alcoholic, the gambler, or the junkie? "Writing is an illness we cannot treat but only recover from," remarks anthropologist Stephen A. Tyler, in a metaphor of writing as disease that could refer either to a malarial-type infection or to a more ambiguous mental malady such as addiction ("On Being Out of Words" 5). Tyler, echoing Walter J. Ong, further conjectures that the implied critique of writing (and, I would add, the graphophobia) evidenced in the currently renewed interest in issues of orality and literacy, may be due to the rise of "new technologies of representation," such as the personal computer and the Internet, which promise (or threaten) to do away with the "key notions of 'book,' 'word,' 'reading,' and 'writing'" (Tyler 6–7; Ong, *Orality and Literacy* 79–81). That may be so in a more general context, but in Spanish America, as I have already pointed out, suspicion of writing runs as deep as the attachment to it and springs not from new technologies but from long-standing grievances that have continued until the present. In the many works of twentieth-century Spanish American narrative that anguish over writing's possible links with evil, the metaphor of writing as addiction underlies four distinct approaches to an ethics of writing. I would like to dwell briefly on these approaches.

Jorge Luis Borges was undoubtedly the main contemporary proponent of the view that writing is so addictive and dangerous that it should be either avoided or severely restricted, and that authors themselves are dubious demiurges who traffic in infamy. The notion of the author as akin to a criminal was first set forth by Borges in *Historia universal de la infamia* (1935) (published in English as *A Universal History of Infamy,* 1972). Borges retells in that book the biographies of famous delinquents of history (some of whom were real, and others apocryphal): Jesse James, Monk Eastman, Lazarus Morell, Tom Castro, the Widow Ching, Kotsuké no Suké, and Hákim of Merv. Parodying Hegel's 1830 *Lectures on the Philosophy of World History*, particularly Hegel's notion of the "great men" who make history, Borges presents us with a mock-heroic rogues' gallery of evildoers, all of whom share not only a propensity for large-scale violence but also an authorial talent for lies and deceit, for creating fictions in order to further their criminal enterprises. The difference between these infamous liars and the law-abiding writers of fiction, Borges suggests, is merely a matter of degree. Significantly, both the written word and the act of writing play important roles in the lives of the criminals Borges describes: the slave rustler Lazarus Morell, we are told, "knew the Scriptures and preached with singular conviction" (Borges, *Obras completas* 297); the impostor Tom Castro used the letters of the deceased Roger Charles Tichborne to his mother in order to impersonate Tichborne (303); the Widow Ching, who was a female buccaneer, wrote down the rules for piracy "in a precise and laconic style" (307); and Hákim of Merv declared himself a prophet and wrote a sacred text titled *The Hidden Rose* (324).

In the prologue to *A Universal History of Infamy*, using largely moral terms, Borges exalts reading over writing: "Reading is, at present, an activity posterior to writing: it is more resigned, more civil, more intellectual" (*Obras completas* 289). In Borges's works, reading may be a cause as much of torment as of pleasure, but writing is consistently associated with egotism, vanity, deceit, and violence. Witness the nature and fates of such varied Borgesian writer-characters as Yu Tsun, Red Scharlach, Jaromir Hladík, Nils Runeberg, Aurelian the theologian, and Carlos Argentino Danieri, to mention just a few. Two notable exceptions to this rule may be Pierre Menard and Herbert Quain, but both are portrayed more as literary theorists and experimenters than as enthusiastic writers. Herbert Quain's works, we are told, are "admirable, perhaps, for their novelty and for a certain laconic probity, but not for their passion" (*Obras completas* 461).

Quain is also said to have argued that "readers were already an extinct species" and that "every European is a writer . . . potentially or in fact" (464). This decline of reading, and the correlative increase in writing, leads to aberrations such as that of Yu Tsun in Borges's "El jardín de senderos que se bifurcan" (The garden of forking paths): during World War I, the Chinese-born German spy, despite his imminent capture, is able to communicate to his superiors the name of a city that is to be bombed—Albert—only by murdering the eminent British sinologist Stephen Albert, a fact that appears in the newspapers the next day and is duly noted by German intelligence. On a more comic note, the vice of writing is lambasted in the character of Carlos Argentino Danieri in "El aleph" (The aleph). The buffoonish Danieri (whose name and Italian provenance make him a parody of Dante) is engaged in writing a wordy, potentially infinite, and aesthetically worthless poem titled *The Earth*.

But perhaps Borges's most awesome portrayal of writing's vacuity and its power to proliferate unceasingly is, of course, "La biblioteca de Babel" (The library of Babel). In this graphophobic nightmare, a dying race of librarians inhabits a seemingly limitless universe of books, most of which cannot be read or deciphered, because they contain all the possible combinations of the letters of the alphabet. This story is but one of several texts in which Borges extols the virtues of textual economy. A desire for scriptural minimalism runs throughout Borges's works, becoming most evident in stories like "The Library of Babel" or in his disparaging comments on the writing of novels in the prologue to *Ficciones* (Fictions): "A laborious and impoverishing delirium is the composition of vast books, dragging on for five hundred pages an idea whose perfect oral exposition only takes a few minutes" (*Obras completas* 429). The elliptical quality of Borges's style is well known, and we know that he never wrote any novels by himself (although he collaborated on one with Adolfo Bioy Casares, *Un modelo para la muerte* [A model for death], 1946). Indeed, Borges's whole narrative oeuvre, although extensive, tended towards ever more compact forms, such as the "short-short stories" collected in *El hacedor* (The maker, 1960) and scattered throughout his books of poetry. The cliché about Borges's teaching us that writing and reading are very much alike, or are two faces of a common experience of literature, is only partially correct. For Borges, the wholesale conversion of readers into writers was in fact a recent historical development, which he deplored. Readers, who necessarily practice a kind of scriptural asceticism, evidently occupied, in Borges's view, a higher moral and intellectual plane than writers.

Borges's notion of the reader's moral superiority was contested, however, by another Argentine author, Julio Cortázar, who posited instead the complicity between writer and reader and made the reader share in the writer's guilt. The idea of the *"lector cómplice"* (reader-accomplice) first made its appearance in Cortázar's novel *Rayuela* (Hopscotch, 1964), where it was viewed in a positive light. Cortázar's reader-accomplices in this book are, in effect, readers-turned-writers, and they help to underpin *Hopscotch*'s supposedly "open" structure, which allows readers to pick and choose, to a limited extent, among the novel's various chapters in order to compose—to write—slightly divergent readings of the text. In *Hopscotch*, the idea of the reader-accomplice is presented as a liberation of the readers, freeing them from the author's tyranny. If reader-accomplices are felonious here, their felony is the relatively minor one of transgressing artistic boundaries in order to subvert traditional novelistic structures.

Decades later, however, in "Recortes de prensa" (Press clippings) one of his most powerful but least-known short stories, from his late book *Queremos tanto a Glenda y otros relatos* (1981) (published in English as *We Love Glenda So Much and Other Tales*, 1983), Cortázar's view of the reader became as gloomy as Borges's view of the writer. In this story, Noemí, an Argentine writer living in Paris, after reading a testimonial text about tortures and "disappearances" in Argentina, responds violently to men's aggression against women. Soon after reading the testimonial text, she comes upon a woman who is being tortured by her husband. Noemí decides to intervene by rescuing her and then helps the tortured woman to turn the tables against her husband by torturing *him*. Whether this occurs in fact or as Noemí's fantasy the story leaves to the readers to decide. Indeed, "Press Clippings" forces readers to confront a fundamental ethical question about themselves: If writing and reading, however different their relation may have been in the past, are now inextricably linked, are we not all—writers as well as readers—guilty of collaborating in the violence that underlies all writing?

The idea of guilt associated with both reading and writing is central to testimonial narrative, a form of Spanish American writing that tries to pass itself off as orality and that uses graphophobia in order to advance an ideological agenda. In testimonial narratives as varied as Miguel Barnet's *Biografía de un cimarrón* (The biography of a runaway slave, 1966), Elena Poniatowska's *Hasta no verte, Jesús mío* (Until I see you, my Jesus, 1969), and Rigoberta Menchú's *Me llamo Rigoberta Menchú, y así me nació la conciencia* (I, Rigoberta Menchú: An Indian woman in Guatemala, 1983), writing is condemned because of its association with power and violence, even as it is being utilized. Like the critic Angel Rama in *La ciudad letrada*, but also like their colonial precursors in the seventeenth and eighteenth centuries, authors of testimonial narratives set up a Manichaean universe in their works, in which writing and literacy are regarded as necessary evils at best, and at worst as extended forms of political and social oppression. However, unlike the colonial texts, with their emphasis on the "demonic" and ambiguous aspects of writing, testimonial narratives seek to escape the contradictions of writing altogether by mimicking orality, the spoken word, and particularly those words spoken by the powerless and the oppressed. Nevertheless, despite their claim to give voice to the voiceless, these works are relentlessly monological and seek to bring readers to their side by playing on the deep-seated sense of guilt about being literate that Cortázar identified in "Press Clippings." Through their appeal to orality, these texts not only seek to produce the impression of immediacy, but also implicitly condemn the ironic distancing and critical reading allowed by the written word. With the best intentions, testimonial texts use ethics as a weapon, forcing readers to judge or be judged, to accept their narrative at face value or risk moral opprobrium. The apparent moral choice offered by testimonial narratives to their readers is in fact no choice at all, since these narratives from the outset make it morally unacceptable to read them as fictions.[13]

A third view of the relation between writing and evil is that of Alejo Carpentier in his last novel, *El arpa y la sombra* (1979) (published in English as *The Harp and the Shadow*, 1990). In that work, the character of Christopher Columbus is presented as an allegory of the writer, and his obsessive quest to cross the Atlantic in search of new lands is compared to the writer's struggle to produce a text whose final outlines can barely be foreseen. Like Borges, Carpentier presents writing in *The Harp and the Shadow* as a kind of compulsion, akin to a demonic possession.

The writer is seen in *The Harp and the Shadow* as a Faustian figure, willing to risk his soul to produce a great work. But Carpentier, like Cortázar, posits the readers' complicity in the creation of his fictional works. *The Harp and the Shadow* abounds in allusions to the interlude *El Retablo de las Maravillas* (The retable of wonders), a metatheatrical text in which Miguel de Cervantes explores, as in the *Quixote*, the complicity of the spectator and the reader. The lesson of Cervantes's play, and of Carpentier's evocation of it, is that the writer's compulsion to write is no different, nor less powerful, than the readers' compulsion to give shape and meaning to literary texts. Writers and readers both share in the Faustian bargain.

Unlike Goethe with regard to Faust, however, Carpentier sees almost no possibility of redemption for either writers or readers. Their only hope—a very slim one at best—may lie in the impossibility of anyone rendering a "final judgment" on them. This is so because for Carpentier writing belongs definitely to "the kingdom of this world"; it is one material thing among the other things of the world, and as such, it does not lead towards transcendence of any kind, whether religious or philosophical. Furthermore, in this world, which is the only one we inhabit and know, everyone is either a writer or a reader, and thus everyone shares in writing's perpetually abject state.

Writing as abjection; writing as addiction; writing as an endlessly proliferating system; writing as an extension of violence and oppression—the list of graphophobic accusations in modern Spanish American literature is extensive, almost reaching the level of paranoia. Still unclear, however, is precisely how, despite all of these negative views, writing becomes "addictive." Where does writing's power to enthrall originate? From where does writing derive its enormous social and cultural authority? On a more specifically literary level, what compels writers to write fictions and readers to read them? These are, of course, vast questions, on which literally thousands of volumes have been written, but they are also pertinent to recent attempts by Spanish American writers to re-

solve the apparent impasse presented by the relation between writing and evil.

Undoubtedly, the most ambitious and daring of these attempts is Gabriel García Márquez's novel *El amor en los tiempos del cólera* (1985) (published in English as *Love in the Time of Cholera*, 1988). The central work in an "amorous trilogy" that also includes *Crónica de una muerte anunciada* (Chronicle of a death foretold, 1981) and *Del amor y otros demonios* (Of love and other demons, 1994), *Love in the Time of Cholera* investigates the possibility of somehow purging writing of its violent and abject elements by means—corny as this may sound—of the redeeming power of love.

*Love in the Time of Cholera* tells the story of two lovers whose relationship, interrupted for over half a century, is mediated by writing. The title suggests a mixture of sublimity (love) and abjection (cholera) that is in itself evocative of the ambivalence of writing. It is also meant to evoke, along with certain passages in the novel, the medieval idea of lovesickness, the so-called *amor hereos* or "heroic love," which is prominent in works such as Rojas's *Celestina*.[14] One supposed cure for lovesickness in the Middle Ages was *logotheraphy*, the use of language to divert the lovesick individuals from their obsessive preoccupations with their love objects (Solomon 59–64). The many allusions in *Love in the Time of Cholera* to the topic of lovesickness, as well as the novel's "open" ending, in which the aged lovers Florentino Ariza and Fermina Daza realize that love is an endless emotional shuttling back and forth, make clear that one of this novel's principal aims is to invoke the curative, regenerative powers of literature—and, by extension, of writing. The powers of the written word are presented as similar, if not equal, to those of love.

Good writing exerts a seductive influence over readers; it makes readers fall in love with it. But reading, like falling in love, is not a state of rest, but a process; it means entering into a cycle of communication, of communion, of sharing. The healing power of reading is in many ways comparable to the psychoanalytic process known as transference, whereby the analyst and the person being psychoanalyzed share in a mutual process of reconstructing and reinterpreting the analysand's past. Moreover, this process for Freud, like love for García Márquez, was potentially interminable.[15] The endlessness common to transference, love, and writing, rather than being a source of anxiety, is seen by García Márquez in a positive light as a form of vitality, a way of deferring death.

Just as significantly, the plot of *Love in the Time of Cholera* is framed by instants of privileged communication symbolized by the religious theme of the Pentecost. García Márquez's frequent and detailed allusions to Christianity in his novels are almost always symbolically associated with questions of writing, authorship, and authority: one example is the obvious evocations of Genesis and Exodus in *Cien años de soledad* (1967) (published in English as *One Hundred Years of Solitude*, 1970), and many critics have noted the symbolic allusions to the Gospels and to the Passion of Christ in *El otoño del patriarca* (The autumn of the patriarch) and *Chronicle of a Death Foretold*. While these allusions are mainly connected to the origins of the Christian religion and to Jesus as both a scapegoat and an authority figure, *Love in the Time of Cholera* evokes the Acts of the Apostles and the Pauline epistles, that is, the moment of Christianity's worldwide dissemination through writing. Through the metaphor of the Pentecost, García Márquez's novel proposes that the curative powers of writing have become democratized, accessible to all. The "good news" about writing is that its potential to create visions of beauty and harmony is no longer limited to an intellectual or social elite. In this regard, García Márquez seems to be echoing Borges's comments in his essay "Sobre los clásicos": "I do not have an iconoclastic vocation. During the thirties, under the spell of Macedonio Fernández, I used to believe that beauty was the privilege of a few authors. Now I know that it is commonplace, and that it awaits us in the chance pages of a mediocre writer or in a conversation overheard in the street" (*Obras completas* 773). Like love, writing thrives with the freedom that makes it accessible to all.

Alas, *Love in the Time of Cholera* also points out repeatedly the peril, even the violence, that underlies love. Just as love can be a source of rejuvenation and vitality when it is freely and equally shared, it can become a source of pain, destruction, and death when it is in any way unequal, as the disturbing episode of Florentino's seduction of the child América Vicuña demonstrates (395–398, 485–486). Love can also be addictive, as Florentino's catalogue of 622 lovers over fifty years attests (226). *Love in the Time of Cholera*, along with the other two works of García Márquez's "amorous trilogy," ultimately recognizes what Plato had observed two millennia before in the *Symposium*: that love is a daimon, a demon, a mediator or "go-between," and that as such it is as unreliable and untrustworthy as that other go-between, writing (*The Works of Plato* 331–334).

Not coincidentally, perhaps, *Love in the Time of Cholera* also abounds in allusions to Dante. The most obvious of these are, of course, the name and some of the traits of Florentino Ariza. Florentino's adoration of

Fermina in the first third of the novel is reminiscent of Dante's relationship with Beatrice in the *Vita Nuova* (1293). But Florentino and Fermina are also evocative of two characters from Dante's *Divine Comedy*: Paolo and Francesca. Florentino and Fermina are in many ways a positive rewriting of Dante's doomed lovers. In fact, García Márquez's text seems to allude to Paolo and Francesca in the tragic news story Fermina hears over the radio of two elderly lovers who had sustained an adulterous relationship for forty years, until the day they were murdered by a boatman in the very same place where they had had their first love encounter (460–461). Unlike these elderly lovers, or Paolo and Francesca, Florentino and Fermina live to old age and manage to freely fulfill their love after the death of Fermina's husband, Juvenal Urbino.

However, Florentino and Fermina resemble Paolo and Francesca in two important respects: they are brought together by writing and reading (in this case, Florentino's letters), and like Dante's characters, they seem to be suspended in a sort of eternal restlessness. But Florentino and Fermina are not carried along, like Paolo and Francesca, by an otherworldly "hellish tempest, which is never stilled" (*Inferno* V, 31); instead, their "goddamned coming and going" takes place in this world, in a ship under their command, paradoxically named the *New Fidelity* (*El amor en los tiempos del cólera* 503). The lesson of this fable about love and writing by García Márquez may well be that writing can not be redeemed by love, because love itself is like writing: a form of mediation that can be foolishly abused or wisely used and can work for evil or for good.

The action in *Love in the Time of Cholera* takes place during the last two decades of the nineteenth century and the first three decades of the twentieth.[16] Not coincidentally, perhaps, it was during this same period that the Spanish American modernists began their inquiry into the ethical dimension of writing. As will be seen in the following chapters, the ethical questioning of writing by the modernists and by subsequent writers first appears in the context of what might be termed "the theory and practice of abuse." I refer here to "abuse" in all of its various but interrelated meanings: as a verb, "to attack in words; to put to a wrong or improper use; to use so as to injure or damage," and as a noun, "a corrupt practice or custom; improper use or treatment; abusive language" (*Webster's New Collegiate Dictionary*, 8th ed., s.v. "abuse"). In such varied Spanish American texts as the short story "La hija del aire" (The daughter of the air, 1883) by Manuel Gutiérrez Nájera and the novels *La charca* (Stagnant waters, 1894) by Manuel Zeno Gandía and *Ifigenia* (Iphigenia, 1924) by Teresa de la Parra, we find some of the earliest descriptions of what might be called "scriptural abuse," of which these texts also serve as examples themselves. By means of female characters such as the "daughter of the air," Silvina, and María Eugenia, who are often thinly veiled personifications of writing, these narratives explore how writing can be alternately a victim and a perpetrator of abuse and oppression. Furthermore, as their recurrent use of the motifs of alienation and captivity also suggests, these works carry out their inquiry mostly without logocentric illusions, without the hope that orality might provide an escape from the paradoxes and violence of writing, the type of hope that Derrida denounces in Rousseau and in Claude Lévi-Strauss (*Of Grammatology* 101–140). The texts by Nájera, Zeno, and de la Parra examined in the following chapters also display a mixture of guilt and resignation towards writing: guilt about the violence of their scriptural origins and resignation to the seeming inevitability of that violence.

As the previous pages suggest, to speak of ethics in the context of Spanish American literature is to invoke a panorama so vast that it encompasses virtually the whole of that literature. If all writing and reading are profoundly linked to ethics, as many contemporary critics and thinkers have argued, Spanish American literature nevertheless seems to overflow with explicit moral and ethical concerns from its very beginnings—in the writings of a Bartolomé de Las Casas, for example—down to the recent vogue of testimonial narrative.[17] The moral condemnation of human injustice and violence in all its forms is one of Spanish American literature's most obvious and recurrent motifs and has already been abundantly explored by critics and scholars from a wide variety of theoretical perspectives. This book, therefore, will not dwell on such thematic aspects, an undertaking which would have been in any case repetitive and potentially interminable. Partly for similar reasons of economy, I have left out of my analysis the undoubtedly fertile field of Spanish American poetry and have made only general observations about colonial and nineteenth-century literature in the introductory chapter. In the rest of the book, I have focused exclusively on Spanish American short stories and novels from the end of the nineteenth century through the twentieth.

My focus on the twentieth century also follows from the particular way in which I have chosen to explore the appearance of ethics in Spanish American narrative. Instead of relying on a thematic approach to issues of violence and social protest, this book seeks to carry out a more theoretically oriented reading of Spanish American texts. Previous theoretical readings have focused fruitfully on questions such as writing's relation to authority in Latin America (as in González Echevarría's *The Voice of the Masters*) or, more generally, on the ethical qualities of narrative fiction (see Booth, Harpham, Hillis Miller in *Versions of Pygmalion*, Newton, Parker) or the ethical implications of reading (Eaglestone, Hillis Miller in *The Ethics of Reading*). My book, in contrast, aims to trace and describe how Spanish American writers have reflected ethically in their works about writing's relation to violence and about their own relation to writing.

For reasons too complicated to enumerate, but that must certainly include the multiple forms of religious and political censorship and persecution that have been part of the Iberian and Spanish American civilizations for centuries, Spanish American writers have developed an intense awareness of the potential dangers of the written word. What is perhaps new in twentieth-century Spanish American narrative is its increasingly overt display of this awareness coupled with the insistence that violence is an intrinsic quality of writing itself, not merely a consequence of the ideas writing conveys. Spanish American writers, as I hope to show, have often viewed and continue to view writing with a mixture of fascination and dread. They have good reason: for these authors, writing's entanglement with duplicity and oppression generates a far-reaching web of complicity from which no one, neither writer nor reader, emerges untainted.

To be sure, this is a grim view that runs counter to a long-standing and powerful discourse in praise of literacy and offers scant solace to those who seek respite in literature from the conflicts and tensions of everyday existence. In its disenchantment, this position displays a force that is at once tragic and strangely seductive, while at the same time remaining faithful to Hispanic culture's more down-to-earth conception of literature, which emanates from the *Quixote* and reaches back to earlier works of medieval literature such as *Celestina* and *The Book of Good Love*.

These last three allusions should also indicate that I am not arguing for the uniqueness of twentieth-century Spanish American letters on the basis of a presumed greater sensitivity to the question of ethics and writing or on any other basis. Clearly, studies similar to this one could be written about most other literary traditions. As I hope to have made clear in this introduction, an awareness of writing's links to violence is found, to a greater or lesser degree, throughout all of Western literature in all of its periods. I focus on the specific case of Spanish American literature mostly because that is the field I know best. In this case, I am simply pointing out the existence in Spanish American letters since colonial times of a tendency to distrust writing that, like so many other aspects of modern literature, has become more self-reflexive in the twentieth century.

One of the chief aims of this book is to call attention to the complex love-hate relationship between writers and writing, a relationship that is mediated to a large extent by ethics. Certainly, long before the international scandal about Paul de Man's wartime articles that, according to some, changed the nature of literary theory (Harpham, "Ethics" 389) and before the current trend towards an "ethical criticism," a great many fiction writers were warning anyone who would listen that writing—to paraphrase Bataille—is not innocent, that it is guilty and should admit itself so (8). However, in the still incipient field of "ethics and literature" only Levinasian readings such as Robert Eaglestone's *Ethical Criticism* have questioned the supposed axiological neutrality of writing. Glossing the Franco-Lithuanian philosopher's career, Eaglestone underscored Levinas's initial mistrust of literature and his antiaestheticism: "Literary critics who have used Levinas's work to provide a basis for criticism have not appreciated the full weight of his arguments against aesthetics, and how this argument in turn reflects his central ethical concerns. For Levinas in these works, it is impossible to speak ethically about art, save to say that art is unethical" (124). Following Derrida's sympathetic yet severe critique of Levinas's ideas in "Violence and Metaphysics" (1978), which pointed out the contradictions inherent in expressing through language an antiaesthetic, antilinguistic philosophy, Levinas subsequently developed a distinction between "the saying" and "the said." The former term stands for the spontaneous and vital use of language by a speaker, while the latter stands for the fixity and ambiguity of the artistic, literary use of language. Nevertheless, this distinction remains unconvincing, largely because it attempts to exempt speech from the ethical ambivalence of both spoken and written language.

My own approach shares many of the concerns expressed in Derrida's fruitful dialogue with Levinas's thought, that is to say, with the ethical turn of deconstruction.[18] Deconstruction is pertinent to my analysis of ethics in Spanish American narrative because it is only in deconstruction that I have been able to find a serious consideration of writing as act and as phenomenon, as well as a rigorous philosophical discussion of the role of violence in writing and of the reasons for the distrust of writing by a certain Western philosophical and critical tradition. Most other current critical modalities, including cultural studies and its Latin American analogue, the sociology of literature, have chosen, often for programmatic reasons, to avoid the close attention deconstruction pays to writing. However, given the demonstrable historical existence of a distrust of writing, that is, graphophobia, it seemed logical to focus my ethical inquiry on writing itself rather than simply on its contents, the ideas and images writing conveys. Graphophobia, after all, suggests that it is not just the meaning communicated but our instrument of communication itself, our writing, that is somehow "tainted," perhaps even immoral. In my view, any attempt to link ethics with literary study should at least try to come to grips with this question of writing's relation to good and evil.

After this introduction, this book is divided into two parts, the first titled "Abuses" and the second "Admonitions." The first part consists of three essays on works by Spanish American authors from the end of the nineteenth century and the early twentieth century: the Mexican Manuel Gutiérrez Nájera, the Puerto Rican Manuel Zeno Gandía, and the Venezuelan Teresa de la Parra. As I have already indicated, my readings here focus on these authors' thematic emphases on various forms of abuse: physical and mental; of children and of women; as well as the abuse of writing itself, and writing as a form of abuse. I view these narrators as pioneers of the ethical questioning of writing in Spanish America because their works display a dawning awareness of the ethical dilemmas writing poses. In my readings in this section of the book I also trace a double-faced metaphor—recurrent as a leitmotif and undoubtedly patriarchal in origin—of writing as both a lost or orphaned girl-child and a femme fatale, as both victim and perpetrator.

The second part of the book, "Admonitions," examines the full-fledged reflections on the ethics of writing found in works by three major twentieth-century authors: the Cuban Alejo Carpentier and the Argentines Jorge Luis Borges and Julio Cortázar. These authors' short stories and novels are not only trenchant meditations on issues such as the relation between writing and evil, but also cautionary tales about writing's morally ambiguous power. I am acutely aware that a great many more Spanish American authors could be studied from a similar perspective (as my extensive comments on Gabriel García Márquez in this introduction suggest), but I consider that an episodic approach centered on a few (and, I hope, well-chosen) examples helps me to make my point more clearly than an exhaustive catalogue.

The works by Borges, Carpentier, and Cortázar studied in this book also display an awareness of their paradoxical situation as written texts that seek to warn us about the dangers of writing. None of these authors, however, seriously argues that it is better not to write, although Borges in particular seems to advocate a sort of textual minimalism. Despite the anguish expressed by Cortázar in his deeply disturbing short story "Press Clippings," he and his colleagues seem resigned to dealing with what one might call the "toxic" aspects of writing, seeking to balance writing's morally dubious qualities with its positive pedagogical and social effects. (In fact, the dual metaphor of writing as girl-child and as femme fatale makes one last reappearance in Cortázar's "Press Clippings.")

At the risk of repeating myself, I would strongly caution readers not to regard the transition posited here from "abuses" to "admonitions" as a dichotomy in which Nájera, Zeno, and de la Parra would be the exponents of scriptural abuse and Borges, Carpentier, and Cortázar the apostles of scriptural asceticism. Strictly speaking, "abusive" texts would be those that displayed no awareness of the ethical problematics of writing, and this is decidedly not the case with the writings of Nájera, Zeno, and de la Parra. I invite readers instead to see these turn-of-the-century texts as initial stages in a process of ethical awareness about writing and violence that Borges, Carpentier, and Cortázar, among others, bring to fuller development.

"Literature is fire," Mario Vargas Llosa said famously in a 1967 speech, on being awarded the prestigious Rómulo Gallegos prize ("La literatura es fuego" 132). He was of course expounding on his neoromantic notion of the writer as a demonic figure, a "perpetual spoilsport" (*un eterno aguafiestas*), and of literature as a "permanent insurrection" (133, 135). The fiery metaphor also alludes to writing's awesome power and to the responsibility such power entails. Like the technologies of fire, medicine, or nuclear energy (all metaphors that have historically been applied to writing and will also be found in this book), writing requires cautious handling.

Spanish American writers have learned to write with care, in the many senses of the term: in "a disquieted state of blended uncertainty, apprehension, and responsibility," as well as with "painstaking or watchful attention," or even with "suffering of mind: grief" (*Webster's New Collegiate Dictionary*, 8th ed., s.v. "care"). No other literature in the world today, it seems to me, so consistently displays the near paranoid degree of perfectionist vigilance (and self-vigilance) found in Spanish American literature. This vigilance includes the very language in which this literature is written: as the Cuban Juan Marinello noted in 1932 (and many critics have since repeated), Spanish, despite its status as the "mother tongue," is always perceived by Spanish Americans as a "foreign tongue" in which they are held prisoner ("Americanismo y cubanismo literarios" 49). If one adds to this sense of linguistic alienation the sense of estrangement that is also part and parcel of writing, one begins to marvel less at the care with which the Spanish Americans write than at their audacity. One also begins to realize the depth of the ethical dimension of Spanish American letters, which goes far beyond the moral denunciation of political or social oppression and violence and becomes instead a reflection on the violent and oppressive aspects of writing itself.

## PART I

*Abuses*

## CHAPTER I

# Writing and Child Abuse in Manuel Gutiérrez Nájera's "La hija del aire"

The seeking of the caress constitutes its essence by the fact that the caress does not know what it seeks. This "not knowing," this fundamental disorder, is the essential. It is like a game with something slipping away, a game absolutely without project or plan, not with what can become ours or us, but with something other, always other, always inaccessible, and always still to come. The caress is the anticipation of the pure future without content.

— EMMANUEL LEVINAS,
*Time and the Other*

Most fierce and capricious is Poetry:
This I've come to tell the honest folk

Muy fiera y caprichosa es la Poesía,
A decírselo vengo al pueblo honrado
— JOSÉ MARTÍ,
*Versos libres*

One evening in 1882, the Mexican poet, journalist, and founder of Spanish American modernism, Manuel Gutiérrez Nájera, went out to the circus.[1] This was in Mexico City, during the Francophile dictatorship of Porfirio Díaz, the era that Mexicans themselves call their belle époque.[2] The Circo Orrin was back in town, and despite his intense dislike of circuses, Nájera attended a performance (*Cuentos completos* 119). He was looking for a little girl-acrobat he had met there the year before whose sad and helpless appearance had struck him deeply. But she was nowhere to be found. In her place was another girl-acrobat whose plight was similar, and this led Nájera to reflect on what might have happened to the earlier one. A few days later, back home, or perhaps at his desk in the offices of the newspaper *El Nacional* (where he often worked until late at night),[3] he wrote one of his deceptively light *crónicas* (chronicles) about this experience,[4] ending with an appeal to his fellow citizens to help stop exploitative child labor practices. The article, with its very slight anecdote, featured a first-person narrator who greatly resembled Nájera and who addressed his readers directly. Titled "La hija del aire" (The daughter of the air), it appeared in *El Nacional* on April 6, 1882 (*Cuentos completos* 119 n. 1).

Seemingly, that is all there is to this very brief text. But the following year, when Nájera collected the short stories for his first book, *Cuentos frágiles* (Fragile stories, 1883), this article was among them.[5] Indeed, as one reflects on "La hija del aire" and its implications, it becomes evident that just as there is more to the little girl-acrobat than meets the eye, Nájera's story itself holds hidden depths. As a chronicle, this text's ostensible purpose was merely to denounce a social problem journalistically, thus requiring a purely referential and "realist" reading. However, by taking it from its journalistic context and placing it in a book of short stories, Nájera clearly invites other, less innocent interpretations. As I will argue here, "La hija del aire" is not only the most striking among Nájera's gallery of child portraits (and there are many in his works), but also a key text for understanding the nature of his literary modernity, a modernity achieved in part through his exploration of the ethics of writing.

Before examining Nájera's story, it is important to understand his background as a Spanish American modernist, and to outline his implicit views on writing and ethics. To speak of ethics in regard to Spanish American modernism may seem surprising and even contradictory, since that literary movement is usually linked to a glorification of artifice and a radically aestheticist position that considers art to be "beyond good and evil."[6] The antinomy begins to dissolve, however, when one recalls major modernist authors who were consummate moralizers, such as the Cuban José Martí and the Uruguayan José Enrique Rodó, as well as the writings of the so-called *mundonovista* or Americanist phase of modernism, which evidence an intense concern with what Ernest Renan called *la reforme intellectuelle et morale*.[7] It should be recalled, as well, that many modernist writers came of age during the latter years of the Victorian period, when in Spanish America, as in Europe, social conduct was ruled by a rigid moral code, and that their works therefore reflect, albeit sometimes polemically, the moralizing tenor of their times. In fact, modernist writings display two opposing attitudes towards morality: on the one hand, the insistence on "honesty" and the tendency towards an uplifting didacticism in the works of modernists such as Nájera, Martí, and Rodó, and on the other, the sensuous, erotically charged writing first attempted by the Cuban Julián del Casal and the Colombian José Asunción Silva that later became a hallmark of the poetry of the Nicaraguan Rubén Darío. It might be argued, however, that this second attitude does not question the validity or the uses of morality, and only differs from the first in its defense of eroticism based on the venerable Platonic tradition that equates the good with the beautiful.

But although many modernists would probably have agreed with Wittgenstein's assertion that "ethics and aesthetics are one and the same" (*Notebooks* 77, *Tractatus* 6.421), more often these writers wavered between aestheticism (which subordinates ethics to aesthetic values) and social responsibility. This ambivalence is evident in the two phases into which critics have divided the modernist movement: the "aestheticist" phase between 1880 and 1898, and the politically committed "mundonovista" phase after 1898. But it can also be seen, synchronically, in a single author's work, as in Rubén Darío's statement in the prologue to his second book of poems, *Cantos de vida y esperanza* (Songs of life and hope, 1905): "I am not a poet for the masses, but I know that I must inevitably move towards them" (*Poesías completas* 625). In any case, the tension between aestheticism and ethics—that is, between the absolute autonomy of art and the view that art has a moral function—constitutes a genuine duality in the literary practice and theory of the modernists, as in much of Western art from the same period. Even as the modernists delved into the nature of art and literature in their works, they also engaged in a parallel quest for an ethics that would guide their literary practice and give it its ultimate meaning. Paradoxical as it may seem, even those modernists who regarded themselves as aesthetes sought to find an ethics of art, that is, an ethics derived purely from artistic principles. Their inquiry naturally tended to focus on the literary art and on the activity that gives literature its specific character: thus, the modernists sought an ethics of writing.

It is not difficult to see the relevance of ethics to the work of Manuel Gutiérrez Nájera. The constant concern with the Other evidenced in the texts of this early Mexican modernist gives them a patently ethical cast.

Language in general, of course, deals predominantly with its Other, with what is not language, and journalistic writings—as many of Nájera's stories were, in the beginning—have a special obligation in this regard, since already by the late nineteenth century the rhetoric of journalism had begun to eschew subjectivity and self-reflexiveness.[8] But in referring to the Other in this context, I am speaking about a person or a personified entity, and my wish is to underscore Nájera's concern with people: in his journalistic narratives, or crónicas, Nájera invents characters—including even himself as one character among others—but he also describes people from his surroundings, and he frequently addresses his readers directly. Nájera's texts are decidedly *relational*, that is, they are primarily concerned with the opinions of others, with the places that the narrator and his characters occupy in society, and with the interactions and dealings among individuals in public spaces such as streets, churches, theaters, or trolley cars. But who is the Other to whom Nájera relates in his writings? Although his work as a journalist obliged him to portray nearly all the human types and social classes in Mexico City during the regime of Porfirio Díaz, Nájera's stories focus their attention preferentially on people lacking authority, people who are in relatively defenseless, even destitute positions with regard to Nájera. Particularly, the category of the Other in Nájera includes women, children, the elderly, and the poor, but also the readers, and ultimately, I would argue, a personified version of writing itself. I agree with J. Hillis Miller's contention, in *Versions of Pygmalion*, that one of the ways in which ethics manifests itself in narrative texts (literary and otherwise) is through the rhetorical trope of prosopopeia, or personification (11, 13, 136ff.). But I would add that the link between ethics and personification is due not only to a tendency to anthropomorphize when speaking of abstractions (Miller 136), but also to the fact—on which Miller does not dwell—that ethics is primarily concerned with intersubjective relations, with relations between people, and not with the question of being. As Harpham notes, ethics' "postulation of the *ought* is uneasy in the company of philosophy's metaphysical, ontological, phenomenological, or epistemological explorations of what *is*" (*Getting It Right* 7). Or, in Emmanuel Levinas's more trenchant formulation, "the question *par excellence* or the question of philosophy" is "not 'Why being rather than nothing?' but how being justifies itself" (*The Levinas Reader* 86). As I hope to show in my reading of Nájera's text, literary works concerned with an ethics of writing frequently give prosopopeia a peculiar twist of their own by taking personification back to its origins in language and writing even as they make use of it. In "La hija del aire," as will be seen, Nájera creates, Pygmalion-like, a "person," a "character," but he then contextualizes it in a way that allows its traits to be interpreted as emblematic of writing.[9] Remembering our discussion of graphophobia in the introduction, a characterization of language and writing as primarily impotent or defenseless would seem debatable (see also Heidegger, "Language" 189–210); but the instrumental and utilitarian aspect of written language is also undeniable, and it was with this initial belief in the malleability of language that modernists such as Nájera set out to write, although experience would soon teach them otherwise. There is a similar paradox at work between Nájera and his reading public: the reader, apparently subject to the narrator's whims, is after all the one who actually *pays* to be entertained and informed by Nájera and his journalist colleagues. In any case, Nájera preferred to imagine that his readers were humble folk. As Nájera himself writes in an 1881 article:

I shall always arrive on time to the cottage in the country where the
cheerful little girl or the sick old man awaits the arrival of my chronicle,
so that, like a good friend, by the loving warmth of the fire and while the
humble dinner is prepared, I can tell them about the plot of the new theater
play, the adventures of a fashionable actress, or the imaginary splendors of
the festivities. (*Obras IV* 198)

As this quotation suggests, despite his apparent weakness and poverty, the Other is not totally powerless, since he manages to oblige Nájera to respond, to attend to him: "I shall always arrive on time," says Nájera, alluding to his obligation towards the "cheerful little girl" or the "sick old man." In terms taken from Levinas, we could say that Nájera recognizes himself as a hostage to the Other, a condition that springs from the remembrance of death provoked by the Other in the observing subject and the consequent ethical need the subject feels to justify himself, to justify his existence before the Other (*The Levinas Reader* 83). The "cheerful little girl" and the "sick old man" mark emblematically the beginning and the end of human existence, and exemplify perfectly Levinas's dictum that "mortality lies in the Other" (*The Levinas Reader* 83). In more literary terms, it is clear that his need to earn a living through journalism served to remind Nájera of the Other's authority, embodied in the reading public. The term "authority," whose meaning straddles the fields of political theory and literature, almost never appears in the discourse on ethics. Yet I believe it is proper to bring it into this context, not only as a rhetorical move that allows me to evoke the literary con-

cept of the "author," but also because of its close association with certain concepts with which ethics deals constantly, such as justice, right,
and responsibility. *The Oxford Companion to Philosophy* defines "authority" as "a person or group having a right to do or to demand something, including the right to demand that other people do something"
and notes that "authority is invariably and justifiably discussed alongside power" (*Oxford Companion to Philosophy* 68). When Levinas, for
example, speaking of the ethical relationship, states that "the Other becomes my neighbor precisely through the way the face summons me,
calls for me, begs for me, and in so doing recalls my responsibility, and
calls me into question" (*The Levinas Reader* 83). When he speaks of our
"responsibility for the Other" (83), a form of authority is implicit, albeit
one that is based less on power than on a transcendental experience of
the Other that decenters the self, "holding it hostage" to the Other (107;
see also Harpham 7–10). Nothing could apparently be further from the
egotism and the *culte du moi* displayed by many turn-of-the-century
writers than Nájera's intense attention to the Other, an attention bor-
dering on devotion or servility, but one that never loses sight of the question of authority.

An indication of Nájera's curiosity about the relation between otherness and authority is his constant use of pseudonyms. It should be remembered that, like most of his modernist colleagues, Nájera almost
never occupied a position of responsibility that was not literary.[10] Unlike their romantic predecessors, who were first and foremost politicians,
administrators, or landowners, and secondarily writers, the modernists
rarely had more power than what they received from their work with the
pen. Despite the fame and popularity achieved by some modernists, these
elegant and refined poets, aristocrats of the written word, were mere
salaried workers, most of whom, like Nájera, earned their keep through
journalism, an institution that turned words into merchandise and writers into laborers. Nájera's best-known pseudonym, "El Duque Job" (Duke
Job), neatly expressed the two contradictory facets of the modernists'
condition: aristocracy in literature, and trials and tribulations in everyday life. It is almost a commonplace of criticism on Nájera to allude to
the exploitation he suffered in his journalistic work. Nájera's critics and
biographers often describe him as a slave or prisoner of his work (see
Nájera, *Escritos inéditos* ix, and the quotations from the poet Amado
Nervo in Margarita Gutiérrez Nájera 37–38), an image that Nájera himself
clearly cultivated, as evidenced in the following fragment of his chronicle
"Un banquete al maestro Altamirano" (A banquet in honor of Altamirano):

I write from six to eight hours daily; four, I devote to reading, because I don't know yet how one can write without reading anything, if only to see which idea or which phrase one can steal. I publish more than thirty articles a month; I pay my weekly contributions to albums; I write verses when nobody sees me and I read them aloud when nobody hears me, because I'm proud of my good manners. . . . And people still call me lazy! (*Obras. Crítica Literaria, I* 365–366)

The nearly thirty pseudonyms Nájera used throughout his journalistic career evidence the defensive situation in which he found himself in matters of authority. Pseudonyms came about in journalism as devices to protect journalists from accusations of libel. Such accusations, at the end of the nineteenth century, were still frequently resolved by means of duels with swords or pistols (Shattuck 13–14). But pseudonyms were also a means to defuse the question of the journalist's authority and the legitimacy of the knowledge he must display. As Nájera humorously observed, "Writing without a pseudonym is like going out on the street without a shirt. For a writer's ideas to be well received, it is necessary that nobody should know him. No one can believe that the friend with whom he has just played billiards is a man of talent" (*Divagaciones y fantasías* 17). Pseudonyms are thus a paradoxical resource, since they allow journalists to recover their authority at the price of sacrificing their personal identity as authors. But pseudonymy has an even deeper implication: by using it, authors acknowledge and abandon themselves to the alterity of writing. Pseudonymous authors leave aside the romantic pretension of stamping their personality into their writing, acknowledging instead that, in setting pen to paper, by entering the game of writing, they automatically become another. "Je est un autre" (I is another): Rimbaud's paradoxical (and ungrammatical) phrase was consistently put into practice by Nájera, for whom the mythical figure of Proteus, the demigod who could turn into anything and foretell the future, was an emblem of the chronicler's métier.[11] In Nájera's case, that Other whom the writer aspires to become has many faces, but ultimately the writer's goal is to metamorphose into writing itself. That would be Proteus's ultimate metamorphosis: the writer turned into words, so conjoined with his writing that they become inseparable in their total harmony—style turned into man, man into style.[12]

But textualization (with all the risks it implies) was still for Nájera a means to achieve or maintain a measure of authority. Nájera's relation to authority, however, whether literary or political, was tense and ambivalent, as can be seen in a well-known fragment of his "Presentación" to the literary journal he founded in 1894, *La Revista Azul* (The blue journal). The text is signed by the "Duke Job." Explaining his journal's lack of an overarching ideological or aesthetic program, Nájera remarks with his usual wit:

> In parliamentary governments, each ministry presents its program as it begins its term. . . . What do programs and we have in common? Do we have the stiffness and the appearance of government ministers? A program? . . . I have never had a program! A program? That sort of thing is never fulfilled! Our program consists in simply not having any. (*Obras. Crítica literaria, I* 533–535)

Unlike other modernists, particularly Martí and Darío, Nájera here denies having any aspirations to literary authority, and assumes instead an apparently frivolous and irresponsible pose. But such a playful literary anarchism might be only a strategy to produce another, more capricious, personalist, and arbitrary type of authority.

Nájera's rejection of authority in the previously cited text certainly provokes suspicion—particularly the suspicion that his presumed respect towards his fellow beings, towards the Other, actually conceals his envy of the authority that the Other is able to exert almost automatically, effortlessly, merely by being an Other.[13] Pseudonymy and antiauthoritarianism are twin aspects of Nájera's writing: pseudonymy is a paradoxical resource used to buttress the writer's literary authority by means of the otherness of writing, while antiauthoritarianism is the expression of a desire for a more radical otherness, an anarchical impulse that questions and denies authority of any kind. Nájera's ethics of writing seems to be based on a questioning of authority understood as obedience to rules or models, that is, as a form of identity; but such a questioning is then followed by a search for another kind of authority, one based contradictorily on a complete *identification* with an Other.

As previously stated, Nájera's writing displays his intense desire to turn himself into that Other that is written language. This desire for conversion, however, is inconsistent with the idea of difference on which the concepts both of the Other and of language itself are based. What this shows is that in Nájera's ethics as a writer there is still a nostalgia for unity and identity that is ultimately antiethical, since it does not respect the Other's integrity and instead seeks to control and assimilate it. However, written language, like an Other, resists such a subordinate role, since the alterity of writing is so great that it escapes the control of the writing subject. Let us recall that Nájera's concept of writing, like that of virtually all nineteenth-century writers, subordinated writing to voice and to a speaker's living presence. Nevertheless, Nájera's experience in journalism allowed him to recognize the authority and power of writing, despite its apparent condition of servitude. Nájera sought to avail himself of that authority by imitating the differential, alterity-bound aspects of writing in the creation of his literary persona, or rather, personae. What he did not foresee was the resistance writing itself could offer to such a project, since, by submitting to the principles and the laws of writing, he inverted the hierarchical relation between voice and writing, and thus risked losing control over his text and becoming his text's servant instead of its master.

This same process of identification and Protean metamorphosis is repeated, on another scale, in the relationship between Nájera and his readers. That relationship is also bound up, despite his protestations to the contrary, with a search for authority. Unlike some of his fellow modernists, however, Nájera does not seek to base his authority over his readers on claims of superior knowledge, or technical mastery, or even the greater perfection and beauty of his writings. Instead, Nájera grounds his authority in a constant appeal to his readers, in a persistent and solicitous attentiveness whose ultimate aim is seduction. Nájera's writing mimics the codes of seduction, in the hope of generating reciprocal feelings. Thus, Nájera strives to capture his readers' attention through the abundant use of pronominal shifters: *yo, tú, ustedes* (I, you, all of you). Phrases such as the following abound in his style: "You are all going to doubt it"; "Do all of you know Juan Lanas?"; "Do you remember?"; "Why do you ask me for verses?"; etc. (*Cuentos completos* 15, 32, 70, 151). A related technique is his use of apostrophe to address the people or things that are the objects of his narrative: "Speak, you poor little girl: Don't you have a mother?"; "O little morning of San Juan, with your clean shirts and your perfumed soaps! . . ."; "Poor woman!"; etc. (*Cuentos completos* 121, 141, 187). The main function of shifters, according to Roman Jakobson's well-known formulation, is to specify and mark the context of communication, as well as to signal the existence of a communicative situation (130–132), but the proliferation of these forms of address in Nájera's prose denotes a further message, which we might render thus: "I am here, with you; I am talking to you; listen to me, and I will listen to you also." It is not surprising, then, that Nájera frequently makes use of epistolary rhetoric (in which shifters play a key role) and that his chronicles often assume an epistolary form. By themselves, it is true, these "dialogic" traits were not unique to Nájera's style: in fact, they were commonly used by most nineteenth-century writers. But they do appear to be more abundant in Nájera's writings than in those of his contemporaries, such as, for instance, José Martí, whose crónicas contain far fewer direct addresses to his readers.

At the risk of sounding overly florid, one might say that there is a caressing quality to Nájera's writing. In the words of Zygmunt Bauman's description of postmodern ethics as a caress, Nájera's writing "remains open, never tightening into a grip, never 'getting hold of'; it touches without pressing, it moves obeying the shape of the caressed body" (92). This caressing nature is a well-known feature of Nájera's style, familiar to his Spanish American readers and critics, for whom the real-life Nájera is indissolubly linked to the gentle, playful persona of his favorite pseudonym, the "Duke Job." The ultimate purpose of that style was to achieve a sort of amorous platonic union with the Other, with the reader: to make two become one. Such a finality is doomed to failure, however, particularly if one conceives of love not in terms of identity but (as Levinas does) in terms of difference: "To say that sexual duality presupposes a whole is to posit love beforehand as fusion. The pathos of love, however, consists in an insurmountable duality of beings. It is a relationship with what always slips away. The relationship does not *ipso facto* neutralize alterity but preserves it" (*The Levinas Reader* 49).

In fact, if Nájera's use of shifters and apostrophe insists on the presence, the proximity, of the two speakers, then the mediation of the epistolary form and its rhetoric underlines the *distance* that separates writers from their readers. It is within this game, this back-and-forth between immediacy and mediation, between proximity and distance, that the seduction of Nájera's writing operates. As Roland Barthes, comparing literature to striptease, observed with his usual perspicacity: "it is intermittence . . . that is erotic: that of the skin which flashes between two pieces of clothing . . . , between two edges . . . ; it is that flashing which seduces, or better yet: the staging of an appearance-disappearance" (*Le plaisir du texte* 19). In this sense, the use of pseudonyms, the assumption of alterity on Nájera's part, must be seen as an element of his seductive strategy of self-concealment and self-revelation.

But this textual game of hide-and-seek is also highly evocative of childhood. It is certainly reminiscent of the infantile game of *Fort!-Da!* described by Freud in *Beyond the Pleasure Principle* (1920), which Jacques Lacan in turn saw as the beginning of symbolization, of the sense of identity, and of desire (103–104). From this angle, Nájera's constant concern with children and infancy can be seen as another important aspect of his ethical reflection about writing, particularly if we recall that the Latin root of infant, *infans*, means "not yet speaking."

Returning to our reading of "La hija del aire," we might proceed by asking: Who is "the daughter of the air" alluded to in the title? Ostensibly, it is a little girl who works as a trapeze artist in the Circo Orrin. Orphaned or abandoned by her parents, she earns her living as best she can, doing dangerous stunts and then begging alms from the spectators (*Cuentos completos* 120). I would nevertheless argue that, with his powerful gifts of allusion and metaphor, Nájera turns "the daughter of the air" into a complex emblem of the ethics of writing.

To begin with, the language and imagery Nájera uses to refer to this child-acrobat are virtually identical to those with which he refers to his process of poetic creation in one of his best-known poems, "Mis enlutadas" (My women in mourning). In that work, Nájera declares that sadness is the source of his poetry. In Spanish, sadness (*tristeza*) is a feminine noun, and it can be pluralized (*tristezas*), as Nájera does. Nájera personifies his "sadnesses," referring to them as "poor daughters of mine [. . .] white little babies, forsaken by their pitiless mother" (Jiménez, *Antología crítica* 110). His "tristezas" are the "women in mourning" to which the title refers, and they rummage through the poet's conscience, where he keeps "all my sins, / all my faults" (109), forcing him to confess them:

And poking silently, like hungry she-wolves
    they find them, take them out,
and going back to my deathbed
    they show them to me
    and say: Speak. (109)

Significantly, the poet presents himself here as a passive and victimized being, to the point of comparing himself with "the helpless martyred girl-child / [who] bites the harpy / who mistreats her" (109), thus suggesting that the "women in mourning" and he himself are one and the same.

It is important to point out in this context—since there is something inevitable about it—that among Nájera's many pseudonyms, at least one, "Crysantema," was feminine (Margarita Gutiérrez Nájera 37). Needless to say, Nájera was a product of his time and place, and like Nietzsche and most of his male contemporaries, he saw in woman not only the Other par excellence, but also an emblem of the alterity of writing and representation in general (Derrida, *Spurs* 57, 67–71). As Nina Auerbach reminds us, both woman and writing, despite their apparent passivity, appear in male nineteenth-century thought as sources of an original and rebellious energy (17). The male writer's struggle to find his style, to gain control over writing, is often metaphorized in nineteenth-century texts as the attempt to submit a particularly defiant or "hysterical" woman to the legality of an organizing male discourse that seeks to coax from her the secret of her vitality (Auerbach 27–29). Frequently, that struggle was fought with the weapon of mimesis, of imitation, and one commonly finds in turn-of-the-century male literature a deliberate imitation of traits stereotypically associated with women and with homosexuals (Molloy, "La política de la pose" 128–138).[14]

In "La hija del aire," Nájera describes the girl-acrobat as an orphan, "daughter of pain and sadness" (*Cuentos completos* 121), and goes on to present her as a "weak, small, and sickly being" (120) who is prematurely aged, battered by her life in the circus, where the audience "that shouts, that howls" turns her into "their beast, their thing" (119). Despite its seeming specificity, however, this character is not necessarily based on a "real" person. As Carolyn Steedman shows in *Strange Dislocations: Childhood and the Idea of Human Interiority, 1780–1930* (1995), the image of the orphaned girl-child, associated with acrobats and the circus, recurs like a leitmotif throughout Western literature and culture during the nineteenth and twentieth centuries. Steedman locates its origin in the character of Mignon in Goethe's *Wilhelm Meisters Lehrjahre* (Wilhelm Meister's years of apprenticeship, 1795–1796), and argues that the long-lasting cultural life span of the figure of the deformed and helpless child-acrobat is associated with the development of the modern concept of interiority and psychical self-awareness (Steedman 3–5). Certainly, Nájera's girl-acrobat could be seen as a portrait of Nájera's "inner self" in which he presents himself, in the manner of the "decadent" poets, as the artist who is misunderstood and mistreated by the masses, by society.

But there is yet another metaphorical level to this text that has larger implications. Although the figure of the girl-acrobat may indeed be derived from *Wilhelm Meister*, the epithet "la hija del aire" is doubly evocative. From the point of view of Hispanists (as well as of cultured Spanish American readers), Nájera's title immediately evokes the homonymous play of the Spanish golden age by Pedro Calderón de la Barca, written around 1653—of which I will say more below. From a more generalized cultural perspective, the epithet can be regarded as a metaphor for language itself: are not the words "daughters of the air" an image whose venerable tradition dates back as far as the Platonic dialogues (and one that is also implicit in Goethe's Mignon)? In *Phaedrus*, for example, Plato reiterates his theory of poetic inspiration (which he also presents in *Ion*) as a divine breath or afflatus (*The Works of Plato* 429ff.). Interestingly, the disquisition on love and language in *Phaedrus* begins with some insistent allusions to the myth of Boreas. According to the traditional version of the myth to which the character of Phaedrus refers, Boreas, the north wind, kidnapped and raped the nymph Orithyia on the banks of the river Illissus. Socrates disagrees with this version and proposes his own, according to which the wind Boreas made Orithyia fall down (382). The similarities between the traditional myth of Boreas and Orithyia and the legend of Queen Semiramis, on which Calderón bases his play *La hija del aire*, are noteworthy (see the account of the sources of this play by Gwynne Edwards in his critical edition: Calderón xxiii–xxvii). Also quite striking is the similarity between the Platonic reinterpretation of the myth of Boreas and the death of Semiramis in Calderón's play: Semiramis, like Orithyia, falls to her death from a cliff (Calderón 264). The figure of Mignon in Goethe's *Wilhelm Meister* may be interpreted as a romantic version of the Platonic metaphor found in the *Phaedrus*, which presents writing as an androgynous, childlike being, incapable of explaining itself (Goethe 3:134–140; Plato 443–444).

If we accept this essentially allegorical identification of the girl-acrobat with the written word, and of the circus with the process of writing, the image of writing Nájera presents in his tale is one of fearful brutality. The circus's founding principle, its law, appears to be, as the narrator himself observes at the outset, that of "abjection":

> I rarely go to the circus. Any spectacle in which I see displayed human abjection, whether moral or physical, is greatly repugnant to me. However, a few nights ago, I entered the tent that was raised in the small plaza near the Seminario. A contortionist dislocated himself (*un saltimbanco se dislocaba*) with grotesque contortions, exploiting his ugliness, his shamelessness, and his idiocy, like those beggars who, in order to stimulate the expected benevolence of the passersby, display their sores and exploit their rottenness. A woman—almost naked—twisted about like a snake in the wind. Three or four gymnasts, muscled like Hercules, threw at each other large weights, bronze balls, and iron bars. What degradation! What misery! (*Cuentos completos* 119)[15]

Like hapless orphans, words are submitted in the circus of writing to the "heavy hand of a wicked gymnast [who] breaks bones, rips tendons, and dislocates legs and arms, until he turns them into elastic rag firedogs" and they feel "how the trainer's whip bites into their raw flesh" (121). The violence of these images is unusual for Nájera: it intensifies the narrator's confessional tone, giving the whole text an air of agonized introspection allied to an overwhelming sense of guilt. "How you must hate us, poor little girl!" the narrator exclaims (121).

From the opening sentences, the narrator has established the ethical mood of the story by stating that "every spectacle in which I see displayed human abjection, whether moral or physical, is greatly repugnant to me" (119). This moral posture is projected not just towards the Other as a person, but also towards that Other with which Nájera has such a close relationship: language. To equate words with children already implies a biologistic, vitalistic understanding of language, as Derrida observes about Plato's *Phaedrus* in *Dissemination* (79–84). From this concept to endowing language with a sense of personhood and agency is but a short step, which few writers—or philosophers—hesitate to take.[16] In a similar fashion, Nájera personifies language but goes one step further by attempting to represent the moment when living speech becomes broken and "dislocated" into writing. The sickly and frail "daughter of the air" exists in the abject environment of the circus, where her flights are rigorously, painfully controlled for the benefit of others. Nájera seems to be asking: What is my duty, my responsibility, towards language? If we recall Nájera's famously Protean wit and his style based on pseudonyms, puns, and double entendres, the Mexican author seems to suggest that there is something fundamentally immoral in his own artistic manipulation of words, in the violence he exerts on the language with which he must configure his text.

"La hija del aire," Nájera's story, adumbrates an ethics of writing, for it contains a moral questioning of literature's mode of being. Paradoxically, however, such a questioning attacks the very heart of Nájera's literary project, which aims to base its authority on an idea of writing as caress. "You are ill: no one heals you or caresses you softly," says the narrator in his apostrophe to the girl-acrobat (121). To caress language, still more, to "heal" it, freeing it from its fundamental lack and its orphanhood, from the violence inherent in its mode of being, is Nájera's ultimate ambition. His aim is to produce a writing that is smooth and limpid, without breaks, defects, or failings, with which he can identify himself, since Nájera's ethics as a writer, as I stated earlier, imply the writer's metamorphosis into language so as to achieve a harmonious and coherent unity. Nevertheless, as a writer, Nájera cannot fully identify with language, nor avoid doing violence to it, because language is the material on which he works; it is "his beast, his thing." The principles embodied in an ethics of the writer are almost invariably mystified and self-deluding, since they are fundamentally opposed to the notion of writing as an autonomous entity with its own rules and principles. In his fateful visit to the circus, Nájera discovers that the founding principles of writing are difference, disjunction, negativity, emptiness—a whole suite of terms that denote the resistance of writing to the logocentric tradition that Nájera still holds dear (Harpham 80–82). Language as an Other resists losing its otherness, resists being assimilated, and the ethics of writing therefore oscillates, as in a circus spectacle, between authority and anarchy.

Nájera's position in the allegory proposed by his story is at the very least equivocal, for it is not that of the disinterested observer, but one that wavers between identifying with the girl-acrobat and identifying with her tormentors. "Why do you pay my executioners and while away your idleness with my suffering?" (121). When the narrator imagines that the girl asks the spectators this (and the tortuousness—so to speak— of the situation is in itself telling), one of those "executioners" could well be the author himself. As Zygmunt Bauman reminds us, the distinction between caress and abuse, between love and oppression, is diffuse (93–94). The author who initially presents himself as a lover can become a paternalistic tyrant, just as the circus spectacle that at first offers delight can end up causing shame and repugnance. To the chain of inversions suggested by Nájera's text, I would add still another: the being who at first seems most helpless, most innocent, can in the end turn out to be a monster of ambition and a bringer of death.

This is indeed what Nájera's allusion to Calderón's drama in the title of his story suggests.[17] At first, the epithet "daughter of the air" might seem an appropriate and "natural" metaphor for a girl who flies on the trapeze; it could even be regarded as an uplifting metaphor (so to speak), one that poeticizes and gives some dignity to the harsh reality of an exploited child. But in Spanish the allusion to Calderón is far too explicit and too strong; it becomes a Derridean supplement that monstrously threatens to usurp Nájera's own frail and delicate text, which has only the barest outlines of a plot. In fact, we have been speaking of usurpations all along, and this is also one of the principal events in Calderón's play, *La hija del aire*, which tells the story of Semiramis, the legendary queen of Babylon. In this drama where phallic symbols proliferate (swords, arrows, towers, scepters), Semiramis is engendered by the rape of one of

Diana's nymphs. The mother dies in childbirth, and the baby is saved from perishing by birds, hence her epithet. She is later rescued by Tiresias, a priest of Venus. The child Semiramis, a product of the violent discord between Venus and Diana, grows up to become a woman of seductive beauty but ambitious and destructive passions. In the second part of *La hija del aire*, having become queen of Babylon through amorous intrigues and deceit, Semiramis is rejected by the people, who clamor for "a male king" (*un rey varón*; Calderón 166). A popular revolt then gives the crown to the weakling Ninias, Semiramis's son. The evil queen's telling strategy to keep herself in power is to kidnap Ninias and disguise herself as him, making good use of their enormous resemblance. In the end, however, Semiramis is overthrown once and for all, and she dies with her body pierced by arrows while falling from a precipice: "Daughter of the air was I, / now in it I vanish" are her last words (Calderón 264).

A detailed comparison with Nájera's story would fall outside the scope of this chapter, and in any case, the supplementary (in Derrida's sense) nature of the allusion to Calderón leads the reader to look beyond the story's present moment, towards the future. The Calderonian allusion may well be Nájera's way of reminding his readers of the subversive potential of writing: like the girl-acrobat, Calderón's Semiramis is an orphan, and this trait, along with her mimetic qualities, her death by a fall, and her total lack of "principles" (in every sense of the word), associates her with Plato's view of written language in *Phaedrus*. But Semiramis is also a baroque prototype of the turn-of-the-century femme fatale; she is what the girl-acrobat may grow up to become. Already, though she is a mere child, the girl-acrobat's power to enthrall is so great that it has drawn the story's narrator back to the circus he dislikes so much. What would she become if she continued to grow and mature? Might this be really what the narrator was trying to find out when he returned to the circus?

The circus is a form of theater, and Nájera was also a theater critic. Theater's highly suggestive function as a perturbing element, as an Other (which will be discussed in greater detail in chapter 5 of this book), threatens the orderly discourse of this story. Theatricality, with its emphasis on performance, on action, may well be regarded as narrative's Other, since narrative seems more closely allied to the belatedness and fixity of writing. In this case, however, Nájera's allusion to Calderón's play mimics the ambivalence of the *lapsus linguae*, for although the story and the play share the same title, Nájera seemingly wishes to repress any parallelism between the two texts. Remember how, from the beginning, the girl he calls "daughter of the air" has already disappeared in the narrative's present moment, and has been replaced by another "girl-martyr" who does acrobatic tricks on a horse (121). Nevertheless, the narrator's unifying mania betrays him, when in the next sentence he states that there is no difference between the girl-acrobat and the girl-rider, since "it is all one and the same" (121).

Who is she, then, this "daughter of the air" to which the text refers? Is she the helpless girl-child (Mignon) or the tyrannical, man-devouring seductress (Semiramis)? And, by extension, who is Manuel Gutiérrez Nájera: a kindly Proteus who pliantly molds and submits himself to every circumstance, or a sadistic exploiter of children? It is shocking to realize how many children die in Nájera's stories, from "La familia Estrada" (The Estrada family) and "La balada de Año Nuevo" (The New Year's ballad) to "La mañana de San Juan" (The morning of San Juan) and "La pasión de Pasionaria" (The passion of Pasionaria; *Cuentos completos* 61–69, 108–112, 141–145, 146–150). The following witticism from Nájera's story "La odisea de Madame Théo" (Madame Théo's odyssey, 1883) takes on ominous resonances after one has read "La hija del aire": "It is a mistake to believe that little girls who die without being baptized go to Limbo: little girls are never innocent when they die" (179). Not the least of the strange effects created by this story's clash of values is its suggestion—prefiguring Borges—that there is always something sinister about author-figures. Authors are "sinister," however, not because they are demonic yet heroic figures (as in the romantic tradition), but because they flourish in a state of abjection: implicitly, they are placed in the same category with liars, thieves, impostors, traitors, perhaps even sexual perverts and murderers.[18] The measure of Nájera's modernity is given by the links between writing and abjection posited in this story. In his awareness of writing's relationship with evil, Nájera opens, in the Spanish American context, a question that would be taken up much more forcefully and explicitly, a few decades later, by numerous twentieth-century writers in Europe and the Americas.

Of more immediate import to our reading, however, is the question of what values govern this story. Nájera's ethical inquiry into what one might call the "ontology" of literature led him to discover a conflict between two concepts of ethics: that of the writer, which in the work of the modernists is based on identity and sameness, and that of writing, which is founded instead on otherness and difference. Like Martí in *Versos libres* (Free verses), Nájera discovers in "La hija del aire" that poetry is "fierce and capricious," but unlike the Cuban poet, he does not wish to "tell it to the honest folk," and instead tries to repress his discovery by means of a moralizing fable about exploited childhood, taking refuge in the harmonizing ideals of an ethics of the writer. But the discordant face of writing resists such repression and returns, as in lapses or dreams, to reaffirm simultaneously the authority and the subversive power of the Other.

As noted earlier, "La hija del aire" may well be regarded as an inaugural text in the Spanish American tradition of literary-philosophical reflection about writing and ethics. Nájera achieves this primarily by means of his personification of writing in the figure of the girl-acrobat. Nevertheless, as in the twentieth-century works of Borges, Carpentier, and Severo Sarduy, Nájera's prosopopeia is subverted even as it is formulated (on Borges and Carpentier, see chapters 4 and 5 of this book). Instead of buttressing the illusion that the girl-acrobat is a "real" person for whom the readers can feel pity and compassion (as they are invited to do at the end of the story), the text, by means of its allusions to Calderón's Semiramis and to Goethe's Mignon as well as to the topic of the femme fatale, once again turns her into an abstraction, an emblem, returning her to the writing from which she came. This does not happen, however, without raising a series of ethical questions about the writer's relationship to language and the link between violence and writing: If writing is inherently violent, is the writer not an accomplice to that violence, as dubious and abject an entity as writing itself? Is there any possibility of justice in the context of writing, or is writing only governed, as in a circus, by a mixture of anarchy and force? If justice evokes a sense of equity and measure, the issue in Nájera's story becomes then a question of balance, a balancing act (like the girl-acrobat's). How can one do good in writing without representing (without repeating) evil? This dilemma may account for the story's laconic style, brevity, and lack of plot, as well as for the paucity of its anecdote. After all, if the encounter with "the daughter of the air" is also a confrontation with violence and evil, it makes sense to limit to the minimum one's exposure, to make the encounter with evil as brief and harmless as possible.

Significantly, Nájera's work, like that of Borges in the twentieth century, consisted mostly of short pieces: his stories and crónicas. He published only one novel—tellingly titled *Por donde se sube al cielo* (Where one climbs up to heaven)—as a newspaper serial in 1882, but it was not printed as a book until 1994, in a scholarly edition. Other modernist contemporaries of Nájera were just as scrupulous with regard to the novelistic genre: Martí and the Colombian José Asunción Silva also wrote only one novel each, both printed posthumously.[19] But not all Spanish American writers at the end of the nineteenth century were modernists. Spanish American modernism coexisted with other literary modalities, such as realism and naturalism, which were exclusively linked to prose fiction and to the novel. The Spanish American naturalists in particular, like their European counterparts, actively sought to confront evil in their works. Although they were mostly concerned with evil in the form of social injustice, in some instances their inquiries became more profound and self-reflexive, directed towards the act of writing itself. This was the case for the Puerto Rican Manuel Zeno Gandía, to whose novel, *La charca*, we now turn.

## CHAPTER 2

## Silvina's Fall

## Manuel Zeno

## Gandía's

## Epicurean

## Ethics of

## Writing in

## La charca

She fell with the heaviness of what would not rise again. She rolled end over end, crashing against obstacles, bouncing from rock to rock, stopping for an instant against a tree trunk until her weight pulled her again. In her fall, she dragged along masses of rocks that, more compassionate than men, seemed to want to follow her, in a funerary cortege, to the bottom.

She fell down the cliff leaving a bloody trail, a red furrow. It was life returning to its origins, the borrowed nourishment rejoining the earth, matter returning its debris to the cradle of all.

— MANUEL ZENO GANDÍA,
*La charca, in fine*

There is something more to be learned about this
matter:
When bodies are borne on down and down through
emptiness
By their own weight, at a moment one cannot fix
At uncertain points in space, they give way a little
To one side or another in a slight deflection.

If they did not, then everything would fall down,
Like drops of rain falling for ever through emptiness,
There would be no occasion for encounters of
elements
And if one did not strike another there would be
no creation.

— LUCRETIUS,
*De rerum natura* II

Silvina's deadly fall in the last pages of Manuel Zeno Gandía's *La charca* (1894) simultaneously marks the end of the story and the beginning of the novel, since, as often happens in novels, the tale can only be told after the story has ended.[1] The double-faced nature of this event (and duplicity, as will be seen, is very much at issue in *La charca*) is underscored in the narrative when Silvina's dead body concludes its fall literally at the feet of her mother, Leandra, as if returning to the moment of her birth: "the creation next to its maker, the tatter next to the rag, the fetus next to its mother's womb, where, with unconscious bestiality, it was formed by chance" (*La charca* 213). Silvina's death also harks back to the very first lines of the novel, where her fall is prefigured: "At the edge of the cliff, holding onto two trees so as not to fall, Silvina bent over the incline and looked impatiently down there, towards the bed of the river, shouting with all her might" (5).

End or beginning? Destruction or creation? The conditions of Silvina's existence, already abject from the beginning, become progressively worse as the novel develops. Dying by falling off a cliff would be simply the nadir (so to speak) and the expected conclusion of a miserable life. And yet, as I will show presently, in the context of the natural symbolism with which this character is fraught (her very name, Silvina, suggests an association with the Latin *silva*, origin of the Spanish *selva*, "jungle" or "forest"), as well as of the underlying Epicurean and Lucretian ideas in the discourse of *La charca*, Silvina's death becomes a beginning, an origin of sorts. The implications of this ambiguity become even more far-reaching when we recall that *La charca* was the first in a projected series of eleven novels, collectively titled *Crónicas de un mundo enfermo* (Chronicles of a sick world). Silvina's death was meant to be the overture to a vast novelistic project.[2]

A still more basic question concerns the necessity of that death. Why must this most innocent of the novel's main characters perish? To reply that she dies in order to close off the novel, or conversely, to begin the novelistic series, is to offer a purely aesthetic justification for an action whose ethical implications are profound. My reading is instead based on the hypothesis that Silvina, like Nájera's "daughter of the air," is a personification of writing, and that her demise at the end of *La charca* is in part an allegory about writing's origins as well as an expression of Zeno's Epicurean-inspired conception of the ethics of writing.

*La charca*'s concern with origins and sources—and in general, with the question of creation—is indicative of its ethical thrust and of the direction of that ethical impulse. Creation as action and concept, as Geoffrey Galt Harpham argues, is inseparable from the ethical notion of responsibility, a responsibility so great that it becomes almost an impediment to creation itself. This burden of responsibility is why "narratives of creation" always disavow the author's authority, usually by telling "the tale of the domination of the creator" by an outside force or entity that is the "true" source of the text (Harpham 188ff.). In Zeno's series of narratives about a "sick world," *La charca* plays the part of

Genesis, or its cosmogony. As such, it clearly bears the burden of all openings, of all beginnings, which is to lay down the principles, the ground rules, for what is to follow. Chief among those ground rules, I submit, is Zeno's inquiry into the ethics of writing. Like Nájera's story "La hija del aire," Zeno's novel contains, at a certain level, an ethical reflection about its own nature as a literary work.

That ethics is one of the main motivations (if not *the* main motivation) for naturalist fiction in Europe and the Americas is hardly a topic for debate today. Despite the scandals that greeted almost every new naturalist work around the turn of the century, which included accusations of obscenity and immorality, the moralizing and socially reformist intent of naturalist fiction was openly declared from the start by its authors.[3] Arguably, the naturalists' notorious descriptive preference for aspects of life considered improper or scatological during their time may be seen as the antithesis of modernism's obsessive cult of ideal beauty. In other words, if both symbolism and Spanish American modernism equated the beautiful with the good, naturalism used the *ugly* for the sake of the good. Naturalism's antiaestheticist attitude seems to imply that for these writers, unlike the modernists, ethics and aesthetics were not, in Wittgenstein's phrase, "one and the same" (*Notebooks* 77, *Tractatus* 6.421). But antiaestheticism is an aesthetic ideology as well, and in practice the naturalists displayed just as strongly as the modernists their belief in what might be called, using Paul de Man's terminology, a "salvationist poetics."[4]

Naturalism's penchant for the depiction of whatever is ugly or distasteful (according to the criteria of its day) also signals that this narrative mode is at least partially produced under the sign of abjection, as the concept is defined by Julia Kristeva: "a crossing over of the dichotomous categories of Pure and Impure, Prohibition and Sin, Morality and Immorality" (18). It might be argued, however, that the naturalists' ultimate faith in science, in science's capacity to "purify" or "redeem" the abject, serves to counterbalance their apparently unflinching descent into the abyss, thus rendering superficial their inquiry into abjection (Kristeva 17). As I will show, this is not quite the case with the work of Manuel Zeno Gandía, whose probe into the essence of naturalism in *La charca* leads him to reflect implicitly about the role of abjection in all writing.

During the twentieth century, the pendulum of opinion about naturalism swung from the condemnation of its presumed "immorality" by right-wing critics, to the denunciation of its discourse as reactionary by Marxist critics such as George Lukács, who remarked that Zola's definition of society as natural makes social change unthinkable (Petrey 776–

777). The contradiction pointed out by Lukács and others, however, is but a surface manifestation of a deeper dilemma caused by naturalism's attempt to ground morality on nature. Clearly, the relative persuasiveness of such attempts depends on one's definition of nature. Nevertheless, despite the claims of social Darwinists on the right, or of works such as Friedrich Engel's *Dialectics of Nature* (1875–1876) on the left, by the end of the nineteenth century and the beginning of the twentieth, a variety of voices in the sciences and the arts, from Darwin himself to Nietzsche and Flaubert, argued that nature does not take sides, or, put in another way, that to attribute moral agency to nature was to engage in gross anthropocentrism (Donato 225). As I hope to show throughout my reading of *La charca*, Zeno's discourse wavers between the two attitudes: like Zola, Zeno attempts to ground a moral argument on nature, but unlike the French writer, Zeno displays an intense awareness of nature's otherness, of its utterly objective, inhuman character. The resulting tension provides the framework for Zeno's ethical inquiry into writing.

At the outset, however, I must point out that my reading of *La charca* differs markedly from the traditional interpretations of this novel. In my view, its significance in Spanish American literary history resides not in being an exemplary naturalist novel in the style of Emile Zola, but, to the contrary, in being a profound and trenchant critique of naturalism from within the postulates of naturalism itself. The most cursory reading of *La charca* shows that it differs noticeably from the novels of Zola even as it invokes them as its models. *La charca*'s epigraph, inexplicably omitted from most current editions, is in fact a sentence from Zola's *Le docteur Pascal* (1893): "Say all to know all, to cure all" (Zola 1222).[5] *La charca*'s rural setting also sets it apart from the novels of the brothers Goncourt, although it does share with their works a more polished and self-consciously artistic style than Zola's.[6] Few Spanish American naturalists, it is true, were blind followers of the theory and practice of Zola or the Goncourts, but Zeno's *La charca* stands out because of its profound questioning of the philosophical principles of naturalism. Even as it translates and critiques the postulates of Zola's "experimental novel," testing them in the crucible of the Spanish American milieu, *La charca* evokes the origins of "naturalism" in the broadest sense of the term by returning to the origins of "natural philosophy," that is, of science, and in particular to the first deliberate attempt in Western literature to link natural philosophy with literature: the poem *De rerum natura* (c. 55 B.C.) by the Roman Lucretius.

Summarizing the details of *La charca*, including its plot, is no easy task, for although it follows the conventions of realism and has a well-defined structure, its narrative, as befits a work dominated by metaphors of water, is as meandering as the course of a mountain stream. The action in *La charca* takes place in the interior mountains of Puerto Rico, where, at the end of the nineteenth century, coffee was king and thousands of landless peasants toiled in the coffee haciendas that belonged to a few landowners, many of whom were wealthy Majorcan or Corsican immigrants. Following the social stratification presented by the novel in its first paragraphs (6–7), the main characters are: the landowners Juan del Salto and Galante, the merchant Andújar, the foreman Montesa, the escaped convict Deblás (who is Andújar's cousin), and the peasants Ciro, Marcelo, Gaspar, Leandra, and Silvina. The most coherent sequence of events in the novel's plot concerns the scheme by Gaspar and Deblás, with the aid of Silvina (whom Gaspar intimidates into doing his bidding), to rob Andújar, the owner of the only "general store," who exploits the peasants mercilessly (I summarize here pages 67–70 and 121–142 of *La charca*). Gaspar and Deblás are moved not by class hatred but by simple greed. Little do they know that Andújar has been warned of their plot by the peasant Marcelo and has run off to the lowlands with his saddlebags full of money, leaving his coffers empty inside his house. On the night of the attempted robbery, in his confusion and nervousness, Gaspar (accompanied by Silvina, who faints at the crucial moment) kills Deblás, whom, in the darkness, he mistakes for Andújar.

The consequences of the crime involve not only Gaspar and Silvina but also Silvina's lover, Ciro, as well as Ciro's brother, Marcelo, and Silvina's mother, Leandra. The subsequent criminal investigation, which is carried out by judges and forensic scientists from the city and is portrayed as laughably inept, is clearly a parody of positivism and, by extension, of Zola's naturalism (*La charca* 143–164; see also Alvarez 193–212). In the midst of this story, long passages are devoted to the solitary musings of the wealthy and honest landowner Juan del Salto about the evils of the island's socioeconomic situation, as well as to Del Salto's conversations with his friends Doctor Pintado and Father Esteban, in which they propose and compare various projects to reform Puerto Rican society, without reaching agreement. While some conservative critics view Juan del Salto as the novel's main character (thus exhibiting a certain class prejudice),[7] it is more accurate to say that Zeno features the two women, Leandra and Silvina, with whom the novel opens and closes. A salient subplot in the novel is the story of Silvina's attempt to escape, through her romance with Ciro, the degradation of her common-law marriage to Gaspar and of the sexual relations she is forced to sustain with Galante by Leandra, who is one of Galante's many mistresses. Indeed, as I will explain shortly, Leandra and Silvina, mother and daughter, are complementary and interdependent characters in terms of their symbolic functions in the novel.

Zeno's greatest achievement in *La charca* is his portrayal of the depressed economic and social situation of what at that time constituted a large and significant sector of Puerto Rico's population (Picó 192–220, Scarano 459–508), which he accomplishes without falling into the crude and mechanical determinism of Zola's brand of naturalism. Zeno seems to have derived his curiously contemporary-seeming version of nonmechanistic materialism from Lucretius's *De rerum natura*. Although Zeno never alludes to *De rerum natura* or to Lucretius in the text of *La charca*, readers familiar with the classic poem cannot but hear strong echoes of it throughout Zeno's novel.[8] The influence of Lucretius is obvious, for instance, in the much-studied and much-commented descriptions of nature in *La charca*,[9] in which nature is seen as a labyrinthine and fecund jungle in constant process of change and renewal, but also as an entity indifferent to the lives of human beings that "offers flowery havens for love, for sleep, for crime" (*La charca* 53). These passages correspond exactly to Lucretius's concept of nature, in which the natural world is an unending vortex of creation and destruction that is totally amoral and completely independent from the designs of gods and men (the questions at the end of the following passage obviously echo in *La charca* as well):

This is the way to see the nature of thunder
And to understand how it produces its effects,
And not by reading books of Etruscan saws
To find out exactly what the gods are up to,
Where they have sent their fire from, or in what direction
It has turned, or in what manner it has entered
Behind closed doors, done what it will, and escaped,
Or what disasters from heaven thunder can bring.
If it is Jupiter and the other gods
Who shake the glittering sky with their terrible crashes
And if they can hurl their fires wherever they like
Why don't they strike at people who have committed
Revolting crimes and make them spew out flames?
Stick them through the middle and make examples of them?
Why must it instead be the innocent,
People whose consciences are as clear as noon-day,
Who get caught up in the whirlwind of heavenly fire? (187)

Lucretius's idea of nature, derived from the writings of Epicurus (c. 341–270 B.C.), is surprisingly modern, as commentators of the poem have continuously observed since the nineteenth century.[10] It is a radically materialist concept of the cosmos, based on the atomistic hypothesis: "The whole of nature consists of two elements: / There are material bodies, and there is empty space" (*De rerum natura* 26). Zeno also is deeply materialistic in *La charca*; the most explicit passage in this respect is the description of the sleepiness that overcomes Deblás while he is ransacking Andújar's store:

Matter surged with its despotic necessities, and lacking the counterweight of reason, that miserable mass succumbed to narcolepsy, and Deblás fell into a deep, overpowering, bestial sleep. . . . He became inert matter that had suspended all form of relation, a gross form of yeast that lacks self-awareness and does not know when, pushed by force, it must pile up to form planets or disintegrate to form pus; a living mass, sunk by sleep into quietism, enfolding the honest man and the evildoer alike; neutral clay that can be used for anything, from embellishing the breast of a Venus to hardening the hoof of a centaur. (186–187)

The allusion to Venus in this passage (with its obvious modernist echoes) is not the only one in the novel. Leandra is clearly a parody of Venus: suffice it to recall that, at the beginning of the novel, answering her daughter Silvina's call, she comes out of the "waterfalls and whirlpools" of the river in which she was washing clothes, in order to feed her son Pequeñín (5–6). In chapter 5, the narrator refers to "her enormous breasts" (81), and at the end of the novel, to her "voluminous belly . . . so many times consecrated to prolific Venus" (213). The significance of these allusions to the goddess of love becomes clearer when we recall that Lucretius begins his poem with an invocation to the "mother of all Romans: moreover, everyone's pleasure, / Comfortable Venus" (15). In Lucretius's fundamentally antimetaphysical conception, Venus works as a metaphor to refer to the generative principle of *inclination*, the famous *clinamen* (which also means "deviation" or "declension" in Latin). Venus's metaphorical link with the clinamen is understandable if we recall that she is always associated from birth with the waters, with the foam of the sea, and if we note furthermore that in Lucretius's cosmogony, chaos is conceived as a current of atoms in perpetual free fall through the void, "like drops of rain" (50). Within that current there are formed occasional deviations and collisions, which in turn produce turbulences, cyclical vortexes that constitute principles of order: by virtue of the clinamen, order issues from chaos like Venus from the sea foam.[11] As Michel Serres has shown, the privileging of hydraulic physics (whose systematization Lucretius derives from Archimedes) over mechanics is evident throughout *De rerum natura*, and this allows Lucretius to display a sophisticated understanding of natural phenomena as diverse as rain and thunder, the evolution of species, epidemics, and magnetism (Serres, *La naissance de la physique* 85–125).

The privileging of hydraulics is in fact the principal way in which Zeno's philosophy differs from and implicitly criticizes Zola's naturalism. Zeno rejects a biological model to structure his novel and instead bases his picture of Puerto Rican life on the older discipline of hydraulics, the branch of physics that deals with liquids and their flow.[12] *La charca*'s recourse to hydraulics as a source of metaphors and as a structuring principle of its narrative is announced in its very title, which can be variously understood and translated as "stagnant waters" or, as I would argue, "the reservoir." Water metaphors appear throughout *La charca*,[13] but water is also a real and concrete presence in the geographic milieu where the novel's action occurs, the Central Mountain Chain of Puerto Rico, which is indeed a Lucretian world of "inclined planes" (*La charca* 30), fertile nature, and abundant rivers and creeks that erode the land on their way to the sea. It is a world wrapped in clouds and frequently threatened by thunderstorms and hurricanes (*La charca* chapter 6). Contrary to the rather static view suggested by the title (in one of its interpretations), the environment of *La charca* is in an almost constant state of flux; the appearance of stagnation comes from the fact that the characters are trapped in socioeconomic cycles, in man-made turbulences, from which only death can liberate them.

The parallels between Lucretius's text and *La charca* go beyond the similarities I have enumerated thus far. There are structural analogies as well,[14] but more significantly, *La charca*'s discourse itself is constituted following the principles of the atomistic and hydraulic physics of Lucretius. According to that physics, as noted above, nature, the world of things, is made up of atoms in constant motion, in constant flux and reflux: matter is a vortex, a turbulence, a cycle of atoms, within the homogeneous flow of chaos. In *La charca*, the nature that surrounds the characters, specifically the forest, stands for that tangled and multiform chaos that, by virtue of the clinamen, the (sexual) inclinations between living beings, becomes fecund and (re)productive. Within that chaos there are islands of order, such as the coffee plantations, where the ceaseless flow of people and things is submitted to the implacable cycle of work, of production. The "charca" to which the title of Zeno's novel alludes metaphorically is made up of the whole social system: plantations, landowners, peons, and everything that makes up and feeds that whirlpool, that vortex that systematically, in a cruel yet orderly fashion, exploits and destroys human beings.[15]

Dispossessed of their lands, the peasants must submit themselves to the rigors of work on the coffee plantations. Their nourishment no longer comes directly from the fecund nature that surrounds them, but instead, in degraded form, through Andújar's store (62). The peasants' dispossession of their lands is the concrete justification, within the text, for the disjunction between nature and human affairs that Zeno underlines throughout his novel, such as when the narrator states that Silvina "looked [at the landscape] without seeing [it]. That poetic exterior, which was so familiar to her, did not lead her into reverie" (6). Nevertheless, this separation is seemingly contradicted or nuanced in other parts of the text—such as the previously cited passage about Deblás's somnolence or the description of Silvina's death (which I have used as an epigraph to this chapter)—which stress the common substrate that links all of the characters in *La charca* with the natural world: their materiality. The social structure depicted in *La charca* tries to keep people and the land separate, but the novel argues that the social structure itself can be understood and interpreted on the basis of the same physical laws that constitute nature.

If one had to characterize *La charca* synthetically in a single phrase, it could be called "a novel of doubt." *La charca* is a hypercritical text, made up of multiple layers that question, interfere, and parody one another without producing positive knowledge. Thus, in a salient example of internal parody, Zeno compares Silvina, when she is lost in her own thoughts at the beginning of the novel, to a "statue" (6). Later, Juan del Salto, who constantly flirts with grossly positivistic ideas and images, develops a mechanistic metaphor in which he compares Puerto Rican society with a statue that must be set in motion by means of "freedom" and "expansion" (187). Finally, in the novel's last pages, the dismembered body of Silvina is compared with "a relief carved in granite . . . [a] funerary statue" (213). In a bitter parody of the statue of which Juan del Salto spoke, Silvina, though freed from the despotism of Gaspar and of her last common-law husband, Inés Marcante, ends up immobile, petrified in death.

The epistemological critique displayed in these passages gives Zeno's novel, despite its eminently modern naturalist lineage, a curiously postmodern air.[16] Paradoxically, however, Zeno's apparent "postmodernity" may also be attributed to his source in Lucretius. Michel Serres's persuasive reading of *De rerum natura* in *La naissance de la physique dans le texte de Lucrèce: Fleuves et turbulences* (1977) argues strongly for Lucretius as a precursor of both postmodern science and postmodern literature (although Serres's book, published two years before Lyotard's *The Postmodern Condition*, never uses that term). Lucretius's postmodernity is double: In terms of his epistemology, he represents a rejection of the global, universalizing pretensions of modern science (which has its roots in Plato and the Stoics, but which emerges as such only after Cartesian rationalism) in favor of a local, non-"imperialistic" model of knowledge (Serres, *La naissance de la physique* 231–237). In literary terms, Lucretius's postmodernity *avant la lettre* is a function of his profound awareness of the material aspect of writing and, more specifically, of his understanding that writing displays the same principles of disjunction and difference as those posited by Epicurean physics for empirical reality (Serres, *La naissance de la physique* 167–193). Writing, too, is composed of two elements, "material bodies and . . . empty space," which, in their nearly endless permutations, reproduce complexities analogous to those of nature. Lucretius even compares atoms with written characters, apparently alluding to the age-old concept of the "book of nature" that was revived centuries later by Goethe and the romantics (Curtius 319–326):

It is not so different as you might think with verses [than with particles],
For so many letters are common to so many words,
Yet the words and verses differ from one another
And that is true of meaning as well as sound. (36)

. . . So that things indeed are made up of a mixture of elements.
And so of course it is in these very verses,
For many letters are common to many words
And yet you have to admit both the words and the verses
Differ clearly enough and are made of different elements:
No two are of identical composition
But as a rule they do not all resemble one another.
And so in other things there are common elements
But that does not mean that, looked at as a whole,
They do not differ widely from one another. (62)

Reading *De rerum natura* in terms of its own Epicurean physics, Michel Serres demonstrates that the disorder attributed by critics to Lucretius's poem is in fact a coherent formal representation of the physics the poem discusses (172), but also that, conversely, Epicurean physics provides

Lucretius with a model of writing as difference that foreshadows Derrida (to whom Serres does not openly allude).

Lucretius's work proposes not only a differential notion of writing contrary to the dictates of nineteenth-century literature (which was still centered on writing as an adjunct to the spoken word), but also an ethics congruent with that notion. This ethics, derived from the teachings of Epicurus and widely caricatured in popular accounts of Epicureanism since Roman times as an egotistic hedonism, was in fact largely manifested as an austere renunciation of the world (*The Oxford Companion to Philosophy* 239). For Epicurus, "the good life is secured by kindness and friendship with those about you, and by moderation of appetite so that, although nothing is forbidden, he who measures his desires by the utilitarian standard and needs least has the firmest grasp on happiness" (*The Oxford Companion to Philosophy* 240). It was a liberal, pluralistic, tolerant conception, always seeking to avoid ambition, and instead striving for equilibrium through an economy of effort.[17] Michel Serres summarizes it thus:

Listen now to the lessons of Epicureanism, which boil down to the following: reduce to a minimum the network of relations in which you are submerged. Live in the garden, a small space, with a few friends. No family, if it is possible, and, in any case, no politics. But especially this. Here is the object, objects, the world, nature, physics. Aphrodite-pleasure is born of the world and the waters. Mars is in the forum and in the armed crowd. Reduce your relations to a minimum and bring your objects to the fore; reduce the intersubjective to a minimum and increase the objective to a maximum. With your back turned on politics, study physics. Peace through neutrality. Such knowledge brings happiness, or at least the end of our worst pains. Forget the sacred; that means: forget the violence that founds it and forget the religious that links men to one another. Consider the object, objects, nature. (*La naissance de la physique* 164–165)

If we now return to the concepts developed in my reading of Nájera's "La hija del aire," it would seem that Lucretius and Zeno share a similar ethics of the writer (distinct from the ethics of writing). Moreover, their ethics of the writer, unlike that of Nájera and the other modernists, is based on an acceptance of difference, not on a search for identity. It would therefore appear to be much closer to the ethics of writing. If that were the case, however, one would expect that as writers Lucretius and Zeno should display a high degree of respect for the Other.[18] But as Serres observes, one of Epicureanism's goals was the attainment of maximum objectivity, which implies a corresponding tendency to objectify people, as well as things. Lucretius's (and, by extension, Zeno's) ethics places difference in the service of objectification.

"Scientific" and dispassionate, the Epicurean and Lucretian vision is inimical not only to religion but also to a sense of tragedy and its emotional impact, as can be seen in Lucretius's condemnation of the sacrifice of Iphigenia:

It is religion that produces impieties.
Think of what happened at Aulis. They took the girl to the altar
—The most respectable men in Greece, the convinced top people—
The blindfold fell from her eyes and she saw her father
Standing there with the executioner priests
Who were trying to keep their carving knives out of *his* sight
And all the bystanders merely blubbered and liked it
Or, dumb with terror, knelt squalidly on the floor. (17)

Nevertheless, banished tragedy returns in *De rerum natura* by means of an original violence through which both critical thought and writing are founded: Lucretius's poem, which sings of the objective contemplation of nature, closes with the chilling description of the plague of Athens, in which "everywhere / the temples of the divinities were piled with bodies" (210). With regard to Lucretius's two key concepts, "atoms" and "void," Michel Serres observes that the Latin term Lucretius uses to signify "void," *inane*, derives from the Greek verb *inein*, which means "to purge or expel," and that "the word 'temple' is of the same family as 'atom'" (Serres, *La naissance de la physique* 165). This etymology suggests that at the root of Epicurean thought lies a quasi-religious concept of nature as a sort of *pharmakos*, or scapegoat, for through its study and analysis humans can purge themselves of their vices and passions. This concept makes the scientific study of nature, or the writing of a poem such as *De rerum natura*, a symbolic repetition of the violent sacrificial act with which physics was founded, an act that Epicureans claimed to repudiate. As Serres concludes:

Nature is still another sacrificial substitute. Violence is still—and always—in physics. Thus the atoms-germs sack Athens and the last survivors kill each other. *Quod erat demostrandum*. It is not politics or sociology that is projected on nature, but the sacred. Beneath the sacred, there is violence. Beneath the object, relations reappear. (*La naissance de la physique* 165–166)

Similarly, although his discourse is highly nuanced and extremely sensitive to alternative points of view (in this sense remaining ethical),

Zeno, like Lucretius, also falls into a near religious "deification" of materialist theory, which leads him towards a view of the world as an ultimately chaotic and indifferentiable universe. In Zeno's novel we observe
many of the same antinomies seen in Lucretius: objectivity versus subjectivity, science versus religion, isolation versus relation, peace versus
violence. These antinomies are openly exposed and explored in the dialogues among Juan del Salto, Doctor Pintado, and Father Esteban in chapters 3 and 9, in which, in an allegorical fashion, each character takes the
position represented by his profession: the physician argues about social
reform from an atheistic, "scientific" standpoint; the priest speaks from
the viewpoint of religion; while the landowner, Juan del Salto, listens to
both and attempts, fruitlessly, to mediate. However, Zeno slyly suggests
the irrelevance of these characters, as well as their constructed, allegorical nature, by means of their names. Doctor Pintado's appellation literally means "painted" and is evocative not only of artistic artifice (such
as a painting) but also of the Spanish colloquialism *estar pintado en la
pared* (to be painted on the wall), which denotes marginality, as in the
English expression "to be a wallflower." Father Esteban's name evokes
Saint Stephen, the first martyr of the Catholic Church, who was stoned
for his beliefs (again, an indication of marginality), and Juan del Salto's
name is emblematic of his own indecisive nature, which "jumps" (*salta*)
from one idea to another.

The antinomies examined self-referentially in the aforementioned
dialogues are also active in *La charca*'s discourse, most noticeably in the
novel's ambivalent use of the traditional categories of tone and point of
view. I am not referring to the contrast, noted by many critics, between
the "realistic" or "naturalistic" passages and the poetic descriptions of
nature in the novel. The ambivalence is of another sort: Throughout
much of the novel, the tone is uninflected, descriptive, dispassionate,
and the point of view is that of Gustave Flaubert's godlike, omniscient,
but invisible narrator. However, there are also numerous instances in
which the tone changes unexpectedly to express astonishment, sadness,
perplexity, or drollery, and the narrative voice emits specific value judgements about the characters, assuming a function analogous to that of
the chorus in Greek tragedy.[19] This ambiguity in tone and point of view,
along with Zeno's use of allegory in the characters' names, also undermines his objectivist stance.

In fact, allegory's effect in this novel moves in two different and opposite directions. On the one hand, it undermines Zeno's objectivism because it reveals the ideological framework of *La charca*, thus showing
that the novel does not spring (as it would have its readers believe)

directly from the observation of reality, but is in fact the embodiment of certain ideas about Puerto Rican society. On the other hand, however, allegory also works to corrode the novel's basis in prosopopeia, or personification. Although allegory itself uses personification (by embodying concepts in humanlike characters), the realization by the reader that the characters in the novel are at least in part allegorical undoes the illusion of personhood created by prosopopeia. In *La charca* we witness the same back-and-forth movement with regard to prosopopeia as in Nájera's "La hija del aire." Like a literary Pygmalion, Zeno uses personification to create his characters, only to subsequently undo the effects of prosopopeia by giving his characters patently allegorical names, or even by referring to some of them, metaphorically, as "statues" (Juan del Salto on page 21 and Silvina on pages 6 and 213). This undermining shifts the novel's discourse back to a certain kind of objectivism, but one that is quite different from Zola's and is partly prefigured by Lucretius: it is what might be called a textual objectivism, which consists in the text's display of its own textual nature as the ultimate expression of its uncompromising objectivity.[20]

What, then, is a reader to make of the narrator in *La charca*? Is he (there is little doubt about the gender) a distanced, dispassionate observer of objective reality, in the manner of both the Epicureans and Zola's naturalism, or conversely, a compassionate individual, concerned with the welfare of his compatriots and moved by the tragedy of his characters? Is this text wholly congruent with the peace-loving, materialist, and atomistic view it espouses, or does a sense of the sacred, and its accompanying violence, intrude? If one identifies the narrator with Zeno, is he simply the "good doctor" who wields his (literary) scalpel in order to diagnose Puerto Rican social ills, or is he, to paraphrase Lucretius, an "executioner priest" trying to keep his carving knives out of our sight?

These questions bear fundamentally on the issue of *La charca*'s intended effect on its readers: clearly, the novel aims to denounce the social situation it describes, but how does it achieve this goal? Arguably, much of this novel's efficacy resides in its presumed objectivity, in its power to persuade readers that its moral lesson comes directly from the observation of nature (or, more concretely, of the social world *as if* it were part of nature), and that it therefore requires no rhetorical supplementation. *La charca*'s discourse, however, constantly insists on nature's supreme indifference to and utter distance from human affairs: nature does not take sides. Nevertheless, after Silvina's tragic fall at the novel's end, the narrator makes his only direct reference to God: "In the mystery of night, God was weeping" (*En el misterio de la noche, Dios sollo-*

*zaba;* 214). Who is this God who weeps? It is certainly not the God of nature, since nature's otherness, its disjunction from human cares and concerns, has been established in the text time and time again. *La charca*'s duplicity appears here in its most profound guise, that of abjection. "In the mystery of night, God was weeping": this deeply ambiguous statement, which is impossible to define as either ironic or earnest, still manages to reduce the deity to the category of the abject. Zeno's God is either useless and impotent, or a hypocrite.[21] Could this be a metaphor for the narrator? Or for Zeno himself?

It is time to examine Silvina, and her fall, more closely. Although Zeno probably never read Nájera's story,[22] the character of Silvina clearly belongs to the same textual genealogy—or antigenealogy, to be more precise—as "la hija del aire." Hers is a fragmented lineage that stretches back to Plato and includes such literary characters as Fernando de Rojas's Celestina, Calderón's Semiramis, and Goethe's Mignon.[23] Like Nájera's nameless "daughter of the air," Silvina is fatherless: "Silvina never knew her father—a scoundrel, perhaps, who in the free polygamy of the forests saw his chance and took it" (*La charca* 9). Her age, as we are told at the beginning of the novel, is fourteen (6), which by the standards of the time meant she was barely out of childhood (the narrator also refers to her as an "adolescent," 10).[24] The physical description of Silvina emphasizes her beauty as well as her suffering, and hints at her inner fragmentation:

Then Silvina appeared among the trees. Her finely molded visage, very beautiful and eternally languid, owed its charm to her black eyes. In that visage were portrayed her frequent moments of anguish and her hours of vexation, which almost always ended in tears. Her impetuousness also appeared, those delirious attacks resulting from deep suffering which, when Gaspar was not present, made her bite her fists with rage and twist her arms cursing her evil luck. Her face showed the effects of the sleepless nights in which, tossing and turning on the floor of her hut, she spent hours of wakefulness without being able to sleep until dawn, and also that vague confusion produced by frequent lapses of memory. Hers was a likable and attractive visage, full of expressions as mobile and variable as the young woman's character. (65)

However, unlike the physical torture endured by Nájera's girl-acrobat, Silvina's anguish is predominantly emotional and psychological. A few months before the beginning of the narrative, Silvina's own mother, Leandra, forces her to sleep with Galante, Leandra's lover, in order to satisfy the landowner's lust and keep his favor. Silvina is later married off to the brutal Gaspar, although the landowner continues to visit her even after the marriage (9–11). Her only solace from this degradation is her love for the peasant Ciro, who returns her love and offers to steal her away from Gaspar. Fearful both of her husband and of Galante, however, Silvina refuses. Her only brief period of contentment occurs after the confused resolution of the murder of Deblás. Gaspar having fled, and Galante having broken with Leandra, Silvina is finally free to live with Ciro. Her happiness is short lived, however, and her moral suffering reaches its peak when Ciro is murdered by his own brother, Marcelo. At the end of the novel—two years after Ciro's death—following the dubious example of Leandra, who has taken another common-law husband, Silvina is living with another peasant, Inés Marcante.

These circumstances tear at Silvina's feeble personality, culminating in epileptic fits, which she begins suffering at the time of the dance in Vegaplana (chap. 6), and which may be seen as the physical expression of Silvina's metaphorically dislocated psyche. Her attacks, although "natural," biological in origin, also take her out of the world, disconnect her radically from her surroundings, to the point that they cause her death. There is thus an ambivalence in the allegorical meaning of Silvina's name similar to the previously noted ambivalence between objectivity and subjectivity, isolation and relation, in *La charca*'s discourse: As mentioned earlier, Silvina's name suggests her link with nature, with the world of forests and jungles that surrounds her. And yet her relation to nature, like that of the other characters in the novel, is extremely distanced, to say the least. Suffice it to recall the first pages of *La charca*, where the setting of the novel is described as seen through Silvina's eyes (6–8) and the narrator states:

Silvina looked without seeing. That poetic landscape, which was so familiar to her, did not lead her into reverie; that quiet afternoon had nothing to interest her fourteen years of age. She thought of her own intimacies, of her secrets and her longings. The regal panorama of the mountains fluttered before her eyes like a band of swallows in front of a statue. (6)

Simultaneously connected to and disconnected from nature, fragmented and divided within herself, Silvina seems already to possess all the attributes that would make her an emblem of writing. But while she is alive, her emblematic ambiguity remains. In my view, the living Silvina may be interpreted as a parody of the romantic concept of writing, which insisted on writing's organicity, its links to the world of living things, and according to which writing, though potentially separated from its meaning, is ultimately reunited with it in the cyclical movement described by M. H. Abrams in *Natural Supernaturalism* (1971). Nevertheless, as Zeno clearly points out, when Silvina finally achieves her longed-for union with Ciro (whose name, along with its orientalist allusion to the Persian king Cyrus, also resembles the Spanish word *cero*, meaning "zero" or nullity), her bliss is muted and short lived, since Ciro is murdered by his brother soon afterwards (193–204). Silvina's story does not end in harmony but continues instead beyond what would have been the conventional romantic ending. The name of Silvina's final common-law husband, with whom she lives in a loveless union, is sufficiently explicit in allegorical terms: Inés Marcante. Not only does his first name, Inés, imply a symbolic sexual ambiguity (in Spanish, it is most commonly a woman's name), but his last name is almost too overt in its association with writing: *marcante* means "one who marks."

However, Silvina's death metamorphoses her into a harsh and uncompromising allegory of writing, freed from any romantic illusions about the harmony of mind and nature. As Silvina falls from the cliff in the throes of her epileptic crisis, she is followed, the narrator tells us, by "masses of rocks that, more compassionate than men, seemed to want to follow her, in a funerary cortege, to the bottom" (212). Her broken body comes to a rest on top of the flat stone where Leandra did the washing, like a victim on an altar. There, the narrator explicitly compares her body to "a relief sculpted in granite. The tenuous light of evening gave it the appearance of a funerary statue, a jacent bust to memorialize the most sorrowful victim of the most cruel pain" (213). Petrified and dislocated, Silvina is now totally congruent with the phenomenal qualities of writing.

The death of Silvina is the birth of writing: in a highly problematical fashion—to say the least—Zeno portrays writing's wrenching, violent face as that of a dead woman.[25] Leandra's presence completes the scene in more ways than one. Not only is she a witness to the metamorphosis, but as Silvina's mother and a symbol of reproduction in the novel, her proximity to her daughter's body, along with her inability to bring it back to life, emblematizes writing's own paradoxical closeness to, yet separation from, its origins.

As the epigraphs at the beginning of this chapter are meant to suggest, Silvina's death resembles the Lucretian clinamen—a sudden, unexpected deviation of a particle from its expected path, which leads to a collision with another particle and the apparition of a vortex, a principle of order and regularity in the midst of formless chaos. For Silvina's fall to be a true clinamen, however, it would have to be a totally random event. But how random can an action described in a text be? Silvina's epilepsy, of course, is an attempt by Zeno to introduce randomness into the narrative, but because of the belated nature of both narrative and language, it can only be a randomness evoked after the fact, and thus it is actually not random at all. This convoluted reasoning (a logical vortex in itself) goes to the heart of *La charca*'s ethics of writing because it bears on the writer's degree of responsibility with regard to his creation. By "responsibility" I do not mean only the writer's authority or power over the text, nor am I merely invoking the hoary question of intentionality. As the etymology of the word suggests, I refer to an action that requires a *response*, an answer, or an explanation. Such a response can only be given, of course, to another subject, another person. But the text—the author's creation—is not a person. Or is it? The very act of writing the novel, as we have seen, and as J. Hillis Miller convincingly argues, depends on the attribution of personhood to a linguistic creation (Miller, *Versions of Pygmalion* 11, 13, 136ff.). And yet writers often find themselves behaving towards that Other whose personhood they have posited in ways that are, at the very least, inconsistent with the moral principles the text claims to uphold.

A fundamental question of the ethics of writing emerges here: Is it possible to represent evil without somehow repeating it?[26] Although the question evokes medieval exercises in casuistry, no author who believes in even the most remote social implications of his or her work can avoid asking it. This is true because if the text is in any way connected to its social context, then it is arguably subject to the most basic of commandments, that which forbids taking another person's life. I am not proposing here that authors whose characters die or are killed are guilty of virtual murder. What I am positing is that a common trait in literary texts dealing with the ethics of writing is their concern with the literary representation of evil and with the fact that, no matter how symbolic, such a representation runs the risk of seeming a tacit assent to evil.

To what degree, then, is Zeno responsible for what he does to his text? I would argue that Zeno himself implicitly poses this question in *La charca*, in the ambiguities surrounding Silvina's fall. In the society described in *La charca*, the crimes of the powerful, such as Galante and Andújar, always go unpunished, in contrast to those of peasants such as Marcelo, who is swiftly incarcerated for the murder of his brother. Is this not also the case in Silvina's death? Although within the narrative her death is presented as accidental, can one say the same from outside the narrative? In other words, is Silvina's death merely the logical outcome of *La charca*'s plot and, as such, a clinamen over which Zeno had little choice or control? Or is Silvina the scapegoat, the Iphigenia-like sacrificial victim whom Zeno kills on the altar of his narrative in order to launch his novelistic series? Is her fall motivated within the narrative, or must readers seek its motivation outside of the narrative, in its creation? As I already mentioned, the text attributes Silvina's fall to a recurrence of her epileptic malady, thus making her death accidental. The haphazard nature of Silvina's demise is further underscored when we are told that during her convulsions she literally teeters on the brink of the precipice: "She shook above the danger like a piece of debris that chance either pushes along or stops. She trembled above death, left utterly to herself, stopped by carnality or pushed by fatalism" (212). From the standpoint of the narrative's creation, however, there is little doubt as to who gives Silvina her final push over the edge. Silvina's death at the end endows *La charca* with an excessively neat circularity that appears determined more by aesthetic considerations than by narrative necessity. In other words, Silvina dies because Zeno as an author *wills* it, since he opts for a tragic ending that gives the narrative a sense of closure.

Zeno's final turn towards tragedy in *La charca* (a clinamen of another sort?), which is parallel to that at the end of *De rerum natura*, is also a turn towards ethics, for as Silvina becomes a (sacrificial) victim who must be mourned, she also recovers the personhood denied her at an allegorical level. *La charca*'s ending seems to be making simultaneously two different points: On the one hand, Silvina is not a person to be mourned but an object made up of words, an allegory of writing. On the other hand, as a victim, a scapegoat, Silvina is indeed a person. Her death therefore prompts a tragic cry of anguish from the narrator, a cry that signals, to use Serres's phrase, the reappearance of relations beneath the object (*La naissance de la physique* 166).

Silvina's fall, I propose, marks the site of a wavering, a vacillation, between Zeno's ethics as an author and the ethics of writing. Zeno's authorial ethics is based on the Epicureans' objectification, which regards writing as an inert, passive medium that the author uses as he sees fit (as Nájera puts it in "La hija del aire," writing is "his beast, his thing"). The ethics of writing, on the contrary, is characterized by a sense of writing as a resistant Other, as a person or a personified entity, towards which the writer must behave responsibly. In the latter context, the enigmatic sentence "In the mystery of night, God was weeping" may be seen as Zeno's tragic admission of guilt for Silvina's death and his recognition that the problematics of evil dwells in his text at the most fundamental level, that of the text's own creation. To paraphrase Genesis: Once their work is done, authors run the risk of finding that it is *not* good—not merely aesthetically, but also in a moral sense. The enormity of this burden, as Harpham points out, is what has led many modern authors to reduce their presence in the text to a minimum, following the example of Flaubert, and to suggest in their "narratives of creation" that the author has virtually no relation to his text, except perhaps that of a passive medium (188). Reminiscent of the doctrine of "due obedience" invoked in recent times by the Latin American militaries to "justify" their human rights violations, these "narratives of creation" claim that whatever happens in the text does so because the author was "only following orders" from a higher authority, be it the Muses, as in antiquity, or the laws of nature, or the rules of a literary genre. In Zeno, this disavowal of authority encouraged by the ethical pressures of creation is further reinforced by the Epicurean ideology of atomistic materialism. Thus distanced from his work, Zeno can simultaneously and contradictorily decry the violence perpetrated by characters such as Galante or Gaspar, while himself doing violence to the character of Silvina in her arguably needless demise.

Zeno's *La charca*, like Nájera's "La hija del aire," culminates in a moment of recognition, when the writer comes face to face with the violence of writing but also with the realization that despite his best intentions he has committed acts in his text that in the everyday world would be considered evil. Such a recognition is fleeting, nevertheless, and in both Nájera and Zeno the writers' consciences are soothed by the belief that their plunges into abjection and violence are meant to serve worthwhile causes: Nájera, as we know, ends "La hija del aire" by calling on his readers to support laws against child labor, and the socially reformist intentions of *La charca* are clear. However, the stage is set for a deeper ethical introspection. Before coming to that, we must still consider how this dawning awareness of writing's apparent complicity with violence and evil was viewed by the emerging female narrators of the early twentieth century.

CHAPTER 3

Ifigenia's

Choice

Teresa de

la Parra's

Demonic

Option

I did not set out to preach morality at any cost when I wrote *Ifigenia*, but *Ifigenia* does not harbor the slightest preconceived intention against the principles of morality. . . . *Ifigenia* is neither moralizing nor antimoralizing; it is simply a portrait, done without further pretensions, of women's souls at the current moment and in all countries. At this moment, two opposite influences stir and fight each other in the souls of women: the right to a complete personal independence, and the atavistic forces of a powerful instinct of social conservation. But *Ifigenia* is above all a defense of a certain type of modern girl one often finds in cities like Caracas, who, though misjudged because she does not obey certain moral principles either in theory or in trivial appearances, nevertheless does obey them in her daily life, even though she finds them unjust, without anybody noticing or praising her for it. [. . .] María Eugenia Alonso is a type of modern woman whose renunciation is the only truly sublime one, because obeying a morality one considers unjust and sacrificing one's life for ideals one does not share is equal to being twice virtuous and seven times heroic.

— TERESA DE LA PARRA,
"Unas palabras más sobre *Ifigenia* y las Aristeigueta"

Mired in stories of our own destruction, stories which we confuse with ourselves, how can women experience creativity?

— SUSAN GUBAR,
"'The Blank Page' and the Issues of Female Creativity"

Manuel Gutiérrez Nájera and Manuel Zeno Gandía, as we have seen in the previous chapters, both display a highly problematical tendency to allegorize writing as a woman, and thus, by extension, to attribute to woman many of the negative traits of writing. Clearly, graphophobia in these male writers went hand in hand with misogyny. For these authors, writing appears as a symbolic act of violence against a female figure who is alternately a victim (Mignon) and an aggressor (Semiramis). The question raised by Susan Gubar in the epigraph to this chapter thus becomes highly pertinent: "[H]ow can women experience creativity?" Do women writers share with men a similar concept of writing? Do they also experience graphophobia, that is, ethical qualms about writing and its attendant violence? And if they do, how is it experienced and expressed? As we saw earlier, in *La charca* Zeno conveys his graphophobia in part by reenacting the myth of Iphigenia, using the death of Silvina as the inaugural scene of his novelistic series. Thirty years later, the Venezuelan Teresa de la Parra also returns to the myth of Iphigenia in her first novel, *Ifigenia*. The ethics of writing she outlines in that work differs in predictable ways from that of the male authors, but it also displays unexpected resemblances to the male writers' reflections about the use and abuse of the written word.

The title of this chapter may at first sound overly paradoxical in its multiple allusions: to the phrase "Hobson's choice," to the title of William Styron's novel, *Sophie's Choice* (1979), and to the myth of Iphigenia. After all, the phrase "Hobson's choice" and the title of Styron's novel both refer to situations in which there is no choice at all, since it is a question of choosing between two equally negative options. And Iphigenia, also, had no choice but to let herself be sacrificed by her father, Agamemnon, so that the winds would speed his fleet onwards towards Troy. Similarly, María Eugenia Alonso, the narrator-protagonist of Teresa de la Parra's *Ifigenia: Diario de una señorita que escribía porque se fastidiaba* (1924) (published in English as *Iphigenia: The Diary of a Young Lady Who Wrote Because She Was Bored*, 1993), finds herself at the novel's end at an impasse that can apparently be resolved only through her capitulation to the demands of a highly conservative, male-dominated society.

But does she, in fact, surrender? Or does María Eugenia's explicit comparison of herself with Iphigenia actually point to an escape hatch, a trap door, leading out of her dilemma? The sincerity of María Eugenia's decision to "sacrifice" herself at the novel's end may well be doubted, but even if one takes it seriously, its implications force one to go back and reread the novel with a far more skeptical and suspicious eye. As I hope to show in this chapter, in *Ifigenia* Teresa de la Parra rewrites the metaphor of writing as an abused (and potentially abusive) woman, which we have already seen in Nájera and Zeno, and seeks to turn it to her advantage.[1]

In *Ifigenia*, de la Parra tacitly accepts the metaphoric linkage between woman and writing, but also inverts its meaning by embracing writing's propensity towards violence and deceit. In consonance with the latter trait, and unlike the works by Nájera and Zeno I have just examined, de la Parra's texts contain little overt violence. On the surface, novels like *Ifigenia* and *Las memorias de Mamá Blanca*, written in a terse, flowing Spanish, seem to be concerned mostly with manners and morals, and whatever is conflictive or distasteful is kept at a distance. Nevertheless, violence does occur in these novels offstage, as in Greek drama, and the threat of violence is always present, although it is mostly psychological or emotional rather than physical.

This seeming acceptance of writing's violent aspects, this demonic option, is conveyed in de la Parra's novel through her allusions to the figure of Iphigenia, whose symbolism in Greek theater and myth goes far beyond that of being a mere sacrificial victim. Anticipating present-day writers such as Hélène Cixous (in, for example, "The Laugh of the Medusa"), de la Parra seems to imply in *Ifigenia* that if woman equals writing, then men would do well to beware of women. At the same time, however, de la Parra appears eager to mitigate the negative ethical consequences of the link between woman and writing by calling on women to be selfless (*abnegada*—a privileged term in her vocabulary) and submissive as a way to help "civilize" men. The question remains, however, as to whether the female meekness advocated by de la Parra is not in itself a strategic ruse meant to deflect criticism of de la Parra's feminist advocacy.

Teresa de la Parra was a Spanish American female novelist at a time (the 1920s) when this role was still highly unusual.[2] Her work, which comprises a narrative of travels in the Orient (*El diario de una caraqueña por el Lejano Oriente*, 1920), two novels (*Ifigenia*, 1924, and *Las memorias de Mamá Blanca*, 1929), and posthumous collections of her speeches and letters, was cut short by her death from tuberculosis in 1936, just as she was reaching full maturity as a writer. Descended from Venezuelan aristocrats, de la Parra possessed conservative instincts that were perpetually at odds with her vocation as a writer, her feminist inclinations, and her sexual preferences. The latter aspect of her life is one over which most of her critics have drawn a veil—or rather, have chosen not to lift the veil that de la Parra herself drew over it—but by now it seems unnecessarily coy not to recognize that de la Parra was lesbian, or at least bisexual, and that this facet of her personality not only complicates but also enriches her work immensely.

To read Teresa de la Parra implies coming to grips with a multilayered writing that is always hesitating between submission and defiance, self-censorship and self-expression. The Venezuelan critic Arturo Uslar-Pietri characterized her in lapidary terms: "She was that monstrously delicate and complex being: a *señorita*, a baroque flower" (*Era una señorita: ese ser monstruosamente delicado y complejo. Esa flor del barroco*; "El testimonio de Teresa de la Parra" 273). Not surprisingly, de la Parra felt an affinity for the women of the colonial period, as she implies in her 1930 lecture series, *La influencia de las mujeres en la formación del alma americana* (The influence of women in the formation of the American soul):

> My feminism is a moderate one. To demonstrate this, my dear sirs, and to treat such a delicate matter as that of the new rights the modern woman should acquire—although not by sudden and destructive revolution but by a noble evolution that conquers through education and by making use of the forces of the past—to treat this subject, I say, I began to prepare three lectures offering a kind of historical overview of women's abnegation in our countries. That is, of the hidden and felicitous influence exercised by women during the conquest, the colony, and the independence period. (*Obras completas* 686)

Indeed, like the colonial male authors I mentioned in the introduction (Poma, Freyle, Carrió, and Lizardi), de la Parra invokes and utilizes the demonic powers of writing to dissemble, confuse, and undo, even as she claims to be reaffirming a certain orthodoxy: "I believe that usually, while politicians, military men, journalists, and historians spend their lives placing antagonistic labels on things, the young people, the common people, and above all we women, who are numerous and so very disorderly, instead devote ourselves to reshuffling the labels and establishing once again a friendly confusion" (*Obras completas* 689). De la Parra was a reluctant rebel, and her untimely death did not allow her to develop a more openly defiant attitude. Nevertheless, today she is recognized as a "moderate" precursor of modern Spanish American feminism, and readers of de la Parra's own time had little difficulty in perceiving that her work contained rebellious aspects, despite her own ambivalent protestations to the contrary.[3]

Like Nájera's "daughter of the air" or Zeno's Silvina, the female protagonist of *Ifigenia* is an orphan and, at eighteen years of age, still regarded as a minor. Unlike the two previously mentioned characters, however, her association with writing is explicit and active, since she is herself a writer: the novel's text consists of a long, unsent letter and a diary, both penned by María Eugenia. Reading these texts, we learn that after the death of her father (her mother died years earlier), María Eugenia is forced to return from her Catholic boarding school in France to live in Caracas with her highly conservative grandmother and her maiden aunt. There she soon discovers that her father's inheritance has been taken over by her scheming Uncle Eduardo, leaving her penniless and at his mercy. María Eugenia's early attempts at rebellion against her grandmother's strict tutelage and the provincial mores of Caracas in the 1920s are aided by her freethinking and alcoholic Uncle Pancho and by her friend Mercedes Galindo, a Francophilic and rather "decadent" character whom María Eugenia tellingly nicknames "Semíramis" (*Ifigenia* 261). It is at the house of "Semíramis" that María Eugenia meets the dashing but opportunistic Gabriel Olmedo, who woos her despite his betrothal to the daughter of a rich and powerful government minister. Ultimately, however, Olmedo follows through with his marriage of convenience, leaving María Eugenia in utter dejection.

In the second half of the novel, which takes place two years later, María Eugenia claims to have undergone a conversion of sorts, from a naïve and frivolous girl who struggled instinctively against the provincialism of Caracas, to a supposedly mature young woman who meekly obeys her grandmother's traditionalist dictates. Rich with ironies, this portion of the novel is also melodramatic to the point of parody. After Gabriel Olmedo's return to María Eugenia, their first and only kiss occurs at the bedside of the dying Uncle Pancho (*Ifigenia* 545–547). At the novel's end, María Eugenia is torn between her love for the untrustworthy Olmedo, who urges her to elope with him, and her marriage commitment to the domineering César Leal. By this time, however, it is abundantly clear that she finds both choices equally unattractive. Gabriel has shown himself to be flighty and unstable, and his passionate offer to take María Eugenia away to New York, promising to respect her personal freedom in an idyllic marriage, does not convince her. César Leal, on the other hand, is the prototype of the overbearing Spanish American macho, for whom María Eugenia is merely another ornament to his life of wealth and influence.

Finally, María Eugenia opts to sacrifice her desire for personal freedom and her identity as a writer by marrying César Leal. In the concluding paragraphs of the novel, as she gazes at her wedding dress lying on a rocking chair, she compares herself explicitly to Euripides's Iphigenia:

> As in the ancient tragedy, I am Iphigenia. We are sailing against adverse winds, and in order to save this ship of the world that, manned by I know

not whom, races to sate its hatreds I know not where, it is necessary for me, branded by centuries of servitude, to yield up my docile, enslaved body as a burnt offering. He alone can extinguish the ire of the god of all men, in whom I do not believe and from whom I expect nothing. Dread ancestral deity, Sacred Monster with seven heads that are called society, family, honor, religion, morality, duty, conventions, and principles. Omnipotent divinity whose body is the ferocious self-love of men. Insatiable Moloch, thirsty for virgin blood, on whose barbarous altar thousands of young girls are immolated! And docile and white and beautiful like Iphigenia, here I am ready for my martyrdom! But before giving myself up to my execution-ers, as I sit before this candid whiteness which is to clothe my body, I want to shout aloud, so that my whole conscious being will hear.

It is not to the bloody cult of the ancestral God of seven heads that I meekly offer myself for the holocaust. It is to another, much higher deity that I feel alive in myself. It is to this great anxiety, much more powerful than love, that moves within me, rules me, governs me, and leads me to high, mysterious purposes that I accept without understanding them. Spirit of Sacrifice, Father and divine Son of motherhood, my only Lover, more perfect Husband than love, you and you alone are the God of my holo-caust, and the immense anxiety that rules and governs me for life.(*Ifigenia* 624–625)

Having foreclosed the option offered by Gabriel, María Eugenia be-lieves she has no recourse but to marry César. With her allusion to Iphigenia, she presents her choice as tragic and attempts to give it a more sublime meaning by arguing that she has chosen "sacrifice for sacrifice's sake," thus portraying herself as the purest of all female martyrs.

One of the main difficulties in reading this novel lies in keeping the narrator-protagonist's opinions separate from those of Teresa de la Parra. Although de la Parra herself warned against this association in articles written after the novel's publication, and although critical readers today may believe themselves immune from such confusions, the novel's dis-course in fact works to foment them. *Ifigenia*'s discourse oscillates con-stantly, in a manner similar to what we have already noted in Nájera and Zeno, between the poles of proximity and distance. Almost all of the novel's text is presented as the private writings of the protagonist, and with its strict use of the first person and a point of view restricted to the protagonist's, its effect is one of immediacy. However, the lengthy and highly ironic descriptive titles of the chapters in the first three parts, which evidently parody Cervantes's similar usage in the *Quixote* and suggest that the whole text is a "found manuscript," already signal an editorial intervention, and are clearly intended to distance readers from the text. In addition, the novel's subtitle mocks any feelings of tragic sympathy by evoking the ambiance of drawing-room comedy: *The Diary of a Young Lady Who Wrote Because She Was Bored*. María Eugenia is furthermore, to a certain degree, a clownish figure, a sort of female Charlot or Buster Keaton (two film comedians popular not only among audiences but also among avant-garde artists of the period), who, like them, displays remarkable vitality and resilience in the face of adversity. In the end, the oscillation between the fictional and the autobiographical in *Ifigenia* persists at all levels of the text and can probably be resolved only rhetorically, by positing a series of parallel oscillations in de la Parra's own life: for example, between her loyalty to the socially conservative principles of her class and her feminist sympathies, or, at an even more personal level, in her ambivalent sexual identity.

Despite her self-comparison with Iphigenia, María Eugenia, unlike the Greek heroine, chooses to marry. For María Eugenia it is marriage that becomes the sacrifice. Nevertheless, the text offers sufficient indications to allow even sympathetic readers to question the sincerity of María Eugenia's final conversion to martyrdom, as well as the substance of her supposed victimization. As Naomi Lindstrom points out, "Iphigenia offers herself to be sacrificed in order to bring justice and glory to Greece, while María Eugenia's motive is a desire for comfort and security" (xii). Support for this assertion is found not only in María Eugenia's rejection of Gabriel Olmedo's offer of escape to New York, but also in her thoughts as she listens to César Leal's arguments against delaying their marriage (a last-minute ploy by María Eugenia to buy time):

> No doubt it was due to these rapid visions of the future that, a few seconds later, when the same concise voice, continuing its enumeration, mentioned the house that "was completely ready and waiting for us," I saw it open in my mind like an asylum to save me, and I said to myself with huge satisfaction, "My house!" (*Ifigenia* 612)

This passage suggests that María Eugenia sees the domestic sphere not only as a refuge but also as a space that offers her some freedom, in accordance with the long-standing male-supremacist convention that allowed women a measure of authority over matters of the home. Moreover, by having her own home, even under Leal's patriarchal rule, María Eugenia would escape the no less rigid and perhaps more insidious control of her grandmother.

Significantly, by this point in the novel, the narrator-protagonist's discourse has become so ironic as to almost suggest an Ophelia-like insanity. This irony is evident, for example, when María Eugenia discreetly mocks her own supposed "conversion" to her grandmother's conservative mores:

> Yes! The moral and material progress I have made in these last two years is immense.
>
> Furthermore, I should declare that I have completely lost the anarchic, disoriented, and chaotic way of thinking that, as Grandmother quite rightly used to say, constituted a threat and a horrible danger to my future. As a result, or as palpable proof that I have lost such a wrong standard of judgment, I no longer paint my lips with *Rouge éclatant de Guerlain*. Instead I paint them with *Rouge vif de Saint-Ange*, whose tone is much softer than *Rouge éclatant de Guerlain*. I never sit on a table but always, always in rocking chairs, or on sofas, chairs, or tabourets, depending on the circumstances. It never occurs to me to hum and much less yet to whistle naughty songs, which are indecencies more fitting for café entertainment, unworthy of being intoned by the lips of a young lady. Likewise I very carefully avoid every kind of interjection, even those that seem quite innocent, such as the French expression "sapristi!" and the Castilian ones "canastos!" "caray!" and "caramba!" for I am convinced that basically they are nothing but hypocritical synonyms for other words that are worse. (*Ifigenia* 402–403)

This ironic tone, which to a greater or lesser degree pervades the whole novel, makes it difficult to take seriously the apparent finality of María Eugenia's surrender to the familial and social pressures at the end of the novel, in spite of the fact that such a surrender seems to agree with many of de la Parra's pronouncements in her writings and speeches after the publication of *Ifigenia*. In her 1930 lectures in Bogotá titled *La influencia de las mujeres en la formación del alma americana*, she declared her ambivalence toward women's suffrage (de la Parra, *Obras completas* 686) and seemed to indicate her approval of María Eugenia's decision when she praised the "*mujeres abnegadas*" (selfless women) of colonial times: "I am left, therefore, only with my selfless women. Frankly, I must tell you that, deep in my soul, I prefer them: they have the grace of things past and the infinite poetry of voluntary and sincere sacrifice" (*Obras completas* 687; see also González Boixó). But if one takes de la Parra at her word in these lectures and regards her as socially and politically conservative, how then does one explain her avowed "feminism" in many of her other writings, including *Ifigenia* (González Boixó 231)? María

Eugenia's wavering between irony and self-sacrifice in the novel certainly resembles de la Parra's indecisiveness about subjects such as feminism and marriage in her own life. Nevertheless, I believe it is essentially correct to regard *Ifigenia* as a feminist work, despite de la Parra's disclaimers and vacillations elsewhere. As I will demonstrate shortly, there is in *Ifigenia* an implicit but indubitable attempt to propose a model of female writing.

It is reasonable to suppose that in alluding to Iphigenia at the end of her novel, de la Parra was aware not only of the ambiguous ending of Euripides's *Iphigenia at Aulis,* but also of the existence of a sequel, *Iphigenia in Tauris,* in which Iphigenia has indeed escaped her sacrificial fate. But how, exactly, would the protagonist of de la Parra's novel escape her own symbolic immolation? De la Parra avoids a direct use of Euripides's *deus ex machina* solution; thus, whatever "salvation" awaits María Eugenia must be surmised on the basis of what the novel itself has already presented. In this respect, the allusions to the myth of Iphigenia and to the related myth of Semiramis offer, between the lines, some suggestive clues for an alternate reading of this novel.

As noted earlier, the explicit comparison of María Eugenia with the Greek tragic heroine actually points to a way out of María Eugenia's impasse. This is so because Iphigenia is by no means solely a figure of victimization. In the work by Euripides to which de la Parra alludes in her novel, *Iphigenia at Aulis,* there is an ambiguous *deus ex machina* ending in which a messenger tells the grieving Clytemnestra that her daughter has been saved from sacrifice by some deity who substituted Iphigenia at the last minute with a deer and carried her off to the heavens:

There the sons of Atreus and the whole army stood
with their eyes fixed on the ground, and the priest
took up the knife,
praying, and looked for the place
to plunge it. Pain welled up in me
at that, and I dropped my eyes.
And the miracle happened. Everyone
distinctly heard the sound of the knife
striking, but no one could see
the girl. She had vanished.
The priest cried out, and the whole army
echoed him, seeing

what some god had sent, a thing
nobody could have prophesied. There it was,
we could see it, but we could scarcely
believe it: a deer
lay there gasping, a large
beautiful animal, and its blood ran
streaming over the altar of the goddess.

. . . . . . . . . . . . . . . . . . .

Agamemnon sent me to say this,
to tell you of this
destiny which the gods have sent
and of the glory which he has won
among the Greeks. I saw it myself. I was there.
It is plain that your daughter
has been taken up into heaven. (94–95)

Clytemnestra's incredulous reply, however, underscores the ambiguity
of this situation:

Oh child, what deity has carried you off?
How may I address you? How can I be sure,
how can I know,
that this is not all a lie, made up
to silence my bitter grieving? (95)

Aeschylus's version of this episode in *Agamemnon* is even more enigmatic. In that telling, a gagged Iphigenia is taken to the altar of sacrifice
"like a figure in a picture, struggling to speak" (42). "What happened
after that I neither saw nor tell," the chorus adds, avoiding any allusion
to Iphigenia's miraculous rescue (42).

Commentators have argued that "Euripides included the rescue of
Iphigeneia in his play partly at least in order to demonstrate its irrelevance from a moral point of view" but also because it was probably an
original part of the myth of Iphigenia (*Iphigeneia at Aulis* 13).[4] As Richmond Lattimore points out:

The slaughter of Iphigeneia is a constant theme in tragedy, but no extant
tragedy recounts that slaughter. The post-Homeric epic *Kypria* told how,
when Iphigeneia was about to be sacrificed at Aulis, Artemis snatched her
away, substituting a fawn in her place, and immortalized her among the
Taurians. The rescue is also attested in a rather recently published fragment of Hesiod. (*Iphigeneia in Tauris* 8)

In any case, Euripides continued to follow the myth in his sequel *Iphigenia in Tauris*, in which we learn that Iphigenia was saved by the goddess Artemis, to whom she was to be sacrificed, and was taken by her to the distant land of the Taurians in the Black Sea, where she served as the priestess of Artemis and, ironically and against her inclinations, even presided over male human sacrifices! Stressing Iphigenia's good nature and her suffering at having to oversee the Taurians' sacrifices, Euripides recounts Iphigenia's rescue of her brother, Orestes (who, after murdering Clytemnestra to avenge her murder of Agamemnon, arrives shipwrecked and pursued by the Furies in the land of the Taurians). Shortly before her reunion with Orestes, Iphigenia reflects on the morality of the Taurians' sacrifices to Artemis:

But the goddess is too subtle. I do not approve.
When she considers any mortal stained with blood,
if only from childbirth or from contact with a corpse,
she keeps him from her altars, thinking him unclean,
while she herself is pleased with human sacrifice.
It is impossible that Leto, bride of Zeus,
produced so unfeeling a child. I myself think
the tale of how Tantalos entertained the gods
by feeding them his son, is not to be believed.
I also think these people, being murderous,
put off the blame for their own vice upon the gods.
I do not think any divinity is bad. (*Iphigeneia in Tauris* 24)

The image of Iphigenia that emanates from myth as well as from Euripides's two plays is that of a former victim who does not harbor grudges or dwell excessively upon her past experience. Exiled from her native land and consecrated to Artemis—remaining, like the goddess herself, virginal—she is able to regard with ironic distance the violent world in which she dwells.

Iphigenia's conversion into a priestess of Artemis is highly significant in terms of her symbolism in de la Parra's novel. Through the allusion to Iphigenia, the novel as a whole is placed under the sign of Artemis (whom the Romans knew as Diana). In Robert Graves's description, Artemis, Apollo's sister, "goes armed with bow and arrows and, like him, has the power both to send plagues or sudden death among mortals, and to heal them. She is the protectress of little children, and of all sucking animals, but she also loves the chase, especially that of stags" (83). Graves further reminds us of Artemis's role as a moon goddess and of her "eternal virginity" (85, 83). And, as the myth of Actaeon underscores, she brooks no advances, real or imagined, from men (Graves 84–85). Artemis is an androgynous deity, and her nurturing, conventionally "female" attributes are always counterbalanced by her warlike and aggressive, conventionally "masculine" side.

Where, exactly, does Artemis intervene in this text, and what is her function? Clearly, since María Eugenia, unlike Iphigenia, will not remain a virgin, María Eugenia's fate after her marriage to Leal can only be analogous to that of Iphigenia if one posits a "spiritual virginity" of sorts in which María Eugenia will be able to preserve some inner portion of herself free from masculine defilement. However, in order to remain "true to herself" even as she submits to marriage with Leal, María Eugenia must of necessity practice dissimulation; she must learn to mask her true feelings and to counterfeit, like an actress, feelings that are not her own. How does she learn this? Her literary inclinations have already familiarized her with some of the skills of dissimulation, but the lessons provided by writing are mediated and deepened by two key figures: Uncle Pancho and Mercedes Galindo, or "Semíramis."

Uncle Pancho, a counterfigure to the scheming Uncle Eduardo, fulfills in the narrative the mediating role that is typical of "uncles": It is he, to begin with, who introduces María Eugenia to Mercedes Galindo, as well as to Gabriel Olmedo. Furthermore, in a conversation with María Eugenia about feminism and the condition of women, he outlines a strategy of subterfuge by means of which women may achieve power and authority in society. The passage is worth quoting in full because it not only prefigures María Eugenia's fate later in the novel but also anticipates some of de la Parra's essayistic pronouncements about the "selfless women" of colonial times:

In human societies, the two sexes dispute dominance or control. Man and woman. Following the law of hierarchies, which of the two is destined to rule the other, and consequently rule all of nature? That is the question. To resolve it in her own favor, while always leaving a man in his vain appearance of command, is the greatest proof of intelligence that a woman can give, and moreover, for the society in which she moves, it is an evident sign of high civilization and high culture. While on the contrary, societies in which men really and truly rule are always primitive societies, barbaric and uncultured. Why, you may ask? Why, for the simple reason that man, in spite of having decked himself out pompously and theatrically from primitive times, with crowns, scepters, and all the other attributes of power, basically is not constituted to command but rather to obey. That is why when he wants to impose his will he always does it badly, with shouts, grotesque and very vulgar gestures like the ones generally used by all those who, not having been endowed by nature with the most precious gift of command, wish at all costs to rule. . . . Those poor women [of Caracas] don't know their power. Dazzled by the idealistic light of mysticism and virtue, they race to spontaneously offer themselves as a sacrifice, and they throw away their prestige by being too generous. They live drunken on the voluptuousness of submission. Like martyrs, their love is excited by flagellation, and they bless their lord in the midst of chains and torments. They live the deep inner life of ascetics and idealists, they finally acquire a great refinement and abnegation, which is without a doubt the highest human superiority, but with their superiority hidden in their souls, they are sad victims. Because they are ignorant of the conquering force of their attraction, they forget themselves; they disdain their power when they neglect their physical beauty, and of course, seeing them worn out and faded, men turn them into pitiful beasts of burden on whose docile and weary shoulders they load all the weight of their tyranny and their caprices, after giving them the pompous name of "honor." (194–196)

It would be easy to dismiss these statements as merely a cynical male ploy to convince women that they are truly the ones who hold the reins of power in an otherwise visibly male-dominated society, if they did not parallel so closely the events that will unfold later in the novel, when María Eugenia seemingly yields to "the voluptuousness of submission" (in Uncle Pancho's phrase). The point about women's civilizing role and their "great refinement and abnegation" is also reminiscent of de la Parra's praise of colonial women in *La influencia de las mujeres en la formación del alma americana.* But more suggestive still is Uncle Pancho's contention that the women of Caracas have yet to learn how to use the inherent power of their physical attractiveness. Uncle Pancho's statements clearly echo the turn-of-the-century metaphor of woman as writing, with its implication of women's mysterious powers that derive from their control of appearances and representation (Nina Auerbach 16–34). For Uncle Pancho, it seems, feminism in Venezuela would be advanced if all women turned themselves into femmes fatales.

However, the closest approximation of a femme fatale in the novel, the Francophilic Mercedes Galindo, turns out not to be quite as *fatale* as one would expect. Although, as the nickname "Semíramis" suggests, she has much to teach María Eugenia about a hyperrefined and theatri-

cal femininity, she is ironically presented by the narrator as anything
but self-centered and perilous to men.[5] In her conversations with María
Eugenia, Mercedes shows herself to be tender hearted and full of compassion towards her vice-prone husband, Alberto, who cheats on her
and mistreats her, although he tolerates her eccentrically "decadent"
behavior:

You don't understand these things, and I hope you'll never understand
them. If I had not found myself in this situation, or if I were as selfish as
some women, I, too, would find this abnegation of mine foolish, and even
unworthy. . . . Alberto, besides tormenting me, needs me morally, materi-
ally, and even physically too. . . . It is true, very true, if I divorced Alberto,
I could live happily and in freedom, but I have seen evidence that he would
sink into the most horrible *débauche*. He has often confessed that without
me, he would indulge in every vice and that only my presence can protect
him from that and save him from destitution and debauchery. Well, what
he says is absolutely true, it seems to me that he is always shouting at me to
stay, and so, *me voilà*! Here I am, and I'll go on sharing his burden of
ignominy so the burden won't grow too great and crush him. [. . .] Do you
think I don't suffer, María Eugenia? Do you think it's not humiliating and
degrading to be the wife of a man who defames himself with every vice?
Yes, it's humiliating, humiliating and distasteful. And your life together
becomes intolerable and hateful. You can't understand it, and Alberto
himself, however much I tell him, doesn't understand it either, because if
he did, he'd be shocked. Women like me who are very weak, very self-
sacrificing, or very contemptible . . . whatever it is, stay in this loveless love
life, suffering all the anguish and repugnance of women who sell themselves to the first man who goes by on the street. (277–278)

Nevertheless, despite Mercedes's confessions of "weakness," her discourse and behavior, like those of the original Semiramis, are seductive,
willful, and self-possessed. Let us recall here that the legendary Queen
Semiramis was the daughter of a nymph of Diana, or Artemis, and that
she was always under the protection of that goddess. The narrator is
enthralled by Mercedes's "silvery laugh . . . , with so many nuances of
meaning, so like her" (282) and describes her as "pretty, swaying, slen-
der, smiling, in her beautiful black dress that fit her body like a silken
glove, the mistress of her castle, among the palm trees on the patio"
(284). Clearly, de la Parra is producing here her own positive counterimage
to the male writers' vision of Semiramis as a symbol of the deceptive-
ness and violence of writing.

The marital situation of "Semíramis" also highlights the fact that, save for María Eugenia's dead father and her unmarried Uncle Pancho (who dies later in the novel), all other men in *Ifigenia* appear in a negative light, as either cads, egotists, or abusers. A strong "misandrogic," or antimasculine, current runs through this novel, paralleled by an emphasis on female friendship and bonding, as exemplified by María Eugenia's relationships with Cristina Iturbe (the addressee of her lengthy letter in part 1), Mercedes Galindo, and the black maid Gregoria (see González Boixó 235). In the world of *Ifigenia*, unlike that of the Spanish American modernists and naturalists, men are usually "fatal" to women, and not the other way around. Besides being a truer picture of the relationships between men and women in Latin America during the 1920s, this is also, to a certain extent, a "woman-centered" perspective: it is the world as viewed through the eyes of Artemis.

Another significant negative male attribute that de la Parra consistently satirizes throughout *Ifigenia* is the tendency to make speeches, particularly the flowery, rhetorical sort dear to Spanish American politicians. Oratorical pomposity is especially evident in Gabriel Olmedo and César Leal, as well as in the Colombian poet with whom María Eugenia flirts on her transatlantic voyage (91–94), and even in Uncle Pancho, who, although we are told that he is "insensible to the magnetic fire of eloquence" (112), is quite fond of speechifying. Significantly, the least eloquent of the novel's male characters is the villainous Uncle Eduardo, whom María Eugenia first knew through the letters he wrote to her father—letters that María Eugenia's father always greeted with expressions such as "From that imbecile Eduardo!" or "What will that fool Eduardo tell me today?" (102). Nevertheless, underscoring the power that comes with the written word—particularly, in this case, through the mastery of legal formulae—it is the "fool Eduardo" who manages to dispossess his brother of his hacienda, thus usurping the family fortune.

It is important to remember that, like every first-person narrative, the text of *Ifigenia*, despite its impression of immediacy, was produced "after the fact." Thus, in a very literal sense, although it speaks about past events, the text itself as an object—a combination of a letter and a diary organized into parts and chapters by an unnamed editor—belongs to the future, and it thus reveals what María Eugenia did after her apparent self-immolation in her marriage to César Leal: she struck back through writing. Writing is not only María Eugenia's consolation, a defensive or palliative measure to alleviate her suffering; it is her counterattack. María Eugenia attempts to retaliate through her writing against both linguistic instances of male domination: the spoken form of oratory and the written form of legal or juridical codes. Against the copious onslaught of male oratory, which is made for public display, María Eugenia unleashes her no less torrential but also intimate verbosity, which often mimics and mocks the rhetoricism of her male interlocutors.[6] Against the dry formulae of the law that Uncle Eduardo has used so effectively, she deploys a discourse evocative of the picaresque genre that is also, by turns, melodramatic and gossipy. It is this linguistic, and specifically scriptural, vitality that is the most telling example of de la Parra's rebelliousness in *Ifigenia*. The copiousness of this novel (in most editions it runs between four and five hundred pages), along with its lively, engaging style, is an implicit statement of de la Parra's literary prowess and fecundity.

In "'The Blank Page' and the Issues of Female Creativity," from which the second epigraph to this chapter is taken, Susan Gubar explains how the experience of literary creation and of writing in general has most commonly been represented by women as a self-sacrifice, "a violation, a belated reaction to male penetration rather than a possessing and controlling" and "not an ejaculation of pleasure but a reaction to rending" (302). The woman-writer sees herself as a victim and equates writing with the shedding of her own blood. Gubar observes that this view of writing in English-language authors dates back to works by Mary Elizabeth Coleridge and Charlotte Brontë in the early nineteenth century and extends to the poetry of Sylvia Plath in the 1960s. At the same time, however, other English-language female writers of the late Victorian period and the early twentieth century, from Florence Nightingale to H. D. and Gertrude Stein, proposed an alternative concept of female writing in which silence and the image of the blank page became emblematic of the creative powers latent in womanhood. These writers sought "to sanctify the female through symbols of female divinity, myths of female origin, metaphors of female creativity, and rituals of female power" (Gubar 308). De la Parra, who was sophisticated and well read and was familiar with the works of French women writers of her day such as Collette and Anna de Noailles (Patout 159–160), was clearly cognizant of those alternative views. Her *Ifigenia*, although superficially a portrayal of the female writer as victim, was in fact covertly proposing the opposite view: that of the female writer as an active and powerful generator of fictions.

On the whole, *Ifigenia*, as its contemporaries clearly understood, was an "outlaw" piece of writing, an instance of writing as rebellion. True, the rebelliousness of this novel's writing is masked by an almost caricatural version of conventional femininity; but this subterfuge is evidently only a strategic move. Instead of invoking the passive, victim-like conception embodied in the figures of Goethe's Mignon, Nájera's "daughter of the air," and Zeno's Silvina, in *Ifigenia* Teresa de la Parra ultimately joins the company of Celestina and Semiramis (and her daimon, the symbolically androgynous deity Artemis), thus taking her chances with the "demonic" tradition of writing.

It is important to note, however, that María Eugenia's "Hobson's choice," her entrapment between two equally undesirable alternatives (whether to elope with Gabriel or to marry César Leal), seems to mirror de la Parra's quandary with regard to writing, since both the patriarchal and the woman-centered views of writing take for granted writing's propensity for violence and deceit. Female writing, it seems, is no less violent than the male version, and therefore it can not claim to be morally superior to it. This graphophobic insight prefigures a similar ambivalence about the relationship among women, ethics, and literacy found in works by other major Spanish American women writers of the twentieth century, such as, for example, the novel *Balún Canán* (1957) and the short story "Album de familia" (Family album, 1971) by Rosario Castellanos; the short story "Los censores" (The censors) in *Donde viven las águilas* (Where the eagles live, 1983) by Luisa Valenzuela; the testimonial narrative *Me llamo Rigoberta Menchú y así me nació la conciencia* (I, Rigoberta Menchú: An Indian woman in Guatemala, 1983) by Rigoberta Menchú; and many of the short stories in *Cuentos de Eva Luna* (Stories of Eva Luna, 1990) by Isabel Allende.

In *Ifigenia*, however, as in the texts by Nájera and Zeno studied in the previous chapters, the implications of graphophobia are left still largely unexplored. If writing is indeed allied to violence, and if all writers, male or female, run the risk of being complicitous with violence, what alternative other than silence (or not writing, to be more precise) is left? Two decades after the publication of *Ifigenia*, the harrowing events of World War II—the Nazi Holocaust and the atomic bombing of Hiroshima and Nagasaki foremost among them—made this question all the more urgent. Theodor W. Adorno's musings about the impossibility of poetry after Auschwitz, which are eerily reminiscent of Jorge Luis Borges's "El milagro secreto" (The secret miracle, 1944), showed how deadly serious the stakes had become for any ethical reflection about literature and writing in general:

Perennial suffering has as much right to expression as a tortured man has to scream; hence it may have been wrong to say that after Auschwitz you could no longer write poems. But it is not wrong to raise the less cultural question whether after Auschwitz you can go on living—especially whether one who escaped by accident, one who by rights should have been killed, may go on living. His mere survival calls for the coldness, the basic principle of bourgeois subjectivity, without which there could have been no Auschwitz; this is the drastic guilt of him who was spared. By way of atonement he will be plagued by dreams such as that he is no longer living at all, that he was sent to the ovens in 1944 and his whole existence since has been imaginary, an emanation of the insane wish of a man killed twenty years earlier. (362–363)

In the following section of this book, we will examine how a trio of Spanish American authors who came to prominence during the second half of the twentieth century responded to the challenge of violence and writing. In Jorge Luis Borges's "The Garden of Forking Paths" (1941), Alejo Carpentier's *The Harp and the Shadow* (1979), and Julio Cortázar's "Press Clippings" (1981), we find, along with a deeper reflection about graphophobia, a return to a strategy of admonitory, cautionary narratives prefigured by Cervantes's *Don Quixote*, in which writing itself is used to warn readers about the perils of writing.

Before proceeding, readers may reasonably ask about the causes of this change in strategy by Spanish American writers. Nevertheless, I must admit to being skeptical of explanations in general and of literary-historical explanations in particular. As David Perkins devastatingly observes in *Is Literary History Possible?* (1992), the search for causes or explanations of literary phenomena tends to dissolve into an infinity of contextual causes and explanations, resulting in banal conclusions and tautologies (121–152). It would be all too easy to repeat here the clichés of twentieth-century cultural history: the crisis of modernist aesthetics and the rise of postmodernism during the 1940s and '50s; the critiques of political ideology, language, and power during the 1960s and '70s; the rise and fall of hopes for revolutionary social change throughout the twentieth century; and so on. All of these well-known phenomena certainly must have played a part in the Spanish American authors' turn toward admonition when writing about writing. It should also be noted, however, that the dawning ethical awareness about writing in the turn-of-the-century texts we have read by Nájera, Zeno, and de la Parra paved the way for this type of response by later authors. We have already observed how Nájera's penchant for brevity and condensation in his narratives seems to foreshadow Borges's textual asceticism. Thus, we are speaking about a change in the literary tradition that is relatively gradual and can be traced back, as I stated in the introduction, to the Spanish American modernists' preoccupation with the ethical implications of artistic form.

More intriguing is the fact that this turn is actually a return to a posture that was already essayed by Cervantes during the period we now call early modern, which was also marked, as cultural historians remind us, by severe social and intellectual crises. As posited in the introduction, graphophobia is a constant in the historical experience of writing, but it also becomes more visible at specific junctures, moments of artistic and cultural conflict such as the baroque, romanticism, modernism and high modernism, and postmodernism. Ethical awareness of the "abuses" of writing, followed by admonitions about writing, also recurs at these moments, but it is eventually suppressed, perhaps because the issues it raises are regarded as insoluble and thinking about them is deemed paralyzing. This might be one of the reasons why Cervantes followed his notoriously self-reflexive *Quixote* with the less self-reflexive, even conservative *Persiles and Sigismunda* (1617).

Is this movement between admonitions about writing and their suppression a truly cyclical occurrence, endlessly repeated in the history of writing? Or am I inadvertently falling into an "immanentist" view of literary history as an oscillation between poles (Perkins 156)? Although I would avoid that extreme position, I would nevertheless point out that the world abounds in repetitive or cyclical phenomena that are nevertheless verifiable. Perhaps the back-and-forth movement I have posited between ethical awareness and ethical oblivion about writing is one such phenomenon.

PART II

*Admonitions*

## CHAPTER 4

# From Fission to Fiction

## Ethical Chain Reactions in Jorge Luis Borges's "The Garden of Forking Paths"

In nuclear fission, a chain reaction is a self-sustaining sequence of fissions. Fission is initiated when a uranium 235 nucleus is penetrated by a neutron; if the nucleus splits, it liberates, on the average, about 2.5 additional neutrons that may cause other nuclei to undergo fission. Some neutrons escape and others are lost to radiative capture. In order to produce a chain reaction, each fission must produce at least one neutron that initiates another fission. The minimum amount of fissionable material required for a self-sustaining chain reaction is the critical mass of the material. The first man-made chain reaction was achieved on Dec. 2, 1942, as part of the Manhattan Project.
— *The Grolier Electronic Encyclopedia* (1993)

Now I am become death, the destroyer of worlds.
— WORDS OF SHIVA IN THE *Bhagavad-Gita*, cited by J. Robert Oppenheimer after witnessing the first thermonuclear explosion at Alamogordo, New Mexico, on July 16, 1945.

At that moment I felt around me and within me something invisible and intangible pullulating.
— JORGE LUIS BORGES, "The Garden of Forking Paths" (1941)

One of Jorge Luis Borges's most perceptive readers, Sylvia Molloy, has observed the ethical tenor that pervades many of his writings:

Any reading of Borges should take into account the ethics that sustains it. For certain readers, the term might seem strange, even dubious. By ethics I mean the honest conduct and conveyance of a text, seemingly deceitful yet aware of its deceptions, admitting to its inevitable traps,

confessing to the creation of simulacra it does nothing to conceal. If a return to Borges, to his entire text, is worthwhile, it is because that text upholds a constant and honest disquisition on writing, his own writing, the writing of others. (*Signs of Borges* 4)

Indeed, the importance of Borges in this regard cannot be overstated. As in many other respects, Borges's work is the touchstone for any discussion of writing and ethics in Spanish American literature in the latter half of the twentieth century.

In the introduction, I proposed that this radical Borgesian honesty, which is unsparing in its critique, led Borges to develop a deeply negative assessment of writing and its effects. By now, it should not surprise us that it is frequently the most thoroughly devoted of writers who offer the most critical and pessimistic views of writing. This apparent paradox is tempered by the realization that like the works of Cervantes, Flaubert, and his other philosophical peers, Borges's negative portrayal of writers and writing has a fundamentally cautionary purpose. Far from advocating the abandonment of writing, Borges seeks to warn his readers about its risks and remind them of the caution with which it should be handled. Borges implies that writing is addictive and deadly, and that if not properly contained, it can have far-reaching and disastrous effects.

In his celebrated story "El jardín de senderos que se bifurcan" (published in English as "The Garden of Forking Paths") Borges suggests another analogy for the "dark side" of writing, one perhaps more appropriate for the twentieth century than the ancient drug/poison dichotomy mentioned in my introduction.[1] It is the metaphor of writing as nuclear power/nuclear destruction. One should not forget that although "The Garden of Forking Paths" is set during World War I, it and the rest of the tales in the collection entitled *Ficciones* were written during World War II, a global conflict that, only one year after Borges penned the last of those stories, would end under the shadow of two mushroom clouds.[2] There is an obvious eschatological tone to many of Borges's narratives, which has as much to do with the fearsome technological advances of the twentieth century as with his view of writing as a sort of archtechnology, the ultimate source of technology and all of its ethical dilemmas.

I am not arguing that Borges anticipates, or displays an unexpectedly great knowledge of, nuclear physics or the atom bomb. Borges's layman's knowledge of atomic theory is obvious from the allusions in his 1936 essay "La doctrina de los ciclos" (The doctrine of cycles), in which he briefly discusses Rutherford's atomic model and even mentions the possibility of "splitting" the atom (*Obras Completas* 385–386). The fact

that already by 1936 the Rutherford model of the atom had been super-
seded by the still current quantum-mechanical model indicates the lim-
its of Borges's knowledge of nuclear physics. "Atom splitting," or nuclear
fission, although hypothesized much earlier, was discovered in 1938 by
Otto Hahn and Fritz Strassman, but I have been unable to determine if,
or how much, Borges knew about it. In any event, the notion of a "chain
reaction," which derives from chemistry and is something of a misno-
mer (since it describes a process that actually branches out in a treelike
formation), was not particularly new by the time Borges wrote *Ficciones*,
and there are many other analogous processes of proliferation in nature
that could have served as models for the chain reactions that appear in
"The Garden of Forking Paths," as well as in "Tlön, Uqbar, Orbis Tertius," "Las ruinas circulares" (The circular ruins), and "Examen de la
obra de Herbert Quain" (An examination of the work of Herbert Quain).

For my purposes, I am less interested in the image of the chain reaction as a possible structural model for "The Garden of Forking Paths"
than for what it suggests about the *explosive* nature of Borges's ethical
ruminations, and about how those ruminations could have been disseminated among the subsequent Spanish American narratives. "The Garden
of Forking Paths" is the closest Borges ever came to a sustained reflection on ethics,[3] and as such, it offers additional insights into Borges's
cautionary views on writing.

In "The Garden of Forking Paths," Borges elaborates on the image
that he first posited in *Historia universal de la infamia* (1935) (published
in English as *A Universal History of Infamy*, 1972) of the writer as a
sinister, treacherous figure. What sets this story apart, however, is that
its emphasis falls less on the figure of the writer-as-criminal, and more
intensely instead on writing itself as a dangerous, and potentially deadly,
phenomenon. Indeed, the deadliness of writing is in effect taken for
granted in "The Garden of Forking Paths," as is its tendency to proliferate and spread.[4] In fact, these notions are arguably more relevant to at
least two of the stories that precede "The Garden of Forking Paths" in
*Ficciones*: the proliferation of writing features in "Tlön, Uqbar, Orbis
Tertius," and the relation between writing and death is important in
"The Circular Ruins."[5] However, in "The Garden of Forking Paths"
Borges gives a new twist to the themes of dissemination, death, and writing by placing them in a context of judgment and justice, thus linking
them explicitly to ethics. An ever-expanding ethical questioning of writing is, in fact, the central theme of this story, as well as the force that
propels the narrative.

"The Garden of Forking Paths," then, tells the story of an ethical chain reaction, a radiating, explosive phenomenon that infuses the past, present, and future actions of every character in the story with moral significance, like the "maze of mazes" that the main character, Yu Tsun, imagines his great-grandfather Tsui Pên built: "a sinuous, ever growing maze that would take in both past and future and would somehow involve the stars" (475). The world described in the story is one in which every decision is inextricably linked to considerations of good or evil, and has therefore a profound moral import. Borges would seem to be offering here a Manichaean view of the world as a stage on which good and evil collide, but unlike the Manichaeans, he does not profess to know where good and evil lie, but is instead concerned with *how* one recognizes and chooses between those two extremes.

An allusion to Borges's story in Geoffrey Galt Harpham's *Getting It Right: Language, Literature, and Ethics* is suggestive of the importance of ethics and of the chain-reaction metaphor in "The Garden of Forking Paths." Explaining the multifaceted, infinitely branching structure of ethical discourse, Harpham uses both the idea of the "chain of command" and the title of Borges's tale as key metaphors in his description:

> Thus ethical problems constitute a theoretically endless chain, a chain of command in which command is always countermanded by alternatives whose recurrence, like a trick candle that refuses to be blown out, resists the commands it calls forth. This resistance is inherited, as it were, from the basic terms of ethical discourse, whose paradigm is the compromised binary. From is/ought, through freedom/obligation, I/one, subjective/objective, integration/permeability, universalism/communitarianism, and other relations yet to be explored, ethics is *a garden of forking paths*, a discourse of mitosis that urges all who will listen to become such gardens themselves, to assume the form of ethics. (48–49; my italics)

For Harpham, the text of "The Garden of Forking Paths" offers a scale model of the branching, proliferating structure of ethical discourse.[6]

In consonance with its title, "The Garden of Forking Paths" is itself organized as a combination of the *mise en abyme* and an arborescent structure that branches out in different directions, creating multiple layers of plot with similar patterns repeated at different scales. Most of the story is presented as a fragmentary document authored in prison by a convicted murderer and spy, the Chinese-born German agent Yu Tsun. This text, we are told, is a "deposition," which was "dictated, read over, and signed by Dr. Yu Tsun" (472). It is therefore, as the text strongly suggests, a signed confession, and as such it is supposed to offer the criminal's explanation of the precise nature of and the motives for his misdeeds, and incidentally, to allow the criminal to reflect on his actions. The principal action to be reflected upon, in this case, is the murder of one Stephen Albert, a sinologist with whom Yu Tsun had conversed, shortly before killing him, about a literary work written by Yu Tsun's ancestor, Tsui Pên: the "chaotic novel" *The Garden of Forking Paths* (477).

In turn, Tsui Pên's novel, which we are told was written in the prisonlike isolation of the "Pavillion of the Limpid Solitude" (476), is a reflection of yet another type: its seemingly senseless proliferation of alternative or contradictory stories is the embodiment, as Stephen Albert proposes, of Tsui Pên's philosophical ideas about time (479). This obvious *mise en abyme* relationship between texts is reinforced by the framing comments of the story's fictional editor, who remarks that Yu Tsun's deposition elucidates an episode that took place during World War I and is recounted on page 242 of Liddel Hart's *A History of the World War*. Yu Tsun's text is essentially a footnote to a military incident that is itself part of a wider-scale conflict, the "World War." Readings of "The Garden of Forking Paths" in the vein of the theory of fractals, or chaos theory (Weissert 232–234), have already elaborated on this aspect, and I will not repeat them here.

It immediately becomes apparent, however, that the branching—and the pruning of those branches (I use botanical images throughout this chapter advisedly)—proposed by the story is not only a metaphor for a certain conception of time, or even for the structure of ethical discourse, but in fact a generalized figure for the process of writing as a whole. Tsui Pên's aptly named novel, *The Garden of Forking Paths*, unveils a hidden facet of writing that is usually regarded as liminal or preliminary, and makes it central to the novel's discourse. As Stephen Albert explains:

In all fiction, when a man is faced with alternatives, he chooses one at the expense of the others. In the almost unfathomable Tsui Pên, he opts— simultaneously—for all of them. He thus *creates* various futures, various times that start others, which will in turn branch out and bifurcate in other times. This is the cause of the contradictions in the novel. [. . .] *The Garden of Forking Paths* is a picture, incomplete yet not false, of the universe such as Tsui Pên conceived it to be. Differing from Newton and Schophenhauer, your ancestor did not think of time as absolute and uniform. He believed in an infinite and vertiginous series of times, an ever spreading network of diverging, converging, and parallel times. This web of time—the strands of

which approach one another, bifurcate, intersect, or ignore one another through the centuries—embraces *every* possibility. (478–479)

If instead of the word "times" one substitutes "plots," or more generally still, "signifieds," Tsui Pên's text can then be read as an unmasking of the consideration of alternatives, the instant of reflection (as in thought, but also as in a mirror), that is prior to the act of writing but inseparable from it. Before one writes, as the pen hovers over the page or the hand pauses over the keys, there is an instant, variable in length, of pondering, of consideration. This suspended moment of reflection is identified by Harpham as the "law that ethical discourse virtually presumes as well as teaches" (42). Ethics, in one of its facets, is precisely this: a potentially interminable and paralyzing process of weighing different courses of action. Furthermore, if writing and ethics share a tendency towards endless proliferation and a tissuelike continuity, they also share a propensity towards discrimination, cutting, or rending. Writing, like gardening, is an art that implies pruning as well as grafting.[7] Similarly, the deliberation of ethics is not complete without a further moment in which reflection ceases and action begins. In the act of writing, this moment occurs as the violent cutting or marking that produces separation and difference. In ethics, it occurs as "morality." As Harpham proposes, in phrases that resonate with Borges's text:

[Morality] designates . . . one name for a particular moment of ethics, not the static passivity of the virtuous will but rather the punctual, purist moment of decision when all but one of the available alternatives, no matter what their claims to rationality or justice, are excluded. The imperative that presides over and legitimates such a moment of decision must be "transcendent," crushing all opposition in its drive to self-actualization and resolution. As the secret agent of the virtuous will, then, morality represents the ethics of ethics. The policeman's gun, morality refuses disarmament. (52)

If one follows this parallel between writing and ethics to its logical conclusion, then it would seem that the two entities are fundamentally inseparable. However, another paradoxical trait shared by writing and ethics is their internal bifurcation: in writing, it is the division between writing as phenomenon and writing as action; in ethics, between ethical reflection and morality. This inner division already signals that, despite their close resemblance, ethics and writing may well have a relationship of incongruence or misalignment, a fact borne out in daily experience by the existence of a variety of texts, some of which are deemed moral, and others immoral. As J. Hillis Miller observes, in a comment that may be

extended to all kinds of writing and not only narrative, "Ethics and narration cannot be kept separate, though their relation is neither symmetri-
cal nor harmonious" (*The Ethics of Reading* 2). Suggestively, Derrida
points out in *Signéponge/Signsponge* that "l'instance éthique travaille
la littérature au corps" (53). This phrase may be rendered in English not
only as "the ethical instance is at work in the body of literature," but
also, more violently, as "ethics works (or forces) its way into the body of
literature" (Miller, *The Ethics of Reading* 133 n). Years earlier, in a well-
known passage from *Of Grammatology*, Derrida had alluded to the specu-
lative notion of "arche-writing" (a concept that would contain both presence and absence suspended within itself without privileging either) and
to the violence that attends the origin of ethical discourse:

There is no ethics without the presence of *the other* but also, and consequently, without absence, dissimulation, detour, différance, writing. The
arche-writing is the origin of morality as of immorality. The nonethical
opening of ethics. A violent opening. As in the case of the vulgar concept
of writing, the ethical instance of violence must be rigorously suspended
in order to repeat the genealogy of morals. (139–140)

It is this paradox of violence and ethics in writing that Borges explores in "The Garden of Forking Paths." Through the extreme instance
of Yu Tsun, the spy who must kill a man so that his superiors may know
which city to bomb, Borges examines writing's seemingly perverse reli-
ance on violence and its collusion with abjection and evil.

A key trait of this story is its consistent use of contrasting but col-
lapsible dualities (or, in Harpham's terms, "compromised binaries"): for
example, the East/West opposition is affirmed and at the same time ne-
gated in the character of Yu Tsun, who is a Chinese-born spy for Germany and a "former teacher of English at the Tsingtao *Hochschule*" (472).
Still more relevant to my analysis is the apparent contrast between Yu
Tsun's manuscript and that of his ancestor, Tsui Pên. The latter text
branches out in a plurality of directions, while the former moves in a
seemingly linear fashion, like an arrow to its target. Tsui Pên's novel, as
noted above, is apparently an attempt to make writing fully congruent
with ethics as a reflection on possible alternatives; as such, it would
seem to be a work that merely presents a certain view of the universe
without deriving any set of values or rules of conduct from that view. On
the other hand, Yu Tsun's text is absolutely permeated by morality and
moralizing. Yu Tsun's deposition, we must recall, is an attempt not to
claim his innocence before the law, but to justify his actions on a higher
moral plane: "I carried out my plan because I felt the [German] Chief

thought little of those of my race, of those uncountable forebears whose culmination lies in me. I wished to prove to him that a yellow man could save his armies" (473). Moreover, while Tsui Pên's novel abounds in sometimes contradictory alternatives, Yu Tsun's narrative recounts a sequence of "irrevocable" decisions: "I foresee that man will resign himself each day to new abominations, that soon only soldiers and bandits will be left. To them I offer this advice: *Whosoever would undertake some atrocious enterprise should act as if it were already accomplished, should impose upon himself a future as irrevocable as the past*" (474). Tsui Pên's novel appears underdetermined, since its controlling principle is so oblique that it has taken centuries to understand, while his descendant's narrative is patently overdetermined, full of expressions such as "should have," "was obliged to," "had to," and "must." The novel *The Garden of Forking Paths* seems to be a benignly tolerant philosophical fable, almost programmatic in its avoidance of violence and coercion (we are told that Tsui Pên "gave up all the pleasures of oppression," among other things, to write it; 476). The "deposition" by Yu Tsun, on the contrary, is a condemned murderer's confession, and it reads like a paean to action and a justification of violence for the sake of misplaced ideals. Finally, Tsui Pên seems to be the very image of the honorable, selfless writer who leaves a valuable legacy that only posterity can appreciate; his descendant, in contrast, appears as a degraded, criminal being whose whole existence is self-described as "abject" (473, 474).

But are these two texts, these two writers, in fact so different from each other? Stephen Albert shows Tsui Pên's novel to be no less rigidly determined than Yu Tsun's text, the only difference between them being, as in an algebraic equation, a difference in sign: the novel relentlessly adds possible worlds to its narration, while Yu Tsun's story ruthlessly subtracts every possibility. Nevertheless, there is negation in Tsui Pên's apparently "open" work—the negation of causality, linearity, and overdetermination, as well as the author's literal separation from the world in the Pavilion of the Limpid Solitude. There is, too, a certain openness in Yu Tsun's narrative, manifested in his dialogue with Stephen Albert and in his incorporation of Tsui Pên's novel into his own tale. Although seemingly amoral, Yu Tsun, as I have already remarked, is deeply concerned with morally justifying his actions in the face of his impending execution. Thus, although his narrative seems to be a linear, objective account of his actions and the order in which they occurred, it is actually a reconsideration, an ethical reflection on those actions. And this reflection is not diminished by its having been undertaken after the fact. "Abominably, I have triumphed": Yu Tsun's ambiguous claim of victory at the story's end strongly implies that ethical introspection has corroded the moral certainties with which he had attempted to strengthen his resolve (480).

More importantly, there is violence in both texts—violence of an epic sort in Tsui Pên's text and of an abject sort in Yu Tsun's, but violence nonetheless. Significantly, the only time Tsui Pên's text is cited indirectly in the story, it refers to an instance of violence. Stephen Albert reads to the spy two versions of the same chapter of Tsui Pên's novel:

> In the first, an army marches into battle over a desolate mountain pass. The bleak and somber aspect of the rocky landscape made the soldiers feel that life itself was of little value, and so they won the battle easily. In the second, the same army passes through a palace where a banquet is in progress. The splendor of the feast remained a memory throughout the glorious battle, and so victory followed. (478)

Yu Tsun then remarks, "I remember the final words, repeated at the end of each version like a secret command: 'Thus the heroes fought, with tranquil heart and bloody sword. They were resigned to killing and to dying'" (478). This moment in the story suggests a point of convergence between these two emblematic figures of the writer, who are joined, not only by genealogy, but also by their common view of writing as violence. Further evidence of this focus on violence appears when Albert, attempting to explain Tsui Pên's novel, uses an example in which a hypothetical character named Fang confronts an intruder and either kills him, or is killed by him, or befriends him, and so on (478). It might be argued that Tsui Pên's novel works as a kind of Derridean "arche-writing": a text that suspends and dissimulates the violence implicit in all moral judgments, but from which such violence can be inferred, as Yu Tsun does when he reads the final words of Tsui Pên's chapters as a "secret command," an implicit moral to the novel's apparently chaotic narrative.

As we have seen, writers are for Borges always associated with crime and violence, and the first target of their aggression is language itself. In "The Garden of Forking Paths" we again encounter the pattern, seen in Nájera and Zeno at the end of the nineteenth century (see chapters 1 and 2), of writing as a treacherous, abject act of violence against language by those who claim to love and respect language the most. The issue is not, it should be emphasized, a question of writing versus speech, of the writer somehow "killing" living speech in order to produce writing, but rather of a deep conflict embedded in writing itself. As was clearly evident in Nájera's text, the pattern is that of a clash between two opposite views of writing that may in fact be aspects of the same phenomenon: on the one hand, writing as a mimetic, lifelike, yet passive and contemplative creation, a victim, vehicle, or servant of others—of the law or of the *logos*—or, on the other hand, writing as a constant Other, as the active prototype of all "secret agents," a dissimulating and aggressive entity that resists being turned into a mere instrument. In order for writing to occur, the latter aspect must triumph over the former, at least provisionally; that is to say, there must be writing-as-action before there is writing-as-inscription. Of course, what is at stake in Borges's story is the force of the "must" in the previous sentence, which is undermined by the ethical chain reaction radiating from Tsui Pên's labyrinthine novel.

In the scene of writing that Borges presents allegorically in this story, the characters of Yu Tsun and Stephen Albert personify the two aforementioned aspects of writing. Indeed, to argue that Yu Tsun is merely an emblem of the writer would be to ignore this character's patently "textual" nature. Furthermore, as Borges proposes in several of his most celebrated stories, from "The Circular Ruins" to "Borges y yo" (Borges and I), all writers are from the beginning so intricately linked to their writing (and to that of others) that they eventually *become* writing. In "Nueva refutación del tiempo" (New refutation of time, 1946), Borges asks, "Are the enthusiasts who give themselves up to a line by Shakespeare not literally Shakespeare?" (763). This statement is reminiscent of Yu Tsun's observation about Albert: "I knew an Englishman—a modest man—who, for me, is as great as Goethe. I did not speak with him for more than an hour, but during that time, he *was* Goethe" (473). For Borges, to write is to play a role. Like the actor, the writer can at different times seem to be himself or another, autonomous or enslaved, writing or written.

Both Yu Tsun and Stephen Albert are textual entities whom we might call "writing-men,"[8] although, as we have seen, usually they are not men at all, but women: Nájera's "daughter of the air," Zeno's Silvina, and de la Parra's María Eugenia, as well as their precursors, Iphigenia, Semiramis, Mignon, and Celestina, among others. To his credit—and perhaps because of the paucity of female characters in his work[9]—Borges breaks with this stereotype; instead, he repeatedly invokes figures of men whose very existence seems to be primarily textual. These characters are all, in the most literal of senses, "men of letters," beings made out of written words. Yu Tsun's name, for instance, comes from one of the characters in the real-world Chinese novel *Hung Lou Meng* (The dream of the red chamber, 1791) by Ts'ao Hsueh-Ch'in (see Balderston 42 and Irwin 88), a fact that suggests that he is already textualized. Stephen Albert's name, which is composed of two first names (thus suggesting the irrelevance of his biological origins), also resonates with cultural allusions ranging from religion and modernist narrative to science and geography: "Stephen" evokes Saint Stephen, the first martyred Christian, as well as Joyce's character of Stephen Dedalus, while "Albert" evokes Einstein's first name (Weissert 231) as well as that of a city "on the Ancre" (Borges 473).[10]

It would be naive to regard these two characters as fixed emblems, however. The topic of time, mentioned in the story as the subject of Tsui Pên's philosophical speculations, becomes relevant here. Yu Tsun and Albert symbolize instead different states, or stages, of the same phenomenon of writing. As Nájera's "La hija del aire" suggests, there is an epigenetic relationship between the images of writing-as-Mignon and writing-as-Semiramis. Given time, all writing, no matter how passive or benign it may seem, becomes resistant, sometimes aggressively so. And the reverse is also true: with the passage of time, the resistances of writing are muted, and writing becomes petrified, monumentalized. As Yu Tsun observes about Albert at one point, "His countenance, in the bright circle of the lamplight, was certainly that of an ancient, but there was something unyielding, even immortal, about it" (478). A Chinese spy among westerners, Yu Tsun, at least at the beginning of his tale, is a personification of writing in its "othering," resistant aspect, an actively dissembling phenomenon that expresses itself through violence; his role is therefore like that of a writer. Albert, on the other hand, who is a former missionary (476), would seem to personify the pliant, beneficent aspect of writing, and although his role at first is that of a reader, he ends up becoming a text, Yu Tsun's text.

Albert's full-fledged conversion into a text occurs, as we know, when Yu Tsun murders him. This is not, it should be stressed, simply a question of the symbolic "murder" of the reader by the writer. Although it is true that Borges constantly posits the moral superiority of reading over writing, the situation here is more fundamental, since it describes the moment when the active part of writing neutralizes the passive, and the dynamic, unstable formation known as a "text" is born: concretely, in this case, the newspaper account read by Yu Tsun's German spy master. The killing of Albert also leads, however, to Yu Tsun's becoming passive himself (he is imprisoned and awaiting execution). He, too, then becomes a text to be read: the branching, complex text of his "deposition," which already begins to mimic Tsui Pên's novel. Albert's murder generates examples of the same two antithetical types of writing (active and passive) that he and Yu Tsun had embodied: the newspaper (writing as action) and the deposition (writing as inscription). Both texts lead also towards death: the newspaper article leads to the bombing of the city of Albert, while the deposition is the preamble to Yu Tsun's execution. In this regard, it should be remembered that Tsui Pên's labyrinthine novel was itself interrupted when he was "assassinated by a stranger" (475).

Ethics enters this context via Tsui Pên's novel, which belatedly leads Yu Tsun (and the story's readers) to realize that events did not *have* to transpire as they did, that there were in fact a number of possible alternative outcomes of the encounter between Yu Tsun and Stephen Albert. This is the case not only within the narrative, but outside of it, in the very act of writing "The Garden of Forking Paths" as a short story, in a manner similar to what we have already discussed with regard to Zeno's *La charca.* As Yu Tsun's narrative itself reminds us, there were other alternatives to killing Albert: Yu Tsun could have befriended him, or not visited him at all, or merely decided at the last minute not to shoot him, and so on. All of these alternatives would have required Yu Tsun to break with the circumstances that he claims determined his actual course of action: he would have had to abandon his career as a spy, as well as the resentment towards Germans and westerners in general that led him to become a spy in the first place. However, none of this is impossible in narrative terms; it simply would have led to a *different* narrative, or perhaps to an altogether nonnarrative text. Other stories in *Ficciones* offer a number of alternative models for such a text. Instead of a crime story, "The Garden of Forking Paths" could well have been written as a bogus book review (like "El acercamiento a Almotásim" [The approach to Al-Mu'tasim]), or as a parodic essay (like "An Examination of the Work of Herbert Quain").

Tsui Pên's *The Garden of Forking Paths* appears in the story as a utopian vision of undifferentiation, contemplation, and reading in a world dominated by differentiation, action, and writing. Things are never quite so simple in Borges, however. It is true that by visibly mobilizing ethics in its narrative structure, Tsui Pên's novel implicitly challenges the moralizing impulse—the "must" that propels and structures all narratives and dictates that all the actions in a story be (or seem to be) necessary, not superfluous or the result of chance. However, as we observed earlier, it is precisely in this sense that negativity enters the ideally pluralistic pages of *The Garden of Forking Paths.* Tsui Pên's text is clearly an antiliterary work. More specifically, it is an antinovel, perhaps a "novel to end all novels," just as World War I was said to be the "war to end all wars." Ironically, that peace-loving book, which refuses to judge or to conclude, thereby avoiding the violence implicit in morality, does not actually escape violence. It can even lead its readers to become writers, because readers can misinterpret (as Yu Tsun does) its invitation to reading, ethics, and quietism as an invitation to writing, moralism, and action. Meant as an antidote to the violence implicit in writing, Tsui Pên's novel only succeeds in generating still more writing, more violence.

How, precisely, does this occur? What else, besides the violence implicit in its negation of narrative, allows this text to be misread so egregiously? How does a text of peace and contemplation become a source of violence and evil? To reply, we must look beyond the drug/poison metaphor that surfaces in the preceding paragraph. We must also recall that Borges's story is concerned with the seemingly unstoppable dissemination of writing's violence, with the apparent impossibility of containing writing and controlling its effects. In this regard, the nuclear power/ nuclear destruction metaphor becomes more apposite. Following that metaphor, if we translate this story into terms of nuclear energy, writing appears in "The Garden of Forking Paths" as the "neutron" that produces a "splitting" in consciousness. This is so because the act of writing immediately implies the reflection upon that act, both before and after the act itself—as one reflects on what one is going to write, and as one reads what one has written. There is thus an inherent doubleness in writing that can turn into duplicity.[11] This duplicity is certainly one of the sources of writing's aura of malevolence, and of the association of writing with the abject.

Nevertheless, there is still another, more profound source of evil in writing. Once the "fissioning" (*fiction*ing?) of consciousness by writing takes place, the process goes on to produce still more "neutrons," more writing, in a cascading, spreading chain reaction whose growth is potentially infinite. "Infinity" is a term that Borges connects more than once to writing (as in "La biblioteca de Babel" [The library of Babel], for example), but also to evil. "There is one concept that corrupts and perplexes all others," writes Borges in an essay about Zeno's paradox ("Avatares de la tortuga" [Avatars of the tortoise], 1939). "I am not speaking of evil, whose limited empire is that of ethics; I am speaking of the Infinite" (*Obras completas* 254). According to Borges, eternity—an infinity of time—is the most horrible attribute of hell ("La duración del infierno" [The duration of hell], 1932; 235–238). Borges's favorite infinity, of course, is the *mise en abyme*, or, as he prefers to put it, "infinite regression" (255). This form of the infinite acts as a kind of logical black hole that can serve to undermine virtually any argument by denying the possibility of ever moving from one term or concept to another. It thus produces a kind of hollowing-out or voiding of thought. Another effect of infinite regression, however, is the production of a dizzying abysmatic perspective, as when one mirror reflects another, which leads to total disorientation because of a lack of any indication of beginning or end. Free-floating

in an infinite textual space whose shape evokes Giordano Bruno's description of the universe as "all center, or that the center of the universe is everywhere and the circumference nowhere" (see Borges's comments in "La esfera de Pascal" [Pascal's sphere], *Obras Completas* 637), both consciousness and conscience lose their bearings. Writing's notorious mirroring qualities, which are linked to its duplicity, can easily produce both of these effects. Tsui Pên's novel, whose ever bifurcating structure of time and narrative leads to infinity, is thus already "contaminated" by this radical negativity and in fact aids in its dissemination.

This voiding of reference points, this emptiness produced by writing, certainly resembles the most common and ancient definition of evil in Western civilization, which dates back to the stoics and neo-Platonists: that of evil as nonbeing (Abbagnano 765). Borges's distaste for the obvious seems to have led him to eschew any overt attempt to define or explain his concept of evil. Nevertheless, following Stephen Albert's riddling technique (479), Borges wrote about evil quite frequently, even as he carefully avoided using that noun. Borges very often alludes in his works to acts of infamy (a favorite word in his lexicon), or to characters who are clearly evil, such as the Nazi war criminal Otto Dietrich zur Linde in "Deutsches Requiem." The latter story, in fact, along with a cluster of related essayistic texts in which Borges discusses fascism and Nazism, is where Borges comes closest to a definition of evil as nonbeing. In "Anotación al 23 de agosto de 1944" (A comment on August 23, 1944) (the date of the liberation of Paris by the Allies), he notes that "Nazism suffers from unreality, like Erigena's hells. It is uninhabitable" (*Obras completas* 728). Zur Linde, the former concentration camp director in "Deutsches Requiem," who uses and abuses the ideas of Nietzsche to justify himself, argues that in defeat Nazism paradoxically has triumphed, because despite the destruction of Germany and the Nazi leaders' deaths, it has managed to enthrone violence and destruction in the world: "There now looms over the world an implacable epoch. We forged it, we who are now its victims. What does it matter if England is the hammer and we the anvil? What is important is that violence should rule, not servile Christian meekness" (581). In another text unrelated to politics, but dealing with the question of nonbeing, of nothingness, Borges denounces as a "fallacy" the idea that "not being is more than being something and that, somehow, not to be is to be everything" ("De alguien a nadie" [From someone to no one], *Obras completas* 739).

For Borges, in any case, both aspects of writing—the active and the passive—are profoundly tinged with negativity, with nonbeing. In both modalities, writing produces a dissolution of consciousness, of the self. Be it through action or through contemplation, the end result of writing is always violence and death. Readers are caught up in this vortex as well, of course, since in modern literature they are constantly being enticed to become writers, as Borges points out in "An Examination of the Work of Herbert Quain" (464). Reading, although still regarded by Borges as a fairly "pure" and disinterested activity, nevertheless entails the constant risk of "contamination" by the nonbeing lurking in every text.

It follows that to avoid writing's deadliness, to contain it (like nuclear weapons and nuclear waste), we must strictly limit our exposure to writing. This limitation applies to reading as well as to writing. It is worth noting that, with the passing of time, Borges not only denied that he had read certain authors (despite evidence to the contrary in his own writings) but began paring down his personal canon to at most a half dozen idiosyncratic names (Poe, Kafka, Chesterton, Schopenhauer, Stevenson, Wells).[12] The encyclopedia—another favorite image of Borges's—paradoxically embodies this attempt to economize reading through summary or synthesis.

Borges's notorious stylistic economy, which he began to develop long before he lost his sight, is yet another manifestation of this strategy to limit the dissemination of evil through writing. Spare and unadorned—after his ultraist beginnings, he avoided metaphors like the plague, so to speak—Borges's writing seeks an austere beauty through a transparency that always allows glimpses of infinity (of nonbeing, of evil) but somehow manages to draw back in the nick of time. The protagonist of "El Aleph" (The aleph, 1949), who resembles Borges himself, fears he has lost his selfhood after gazing upon the "infinite Aleph" (624). However, he adds, "Happily, after a few sleepless nights, oblivion again did its work on me" (626).

All subsequent Spanish American writers have gazed upon Borges's aleph, or trod the forking paths of his garden, and have thus become part of Borges's ethical chain reaction. After Borges, it becomes impossible not to reflect ethically on writing, and on the evil void at writing's core.

In his essay "Sobre Chesterton" (On Chesterton, 1952), Borges considers the paradox of an English author who was widely regarded as an optimist and a purveyor of Catholic dogma but who regularly wrote stories and novels that evoked the horrors of Poe and Baudelaire and prefigured the nightmares of Kafka. Alluding to Kafka's famous parable of timidity and judgment deferred in "Before the Law," and comparing it to an episode in Bunyan's *Pilgrim's Progress* in which a fearless pilgrim fights his way into a castle, Borges concludes that "Chesterton devoted his life to writing the second of those parables, but something in him always tended to write the first" (696).

This reading of Chesterton as a seemingly moral writer who was fascinated by atrocities and evil may well be interpreted, as is frequently appropriate in Borges's work, as a self-reflexive statement, one that alerts us to the depth of Borges's ethical questioning of writing. Among the various examples he offers of Chesterton's fascination with malevolence, one is particularly suggestive: Chesterton, states Borges, "imagines . . . that in the Eastern confines of the world there may exist a tree that is already more, and less, than a tree, and in those of the West, something, a tower, whose very architecture is wicked" (695). The paradoxical notion of an inherently "wicked" building, which implies that things may be as subject to moral judgment as people, is clearly reminiscent of the all too frequent moral condemnation of writing and literature. It also reminds us of the unexpected twists and turns—the forking paths?— that writing often imposes upon the moralizing intentions of writers.

Literature, of course, abounds in protestations of innocence by writers who claim they were misread or misinterpreted, and who seek to blame writing for their own transgressions. Thus far, in our readings of Nájera, Zeno, de la Parra, and now Borges, we have dealt with the writer's relation to writing and violence and pointed out how that relationship is often portrayed as one of complicity. The following works we will examine, by Alejo Carpentier and Julio Cortázar, elaborate still further on the idea of complicity and writing. In both, the context of justice and judgment already implicit in "The Garden of Forking Paths" is made more explicit through direct allusions to trials and judicial proceedings of various sorts, as well as to the context of religion. Also in both, the issue of the writer's accountability is of paramount importance. Unlike Borges, Carpentier and Cortázar do not assume the writer's guilt from the beginning, but instead dramatize how a nominally innocent although fallible person becomes enmeshed, through writing, in a world of violence and evil. Evoking the figures of Don Quixote and Goethe's Faust, Carpentier and Cortázar portray the archetypal writer as the man or woman who dares to enter the endlessly ethical "garden of forking paths" even at the risk of being led astray.

## CHAPTER 5

# Ethics and Theatricality in Alejo Carpentier's The Harp and the Shadow

One of my favorite entertainments was the
theater, the two theaters: the true one and the
false one. The true one was the one in La
Comedia; the false one was of cardboard, and
showed *The Merchant of Venice* or whatever I was
writing in imitation of the plays I had seen in
La Comedia. [. . .] The false theater was more
beautiful and truthful than the true one.
—NILITA VIENTÓS GASTÓN,
*El mundo de la infancia*

devil: Permission to enter I demand . . .
providence: Who is it?
devil: The king of the West.
—LOPE DE VEGA,
epigraph to Carpentier's *El reino de este mundo*

Published shortly before his death from cancer in 1980, Alejo Carpentier's
novel *El arpa y la sombra* (1979) (published in English as *The Harp and
the Shadow*, 1990) has generally been read as a covert autobiography and
as an anticipatory reflection on the ultimate fate of his literary works.[1]
But there is more to *The Harp and the Shadow* than Carpentier's reas-
sessment, carried out with as much ironic humor as sangfroid, of his life

and career. Faced with his personal mortality and with the uncertain survival of his authorial self, the Cuban novelist also reflects, in this seemingly minor work, on the ethics of his craft. More concretely, Carpentier asks in this novel whether in the end, in his struggle to be faithful to the ethics of writing as he understood it, he did not strike a Faustian bargain of sorts, a deal with the Devil—the Devil being, in this case, writing. Following Hegel (in his *Lectures on the Philosophy of World History*, 1830–1831) as well as Borges, Carpentier in *The Harp and the Shadow* portrays fiction writing as complicitous with evil and worries whether his devotion to—indeed his zeal for—writing has resulted in good or evil. Ultimately, what is at stake in *The Harp and the Shadow*'s ethical meditation is a questioning, similar to Borges's in many respects, of the values and principles inherent in writing.

Carpentier's ethical reflection about writing (his own writing and that of others) in *The Harp and the Shadow* takes the form of a fictional narrative about the life of Christopher Columbus and his subsequent destiny as a historical figure. The novel's first chapter, titled "El arpa" (The harp) tells of the voyage to Latin America by the young Italian priest who would later become Pope Pius IX and who would set in motion the attempt to canonize Columbus in the late nineteenth century. The second chapter, "La mano" (The hand) contains an interior monologue by Columbus himself in which, on his deathbed, he offers a highly self-critical account of his life. A burlesque portrayal of Columbus's failed canonization hearings in the Vatican is the substance of the third and final chapter, "La sombra" (The shadow).

In typically Carpenterian fashion, this narrative is laden with allusions to the Western literary tradition, from classical antiquity to the twentieth century. Among these allusions, some of the most striking and constant are to Cervantes and his works, particularly the *Quixote* (1605–1615), *Los trabajos de Persiles y Sigismunda* (The adventures of Persiles and Sigismunda, 1617), and the *entremés* (interlude) of *El Retablo de las Maravillas* (The retable of wonders, 1615).

Roberto González Echevarría has underscored the importance of this symbolic linkage between Columbus and Cervantes, posited in *The Harp and the Shadow* by the many anachronistic allusions to Cervantes and his works made by the character of Columbus ("The Pilgrim's Last Journeys" 292–295).[2] Presenting Columbus as one link in a genealogy of "authors" of which Cervantes, and Carpentier himself, also form parts, Carpentier evidently seeks to connect the origins of Latin America with those of the novelistic genre. Indeed, throughout this novel there is an implicit parallelism between the New World and writing in which, among other things, America's relation to Columbus is compared to that between a text and its author. This symbolic connection between writing and America, as I will demonstrate shortly, is a key element in Carpentier's ethics of writing as it appears in *The Harp and the Shadow*.

The allusions to *El Retablo de las Maravillas* and to the episode of Master Peter's puppet show in the *Quixote* allow us to probe the ethical problematics of writing that lies at the core of *The Harp and the Shadow*. To begin with, much as Calderón's drama worked in Nájera's "La hija del aire," these allusions allow theatricality to enter Carpentier's text and to contribute to its intensely self-critical discourse. If critics have consistently viewed *El Retablo* as a metatheatrical play (see Molho, Meléndez), it can also be interpreted more broadly as a metaliterary text, particularly in view of its connection with the notoriously self-reflexive *Quixote*. Let us recall that in Cervantes's interlude, the male/female duo of Chanfalla and La Chirinos tricks the notables of a country village into claiming to see in the middle of an empty stage, as if they were real, the mythical and historical characters that Chanfalla verbally evokes. Whoever admits to being unable to see them is immediately accused of being a *converso* (a converted Jew). An analogous situation occurs in the episode of Master Peter's puppet show (*El ingenioso hidalgo Don Quijote de la Mancha* pt. 2, chap. 26), when Don Quixote mistakes the chivalric adventures portrayed by Master Peter's puppets for the real thing.

In both instances, Cervantes explores the complex relationship among the author, language, the space of the text, and the reader. In *El Retablo*, Chanfalla and La Chirinos entice the naïve villagers into visualizing a spoken text. Manipulating the villagers' fears and desires, they make the verbal images enunciated by Chanfalla materialize for the villagers on the blank space of the stage. They effectively turn all the villagers into writers, in the process mocking the town's governor, who is the only one who claims to be a poet. In a parallel though converse fashion, Don Quixote in his madness pits the chivalric texts he knows by heart against their theatrical representations by Master Peter's puppets, thus uncovering the conventional traits of both theater and the romances of chivalry. In both cases, theater helps to unveil, by means of its own illusion, the delusions of writing.

Beyond Cervantes's obvious exploration of the shared artificiality of stage and text, it is worth remarking that in both *El Retablo* and the *Quixote*, textual production is in the hands of authorial figures of dubious quality. In both instances, Cervantes presents authors as ethically and ontologically ambiguous figures. In *El Retablo*, Chanfalla and La Chirinos are literally a duo of tricksters, and, furthermore, they are demonic rather than picaresque figures, since their "new trick" (*nuevo embuste; Entremeses* 169) appears to be entirely gratuitous, motivated by a desire neither for wealth nor for status. The town's governor, for his part, is a fake poet, a poetaster. In the *Quixote*, not only are Don Quixote's authorial pretensions motivated by insanity, but Master Peter is none other than the galley slave and bandit Ginés de Pasamonte, who assumes various identities to flee from justice and is also literally an author, since, as the narrator of the *Quixote* tells us, his "endless outrages and crimes . . . were so many and of such a nature, that he himself composed a huge volume to tell about them" (*El ingenioso hidalgo Don Quijote de la Mancha* 461). A similar ambiguity is shared by other authorial figures in the *Quixote*, from Cide Hamete Benengeli, whom the narrator tells us is probably a liar because he is an Arab (52), to the numerous magicians who supposedly write down the deeds of the knights-errant, and who can just as easily help the knights as try to harm them (43).

Cervantes's use of theatricality as a device not only to unmask literary conventions but to posit ethical questions about narrative fiction derives from the age-old association between theatrical discourse and morality. Traditionally, because of its societal functions and its inherent self-reflexiveness as a spectacle, theater has made stronger claims to morality than narrative. Since the days of the Greek chorus, the presence of a spectator within the drama has always signified the inclusion of a "third party," an "other" to the dramatic text and to the rest of the play's characters (Bernard 932–938) This Other's function has often been to pass judgment on the people and events described, to bring into the drama the dimension of ethical judgment. The close resemblance between theatrical representation and judicial proceedings is already a commonplace observation, but it serves as a reminder of theater's overt concern with rules and regulations, with "law" in its most general sense.[3] In *The Harp and the Shadow*, I would argue, as in Nájera's "La hija del aire," theatrical discourse itself becomes the "third party" that is brought in, along with the rest of the text and the reader, to pass judgment not only on Carpentier as a writer but also on writing as a phenomenon and as an activity.

Later in this chapter I will say more about the ethical implications of theatricality, but before proceeding to that discussion, it is important to review those aspects of *The Harp and the Shadow* that can be deemed "theatrical." Carpentier makes full use in this novel of all the metathe-atrical implications of *El Retablo de las Maravillas* and adds some others of his own invention. The first and most detailed allusion to Cervantes's interlude appears in the section titled "The Hand," in which the character of Columbus, on his deathbed, mentally reviews his life history before his confessor arrives. The passage is worth quoting in full. Speaking of his attempts to convince European monarchs to give him ships to sail west across the Atlantic, Columbus remembers:

So I contrived a workshop of marvels (*un tinglado de maravillas*), like those the goliards make in Italian fairs. I launched into my theatrics before dukes and monarchs, financiers and friars, rich men, clerics and bankers, the great men from here and there; I erected a curtain of words, from behind which appeared, in a dazzling procession, the grand illusions of Gold, Diamonds, Pearls, and especially Spices. Dame Cinnamon, Dame Nutmeg, Dame Pepper, and Dame Cardamom entered on the arms of Sir Sapphire, Sir Topaz, Dame Emerald, and Dame Silver, followed by Dame Ginger and Sir Clove, to the beat of a tune whose musical harmonies resonated with the color of saffron and the smell of malabar and the names of Cipango, Cathay, the Golden Colchis, and all the Indies (which, as everyone knows, are many), the numerous, proliferous, epicene, and beautiful Indies, indistinct but moving toward us, wanting to reach out to us, to annex themselves to our laws, close—closer than we thought, though they still seemed distant—the Indies that we can now reach straightaway, sailing to the left-hand side of the maps, scorning the ill-fated route of the right hand, which was plagued in those days by Moslem pirates and buccaneers sailing Chinese junks, while on the land route they imposed outrageous tolls, transit fees, impositions of weights and measures, in the territories ruled by the Great Turk. . . . Left hand. Right hand. Open them, show them, move them with the dexterity of a juggler, with the delicacy of spun gold, or instead, be dramatic and raise them in prophecy, quoting Isaiah, invoking the psalms, lighting Roman candles, exposing the forearm as the sleeve falls back, suggesting the invisible, signaling the unknown, scattering riches, holding up treasures as numerous as the imaginary pearls that still appeared to slip through my fingers, falling to the ground and bouncing in an oriental play of light from the amaranth of the rugs. The nobles and counselors applauded, praised my original notions, momentarily considered my promise of visionary goldsmithery, of alchemy without retorts, but in the end they showed me the door, leaving me in port with neither ships nor expectations. (77–79)

Like that of Chanfalla and La Chirinos, Columbus's retable is a purely verbal creation that works by exciting the desire and greed of its spectators. Unlike Cervantes's characters, however, Columbus fails at first in convincing the European nobles to finance his project. Eventually, nevertheless, it is desire itself, along with his improving theatrical and narrative abilities, that allows Columbus to convince and seduce Queen Isabella (88–95). Closely paralleling Cervantes's interlude, Columbus refers to Isabella as Columba (91), thus turning her into his feminine double (like La Chirinos), a demonic accomplice and joint partner in his deception.

The play of doubles present in Cervantes's interlude is intensified in *The Harp and the Shadow*. A neobaroque tour de force, this novel's allusions to *El Retablo de las Maravillas* evoke, as in a *mise en abyme*, Cervantes's suggestions about the literary text as artifice and about the ontological and ethical ambiguity of the author, and extend them further, self-critically, to Carpentier's own life and work. It is a strategy similar to that of Borges's "The Circular Ruins" (1941). Like the wizard of that story, Carpentier discovers that as an author, he too is a fictional creation, produced by another's imagination—another who might be himself in an earlier instant or stage of his own life. In *The Harp and the Shadow*, Carpentier, in the guise of Columbus, passes judgment on prior episodes of his literary trajectory, such as his famous prologue to *El reino de este mundo* (The kingdom of this world, 1949), in which he coined the concept of "the marvelous American reality" (a notion that anticipates "magic realism"). Clearly, the word "marvels" (*maravillas*) in a Carpenterian context cannot but evoke the thesis of "the marvelous real," in which Carpentier insisted that faith, the belief in miracles and prodigies, was the key to creating a writing proper to the New World ("De lo real maravilloso americano" 116–117). In *The Harp and the Shadow*, however, "the marvelous" is unequivocally associated with Columbus's deceit, with an act of trickery that originates the New World itself. Furthermore, if the New World is in part a fiction, then "the marvelous American reality" can only be a second-order fiction, another deception in a potentially endless sequence. Here we begin to glimpse how writing and the Americas are associated in Carpentier's text, but the full implications of that parallelism will become clearer as our reading proceeds. Suffice it to say, for the moment, that in *The Harp and the Shadow*, Carpentier rereads his life and work in a Cervantine (and Borgesian) key, and the end result of that process is a profound self-questioning that leads him to repudiate a large portion of his earlier work, in the manner of Alonso Quijano at the end of the *Quixote*: "I have good news for you, kind sirs. I am no longer Don Quixote de la Mancha but Alonso Quijano, whose way of life won for him the name of 'Good.' I am the enemy of Amadis of Gaul and all his innumerable progeny; for those profane stories dealing with knight-errantry are odious to me, and I realize how foolish I was and the danger I courted in reading them; but, by grace of God, I am in my right senses now and I abominate them" (Cervantes, *El ingenioso hidalgo Don Quijote de la Mancha* 670).

The very structure of Carpentier's novel seems to reproduce that of a retable or stage as described in Cervantes's interlude. Divided into three chapters ("The Harp," "The Hand," and "The Shadow"), the "spatial form" of this novel is reminiscent not only of the retables of medieval religious painting[4] but also of a theatrical space: the first and third chapters frame the second as if it were a stage on which the character of Christopher Columbus delivers his monologue. This soliloquy is highly problematic, however, since it consists of Columbus's thoughts while on his deathbed, thoughts that the admiral at first plans to tell the confessor who comes to see him but at the end decides not to communicate (51, 168). The ontological status of this text is nebulous, to say the least, since its existence is simultaneously affirmed and denied, turning it into a text that is never written or enunciated in terms of its own fictional setting. Neither can it be stated with certainty that it is an interior monologue presented by an omniscient author, or that it is simply—as the text also suggests—a discourse imagined within the fiction by Pope Pius IX (also note here the oblique allusion to the *Retablo de las Maravillas*):

> The pope remembered that, just as he himself had, Columbus had belonged to the Third Order of Saint Francis, and that it was a Franciscan who had been his confessor one afternoon in Valladolid. . . . Oh, to have been Him, that obscure friar, who *that afternoon* in Valladolid had the immense joy of receiving the confession of the Revealer of the Planet! How the cosmic images must have overflowed that afternoon in a poor room in an inn, transformed by the words of the One who spoke into a veritable Palace of Marvels! (47)

Although Columbus's discourse in "The Hand" ends up contradicting the beatific image Pope Pius IX has of him, one cannot wholly discount the possibility that this text might be a figment of the pontiff's imagination, especially given the "Russian dolls" structure of the novel, already announced from its first paragraph.[5] Like Chanfalla in Cervantes's interlude, who makes the villagers see historical figures (such as Samson or Herodias; *Entremeses* 179) in the empty space of the stage, Carpentier persuades his readers to accept the reality of a fictional text—Columbus's supposed deathbed confession. The figure of Columbus in this novel, like those of Samson and Herodias for the villagers in the interlude, is largely a projection of the desires, fears, and prejudices of the readers, who ultimately must judge if the narrative that the novel ambiguously offers is trustworthy.

In this sense, the absence of the term "the hand" (which is the title of the second chapter) in the novel's title is significant. In the novel's epigraph, taken from the hagiographic work *Leyenda aurea* (The golden legend, 1260) by Jacobus de Voragine, "the hand," along with "art" and "the string," is mentioned as one of the indispensable elements required to make the harp produce its harmonies, and it is an evident synecdoche for the figure of the artist or the author. Its absence in the novel's title prefigures the semantic void that opens in the second chapter, which is an *aporia* or literary black hole through which the game of absence/presence of Columbus, Carpentier, and authorial figures in general is represented. As in Cervantes's *El Retablo de las Maravillas*, Carpentier's retable is also empty; the endless chain of images that appears in it vanishes as soon as we stop to examine it. The text of the novel presents us with a lineage of "magicians"—Columbus, Cervantes, Borges, Carpentier—who are themselves mirages produced by the reader's anxious desire to recover an authorial presence behind the words he or she is reading. Ultimately, we too, as readers, become evanescent figures when we are unable to find a firm ontological grip (a "hand"?) in the midst of the text's semantic back-and-forth movement.[6]

The implicit theatricality in the allusions to *El Retablo de las Maravillas* in the second chapter becomes an even more visible element in the third chapter, "The Shadow." A noticeable departure is its use of an element rarely found in Carpentier's style: dialogue. In fact, this chapter has many comedic or farcical qualities, some of which are reminiscent of the circus atmosphere evoked in Nájera's "La hija del aire"; examples include the use of comic figures such as The Curator and the seminarian, and the irreverent, colloquialism-laden conversation between these two about the bones of saints stored in the Lipsonotec and about the renewed attempt to beatify Columbus (172–178). Abandoning all referential pretense, this chapter of the novel anticipates critical commentary by becoming explicitly metaliterary. Thus, Columbus's ghost, who returns to witness the discussion of his case, is referred to as "the Invisible One" (171), "the man of paper" (171), and the "present/absent Protagonist" (178), and the beatification hearing is called a "Morality Play" (*un Auto Sacramental*; 178). With a Cervantine wink to his readers, the narrator refers to Saint Peter's Basilica as a "Palace of Marvels" (171). The debate over Columbus's beatification, in which characters such as Fray Bartolomé de Las Casas, Lamartine, Victor Hugo, and Jules Verne anachronistically participate, shares with the rest of the chapter a farcical tone and an overall metaliterary quality.

As we have seen, *The Harp and the Shadow* incorporates theatrical elements in its discourse to a high degree, more than probably any other of Carpentier's narratives.[7] Using Cervantes as his principal model, Carpentier pits theatricality against textuality, so as to lay bare the conventions and presuppositions that give his narrative a coherent appearance. The presence of theatricality in Carpentier's text signals, first of all, a desire to tell the truth about the text's own constitution—about its fictionality, for example, or more generally, its artifice—in much the same way as the character of Columbus proclaims his intention to "tell . . . everything, everything" (79). Theatricality is first and foremost in this novel a gesture of honesty, a way to tell the truth about fiction, or, more concretely, to investigate fiction's ultimate truth.

What such an "ultimate truth" might be, at least for Carpentier, is suggested by the specific emphasis in the last section of the novel on the theatrical genre of farce. Despite farce's reputation for frivolity, specialists point out its potential for dealing irreverently with many of the harshest issues of human existence: from the abuses of power, to the myths of the family, to the rituals of death (Bentley 219–256; Bermel 13–14). The inherent antinomy of farce—its conjunction of laughter with violence and pain—is already suggestive of its profound ethical import. Despite its apparent unconcern with morality, its proverbial irresponsibility, farce deals constantly, much as ethics does, with otherness and with the response to otherness.[8] Moreover, in exposing the violence that lies beneath both theatrical and social convention, farce is the most extreme and most unruly form of theatricality.

The unruliness of farce extends also to textuality, to writing, of which it is very nearly the polar opposite. As Albert Bermel notes, "farce . . . takes leave of comedy not only in its written material but also, and more manifestly, in its enactment. It is primarily a performer's art, not a writer's" (56). The presence of farcical elements in *The Harp and the Shadow* is but one of the many signs of this novel's overall critical and negative view of writing.

What is at stake in Columbus's "beatification hearing" is an indictment less of the discoverer than of the writer and of writing. The farcical trial at the end of the novel resembles a "morality play" in more ways than one: not only is it allegorical (since it uses a discussion of Columbus's life and work to address those of Carpentier and of authors in general), but, like the *autos sacramentales* of the Spanish golden age, it deals with questions of good and evil in the context of a polemic between free will and divine providence. Was Columbus—and by extension, Carpentier and all other modern authors—heroic or infamous? Could he have acted otherwise, in the circumstances in which he found himself? Was his work ("discovering" and conquering other nations, or in Carpentier's case, writing novels) inspired by good or by evil? Were the effects of his work, in historical perspective, beneficent or malevolent?

Columbus's beatification case is closed when the Holy Congregation of Rites decides he cannot be beatified because of two grave accusations against him: "the first, extremely serious, of having a mistress—all the more inexcusable when we consider that the navigator was a widower when he met the woman who gave him a child—and the second, no less serious, of having instituted and promoted an inexcusable slave trade, selling, in public markets, several hundred Indians captured in the New World . . ." (193–194). However, the closing of his case does not lead, in the text, to a definitive judgment against the admiral. Immediately following this scene, we find in parentheses a monologue in which Columbus's phantom tries to justify himself and to respond to the criticisms of the Holy Congregation of Rites (195–198). Invoking the code of chivalry in terms that clearly refer to the *Quixote*, "the Invisible One" argues that his concubinage with Beatriz was caused by his amorous fidelity to Queen Isabella, and he insists on the purity of his ideals (197–198). In any event, there is in this text no judgment of Columbus more severe than the one the admiral passes on himself in the second chapter—although, as we have seen, this judgment cannot be admitted as evidence against him, since even as the text seems to offer it to us, it takes it away.

Undoubtedly, although *The Harp and the Shadow* avoids offering a definitive moral judgment of Columbus and of authors in general, it portrays them as profoundly ambiguous beings. Beneath their heroic façade, authors appear as *pícaros*, delinquents, abject individuals. Columbus's heroism in crossing the Atlantic is countered by his infamy in fomenting the enslavement of the Indians (149–152). Bewildered by the injustices that frequently result from the actions he carries out with supposedly elevated motives—although he recognizes his partial responsibility due to weaknesses and greed—the character of Columbus even wonders if he has not inadvertently made a deal with the Devil:

But, in the first line of those who pressed forward to join me in my return to shore I saw the face, wry, ironic, and condemning, of that Rodrigo de Triana whose ten thousand reales of royal reward I had taken to give to Beatriz, my spurned lover. I detected in his look a note of accusation, and I also observed that the sailor still carried, as a sign of his contempt, the silk doublet that I had given him *that day*—now worn and mended all over, but still with its ostentatious red color, the color of the Devil. And, terrified, I asked myself whether the presence of Rodrigo, here, today, was not the Presence of He Who, lying in wait to drag me to the Kingdom of Shadows, was already beginning to call me to account. I had made no pact with him. But there are pacts that do not require a parchment signed in blood. They remain written, in indelible ink, when with lies and deceit, inspired by the Malignant One, we enjoy wonders denied to other mortals. (153)

In *The Harp and the Shadow*, the picaresque image of the author has decidedly Faustian overtones: like Faust, authors are capable of placing their souls at risk in order to produce a great work, and their powers are borrowed, since their "authority" has been granted to them by a more powerful, though malevolent, being. The parallelism between Columbus and Faust suggested in these lines should be extended, of course, to Carpentier as well. Like Faust, both Columbus and Carpentier have made, or fear they have made, the proverbial deal with the Devil. But who is the Devil for the latter two? For Columbus, according to the text of *The Harp and the Shadow*, he is not so much the theological Prince of Darkness as he is an emblem for the act of deceit, of lying, and by extension, of fiction writing. Columbus is an author figure, specifically a fiction writer, and his grandest fiction, produced in collusion with "the Malignant One," is the New World itself. As in Cervantes's *El Retablo*, Columbus's "invention" (a term etymologically linked to "discovery") of the New World (*Nuevo Mundo*) is a *"nuevo embuste"* (new trick; *Entremeses* 169), a fiction. But it could also be argued that Columbus's Mephistopheles is, in fact, the New World itself, which—like the dimly glimpsed shadow of a work still to be written—beckons temptingly and obsessively, with promises of glory and riches, from the text of Seneca's tragedy *Medea* and from the saga of Leif Ericson. What is clear is that in *The Harp and the Shadow*, the New World functions simultaneously as Columbus's demonic obsession, as his created fiction (his "writing"), and as the source of his damnation.

Similarly, Carpentier's whole oeuvre deals almost exclusively with the New World, its identity, and its history. For Carpentier, too, America is conflated with writing; his desire to inscribe the New World is but one aspect of his overall aim to master writing and its mysteries. In this context, one might wonder if Columbus's enslavement of the Indians in the novel is not parallel, allegorically, to Carpentier's "use and abuse" of "American" themes and topics for his own literary ends, which, from the standpoint of the Cuban Revolution's view of literature as an adjunct to social struggles, would be morally reprehensible.

However, both America and writing possess "demonic" qualities. Both are epistemologically elusive entities; both are best understood in differential terms (that is, as what they differ from rather than as what they *are*); and both are symbolically associated with violence.[9] In Carpentier's case, the analogy with Goethe's romantic triangle of Faust-Mephistopheles-Gretchen breaks down when America-as-Gretchen dissolves into a devilish illusion. Writing is not only the Devil's work; writing *is* the Devil. Carpentier's awareness of this dilemma led him to posit Satan, in his early fictions, as the figure that presided, explicitly or implicitly, over the writing of those works. The epigraph to *The Kingdom of This World*, taken from an *auto sacramental* by Lope de Vega, presents a dialogue between God and the Devil that evokes the idea, current in Lope's time, of the New World as part of Satan's kingdom; and the character of Mackandal in that same novel is surrounded by the attributes of a wizard or witch doctor. In "El camino de Santiago" (The high road of Saint James) in *Guerra del tiempo* (War of time, 1958), the figure of Beelzebub appears explicitly as the mysterious entity that propels the story's plot. Starting with *Los pasos perdidos* (The lost steps, 1953), however, the Devil disappears from Carpentier's subsequent fictions, along with the ideas about cyclical time and the "magical" concordance between writing and history. This disappearance, I would argue, is essentially a substitution in which the demonic function is taken over by America itself, in all the confusing and contradictory aspects of its geography and its natural and social history. America becomes for Carpentier a generalized metaphor for writing, and in the process, the theological and moral implications inherent in the earlier allusions to Satan recede to the background. In the novels that followed *The Lost Steps*—*El siglo de las luces* (Explosion in a cathedral, 1961), *Concierto barroco* (Baroque concert, 1974), *El recurso del método* (Reasons of state, 1974), and the ponderous *La consagración de la primavera* (The rites of spring, 1979)—Carpentier investigates writing through an exploration of the complex systems of signs with which America has been represented and interpreted.

I am not arguing that Carpentier, like his golden-age counterparts, anachronistically views America as the kingdom of Satan. What I propose is that America is for Carpentier a metaphorical stand-in for writing, and that Carpentier further views writing as complicitous with evil. It is in part writing's devilish character that turns Carpentier's well-intentioned attempt to harmonize history with fiction in his novels into a falsification of history.[10] Of course, through the example of Columbus's greed, *The Harp and the Shadow* questions even the seeming nobility of the author's aims, and points to self-aggrandizement as a more likely reason for an author's novelistic enterprise. In any case, the work that results from the author's Faustian bargain is always morally dubious. Just as Columbus's achievements are impugned by proponents of the so-called black legend of Spain's deeds in the New World, and by figures such as Father Las Casas (*El arpa y la sombra* 190), Carpentier's own fictions, like those of so many authors, are open to moral condemnation. This vulnerability is due not only to his rejection of moralizing attitudes (which is typical of much of twentieth-century literature) but also, and more problematically, to the fact that his works seem to depend, for their very existence, on evil. Evil in Carpentier's works, as in Hegel's *Lectures on the Philosophy of World History*, is embodied in the "infamies" of history, in the "panorama of sin and suffering" that history presents to us (Hegel 22), without which novels and narratives such as *The Kingdom of This World, War of Time, Explosion in a Cathedral, Reasons of State*, and, of course, *The Harp and the Shadow*, could not have been written. In the latter work, Carpentier goes much further, arguing that it is *representation* itself that is evil, that writing and the theater are both dubious, malignant activities, closely allied to deceit and trickery.

This idea is the most profound ethical ambiguity embedded in *The Harp and the Shadow*, one that connects this work to the long graphophobic tradition I discussed in the introduction. The Platonic origins of this tradition are explored at length by Derrida in his well-known essay "La Pharmacie de Platon" (1972), and they do not need to be repeated here; it is worthwhile, nevertheless, to cite Derrida's gloss of Plato's view of writing in the *Phaedrus*:

Writing is not an independent order of signification; it is weakened speech, something not completely dead; a living-dead, a reprieved corpse, a deferred life, a semblance of breath. The phantom, the phantasm, the simulacrum . . . of living discourse is not inanimate; it is not insignificant; it simply signifies little, and always the same thing. This signifier of little, this discourse that doesn't amount to much, is like all ghosts: errant. It rolls . . . this way and that like someone who has lost his way, who doesn't know where he is going, having strayed from the correct path, the right direction, the rule of rectitude, the norm; but also like someone who has lost his rights, an outlaw, a pervert, a bad seed, a vagrant, an adventurer, a bum. (*Dissemination* 143)

Derrida's gloss resembles so much the description of Columbus's phantom in the last chapter of *The Harp and the Shadow* that one suspects there is in the latter work a dialogue between Carpentier and the contemporary French theorist, or at least a parallel reading of Plato's text. For Carpentier, the enigma of Columbus—as historical figure and as allegory of the author—is analogous to the enigma of the text as presented by Plato in *Phaedrus*, although for Carpentier it is not true that the text "signifies little, and always the same thing" but, to the contrary, the attempt to decipher the text, to pass judgment on it, generates a plurality of meanings. In any case, the ethical ambiguity Carpentier identifies in narrative fiction—the dependence on evil, hypostasized in writing, in order to produce a work of art—becomes also a productive contradiction, whose attempt at resolution brings about the creation of the novel's text.

However, as with the cases of Borges and other writers, one might reasonably ask why an awareness of this link between writing and evil did not prove paralyzing for Carpentier. One possible answer might be, as the deferral of any final judgment about Columbus in *The Harp and the Shadow* suggests, that even in so late a work, Carpentier still adheres to the Hegelian (as well as Marxist) view of history as a process. From this standpoint, one might argue that it is impossible to render judgment on individual acts that are part of an ongoing process whose final outcome is not yet known, or as Hegel sanguinely argues in *Lectures on the Philosophy of World History*, that from the point of view of the present, history and its attendant violence always seem preordained, and that there is nothing to be done about it. In a notorious passage about the "great men" of world history, Hegel states:

A World-historical individual is not so unwise as to indulge a variety of wishes to divide his regards. He is devoted to the One Aim, regardless of all else. It is even possible that such men may treat other great, even sacred interests, inconsiderately; conduct which is indeed obnoxious to moral reprehension. But so mighty a form must trample many an innocent flower—crush to pieces many an object in its path. (32)

A literary version of this Hegelian thesis would argue that authors enjoy a special dispensation from society that allows them to undertake the dubious practices associated with writing, as long as some good to society results from their actions. Writing would be, in these terms, the lesser evil, a peccadillo, a risk worth taking, compared to the evil that would ensue without it. Such casuistic distinctions, however, sound too much like special pleading, a request to exempt writing from the very sort of moral judgment frequently espoused by narrative fiction.

Another possibility, also suggested in *The Harp and the Shadow*, is that for writers, writing is a compulsion, a vice, or—like alcoholism or any other addiction—a kind of disease, and as such, an activity that is beyond the author's rational control. As we have seen in our reading of Zeno's *La charca*, however, claims by fiction writers that their subjects were given to them or even imposed upon them by an external agent are frequent in the history of literature, and may be seen as a way of avoiding the risks and responsibilities of creation (Harpham 184–197). To accept such a view uncritically would lead one to regard the writer not only as a passive transmitter, but also as a victim of writing, a figure as tragic as the very characters he or she creates. This rather tearful scenario is ironically evoked in *The Harp and the Shadow* by means of a direct quote from Columbus's pathetic 1503 letter to the Catholic monarchs recounting the travails of his fourth voyage: "Haya misericordia agora el cielo y llore por mí la tierra" (May the heavens now have mercy upon me, and the land weep for me; C. Colón 168; see also 501). The context in which this quotation appears makes it clear that the narrator regards this view of the writer-as-victim as an imposture, a theatrical gesture aimed at self-justification.

If neither a theory of history applied to writing, nor the notion of the writer as a passive agent, as a victim, explains why persons would choose to write despite their awareness of writing's links to violence and abjection, then the writer is left exposed, unprotected, and fully accountable as the only person responsible for the text. This "return to the author" as a generator of the text might seem to be a restatement of the obvious, but given the prior history of intense questioning of the concept of the author, it in fact raises new problems, or rather, raises old problems anew. Particularly, it is a reminder that claims of authorial passivity and even of victimization are not merely attempts by writers to evade responsibility for what they create; these claims also reflect the subject's fate in the act of writing, a fate that leads inexorably to a dissolution of the self in language, to a loss of identity. It is all too easy, then, to state that responsibility for the text rests solely on the author; but it is much less simple to locate the authors in the texts for which they are supposedly accountable. Like spectators before an empty stage set or visitors to an abandoned palace (and Carpentier's penchant for similar architectural images is well known), readers find in the text only traces and residues of other subjects, one of whom, perhaps, was the builder, but is no longer there to be called to judgment.

In any case, it is doubtful that the reader is in any position to pass judgment on the author, since the question about why one should enter into a relation with writing applies to the reader just as much as to the writer. If writing is, at least potentially, evil, then reading becomes as dubious an activity as writing. Complicity may perhaps be even more visibly at issue in reading than in writing, as Julio Cortázar posited in his theory of the "reader-accomplice" (*lector cómplice; Rayuela* 453–454). We have already seen how *The Harp and the Shadow* both uses and exposes the notion of complicity in the novel's second chapter, when it manipulates the readers' servile obedience to the text through their desire to recover an image of the text's emitter, much as Cervantes's Chanfalla and La Chirinos do with the villagers in *El Retablo de las Maravillas*. But the complicity between readers and the text is not subjected here to intense scrutiny, probably because Carpentier was more preoccupied at this stage with the fate of his works and his own fate as an author.

*The Harp and the Shadow* explores the complicity of the writer and the written word with violence and evil, but Carpentier does this, it must be stressed, in the ironic, playful mode of farce, of a divertimento, which produces a sense of detachment between the author and his text. It is true (Carpentier implies) that writing belongs to "the kingdom of this world," that it is but one thing among others in the world; at the same time, writing is inextricably bound to a devilish principle that distorts and sometimes undoes every good intention, making the gulf between the written word and the world to which it refers as wide and deep as the Atlantic Ocean must have seemed to Columbus. The writer as subject is always bound to become lost or drowned in that sea, like Seneca's Tifis (*El arpa y la sombra* 203–204), and that fate may be punishment enough for his sinful audacity.

For Julio Cortázar, however, as we will see in the final chapter, writing's web of complicity is virtually seamless. Neither the writer's virtual death through inscription, nor the readers' ultimate victimization by the text—as in Cortázar's celebrated story "Continuidad de los parques" (Continuity of parks, 1956)—suffices to atone for their guilt. Harking back to Nájera's "La hija del aire," Cortázar's "Press Clippings" also describes a writer's conflictive encounter with the ethics of writing. It is difficult to determine if Cortázar ever read Nájera's story. There are of course significant differences between the texts: in "Press Clippings," the writer-protagonist is now a woman, signaling Cortázar's attempt to break with the patriarchal imagery frequently associated with the ethics of writing; and the circus metaphor is gone, replaced by the no less sinister Borgesian image of the garden of forking paths. Nevertheless, there are also many uncanny similarities: both stories make use of or allude to the context of journalism; both are concerned with torture, abjection, and the question of guilt; both tell of an encounter with a girl-child that leads to the witnessing of an unspeakable violence. (And could it be simply a coincidence that the author of one of the "press clippings" is exiled in Mexico?) It seems appropriate to close this book with a text that collects and synthesizes so many of the various themes and images that we have been following in the previous pages: Nájera's use of Mignon and Semiramis as emblems of writing, Zeno's inquiry into authorial responsibility, de la Parra's "demonic" attempt to establish a female writing, Borges's ethical chain reaction, and Carpentier's meditation on writing and justice.

## CHAPTER 6

# *Shared Guilt*

## *Writing as Crime in Julio Cortázar's "Press Clippings"*

Call me no longer Naomi, call me Mara, for the
Almighty has dealt bitterly with me.
I went away full, but the Lord has brought me
back empty.
—RUTH 1:20–21

Evil, therefore, if we examine it closely, is not
only the dream of the wicked: it is to some extent
the dream of Good.
—GEORGES BATAILLE,
*La littérature et le mal*

There was something that made comment impos-
sible in his narrative, or perhaps in himself.
—JOSEPH CONRAD,
"The Secret Sharer"

As I discussed in the introduction to this book, since the late nineteenth
century it has often been assumed that literature is written, in Nietzsche's
phrase, "beyond good and evil." In fact, this thesis was advanced mostly
by literary critics who wished to distance themselves from the fruitless
moralizing of much nineteenth-century criticism (which, in Hispanic
letters, reached its nadir in the work of Marcelino Menéndez Pelayo)

rather than by the fiction writers themselves, whose texts—as we have seen in our readings of Manuel Gutiérrez Nájera, Manuel Zeno Gandía, Teresa de La Parra, Jorge Luis Borges, and Alejo Carpentier—continued to display ethical concerns about the act of writing and about the relationship between the writer and society.

Julio Cortázar's writings of the 1970s and early 1980s, like those of Carpentier and other novelists in the Spanish American narrative "boom," evidence concerns with the nature of authority and authorship and with the writer's civic duties as an intellectual, as well as a general questioning of the role of the writer in the power relationships that are at work in literary texts. Novels such as *Libro de Manuel* (A manual for Manuel, 1973), short stories like "Apocalipsis en Solentiname" (Apocalypse in Solentiname, 1977) and "Recortes de prensa" (Press clippings, 1981), and poems such as "Policrítica a la hora de los chacales" (Polycriticism in the hour of the jackals, 1971), among others, offer some of Cortázar's most significant ethical meditations about writing. However, in contrast to the more distanced and ironic stance favored by Borges, Carpentier, Gabriel García Márquez, Mario Vargas Llosa, or Elena Poniatowska, Cortázar's search for an ethics of writing is frequently presented as a gut-wrenching, intimate experience, similar in scope and intensity to a religious conversion.[1] A conveniently brief but richly suggestive example is his late short story "Press Clippings," collected in *Queremos tanto a Glenda y otros relatos* (1981) (published in English as *We Love Glenda So Much and Other Tales*, 1983). In this story, far more pessimistically and skeptically than in his previous fiction, Cortázar comes face to face with the "heart of darkness" that lies at the core of writing.

Regarded by some of his critics as one of Cortázar's most disturbing stories in a realistic and political vein, "Press Clippings" has also been seen as "the culmination of his overtly political writing, which began with 'Reunión' in *Todos los fuegos el fuego*" (Boldy 126; see also Peavler 93).[2] One salient characteristic is that "Press Clippings" has a female protagonist and first-person narrator who is also an author figure. This is something of a departure in Cortázar's oeuvre and clearly indicates his intention to explore issues of gender in society and literature. As was also mentioned in the previous chapter, this story summarizes many of the themes and motifs that we have previously examined in this book— themes and motifs that may well be parts of a widely disseminated symbolic discourse about ethics and writing.

Briefly, "Press Clippings" is the first-person narrative of Noemí, an Argentine woman and a successful author living in Paris, who is asked by a fellow countryman, a sculptor who has done a series of works on the subject of violence, to write a text to accompany a collection of photographs of his works. They meet in his apartment in a seedy neighborhood, and while Noemí studies the sculptures, she shows the artist a press clipping of an open letter, written by an Argentine woman living in Mexico, denouncing the kidnapping and murder by the military junta of the woman's oldest daughter, husband, and other close relatives. Noemí and the sculptor discuss their anguish and their feelings of impotence in the face of the facts contained in the clipping. Noemí agrees to write the text about the sculptures and goes out into the street to take a taxi. As she walks to the taxi stand, she encounters a little girl crying alone in the street. "My papa is doing things to my mama," the girl tells Noemí, and, reaching out, practically pulls the writer into a labyrinthine courtyard and towards a shack where Noemí comes upon a dreadful scene: the father has tied the mother to a bedstead and is torturing her by systematically burning her nude body with a lighted cigarette. Following an uncontrollable impulse, Noemí knocks the man unconscious with a stool, unties the woman, and then helps to tie the man to the bedstead. Without exchanging a word with the woman, Noemí, an intellectual who abhors violence, helps her torture the man. Noemí returns to her apartment in a daze, drinks several glasses of vodka, and passes out. That afternoon, she writes down her experience, which will be the text to accompany the sculptor's works. She then phones the sculptor and, without giving him a chance to interrupt, tells him her story. Several days later, the sculptor sends Noemí a letter with some press clippings from the tabloid *France-Soir* that tell the story of a crime that occurred not in Paris but in Marseille, presumably a few days before, in which a man was tied to a bed and tortured to death. The man's mistress, the clipping says, is a suspect in the crime, and the couple's little girl has been reported missing. The part of the clipping describing the exact details of the man's torture is absent, but the photographs show the shack Noemí visited. Noemí rushes back to the sculptor's neighborhood, trying in vain to locate the place where, in defiance of space and time, she had her experience. However, she does find the little girl and is told by a concierge that the girl was found lost in the street and that a social worker will come to get her. Before leaving, Noemí asks the little girl her last name; then in a café she writes down the ending to her text on the back of the sculptor's letter and goes to slip it under his door "so that the text accompanying his sculptures would be complete" ("Press Clippings" 96).

The complexities in this intense and gloomy story are evident from the beginning, when, after the title, an author's note diffidently advises the reader: "Although I don't think it's really necessary to say so, the first clipping is real and the second one imaginary" (81). The story is indeed constructed, in typically Cortazarian fashion, following a series of polar oppositions that are later collapsed: reality/imagination, past/present, literature/journalism, male/female, France/Argentina, Paris/Marseille, etc. In terms of its structure, binarism and a *mise en abyme* effect also prevail. "Press Clippings" contains two sets of stories, one placed inside the other. The first set comprises the story "Press Clippings" in *We Love Glenda So Much and Other Tales*, written by Julio Cortázar, and the text Noemí writes to accompany the sculptor's works, which is contained in "Press Clippings" and is essentially coextensive with it. The second set of stories includes the two press clippings, each of which presides over one-half of the narrative: the Argentine mother's press clipping in the first half, and the clipping from *France-Soir* in the second half. Cortázar's choice of a female first-person narrator also places the question of narrative authority within a *mise en abyme*: do we read the story as if it were written by Noemí? . . . or by Cortázar writing as Noemí? . . . or by Cortázar writing as Cortázar writing as Noemí? . . .[3]

As my analysis of the story will show, the principal rhetorical device Cortázar uses to coordinate the binary elements and the *mise en abyme* is the chiasmus. This figure, as Richard A. Lanham explains, names "the ABBA pattern of mirror inversion" (33). (A well-known instance is a quotation from Knute Rockne: "When the going gets tough, the tough get going" (Lanham 33).) Lanham observes that chiasmus "seems to set up a natural dynamics that draws the parts [of the construction] closer together, as if the second element wanted to flip over and back over the first, condensing the assertion back toward the compression of *Oxymoron* and *Pun*" (33). Chiasmus may also be seen as a figure that tends to create indifferentiation, since it "seems to exhaust the possibilities of argument, as when Samuel Johnson destroyed an aspiring author with, 'Your manuscript is both good and original; but the part that is good is not original, and the part that is original is not good'" (Lanham 33).

Journalistic discourse is another important element in this story, since it serves to spark the narrative's ethical interrogations. Although the first press clipping does not, properly speaking, belong to any genre of journalism—it is, as I have already indicated, an open letter, written in the style of an affidavit or legal deposition—it is nevertheless disseminated through the newspapers. The clipping's use of legal discourse further heightens its journalistic impact: it is an immediate, direct appeal for justice, and its language therefore carries a powerful performative element. It is not merely a piece of journalistic reporting but an action carried out by a victim of violence seeking redress. When Noemí and the sculptor read it, the clipping not unexpectedly makes them painfully aware of the futility of their own activities to stop the violence:

> "You can see, all this is worth nothing," the sculptor said, sweeping his arm through the air. "Worth nothing, Noemí, I've spent months making this shit, you write books, that woman denounces atrocities, we attend congresses and round tables to protest, we almost come to believe that things are changing, and then all you need is two minutes of reading to understand the truth again, to—" [*sic*] (85)

Noemí responds in a reasonable and worldly-wise fashion to the sculptor's passionate exclamations, reminding him that writing and making art are what they do best and that their relative weakness and marginality "will never be any reason to be silent" (86). She regards the sculptor's expressions of anguish as a form of "autotorture" and in fact is pleased that the man's works are "at the same time naïve and subtle, in any case without any sense of dread or sentimental exaggeration" (87, 82). She is leery of any sort of sensationalism or directness in representing the subject of torture and is sophisticated enough to realize that she herself feels an "obscure pleasure" when evoking images of torture (83).

The second half of the story, which begins when Noemí leaves the sculptor's apartment, is controlled—fittingly, as it turns out—by a hidden journalistic subtext: the crime story in *France-Soir*, in which Noemí unknowingly and mysteriously participates. This section of the narrative is a descent into darkness, literally and metaphorically: the darkness of the passageways that lead from a street in Paris to a shack in Marseilles and the darkness of Noemí's unconscious, which yearns to pay back the torturers in their own coin, in a version of talionic justice like the Old Testament's "an eye for an eye, a tooth for a tooth." (There are other, more direct links with the Bible in the story, as I will explain shortly.) In essence, this section's discourse combines, in a volatile mix, sensationalist journalism with psychoanalysis.

But why journalism? Why not deal more directly with the question of art and violence, or art and crime, as in De Quincey's *On Murder Considered as One of the Fine Arts* (1827) or, to mention a more recent example, Patrick Süsskind's *Perfume* (1985)? There is more here than merely a reminiscence of, or a coincidence with, Borges's use of journalism in "The Garden of Forking Paths." Journalistic discourse appears in many works of contemporary Latin American narrative as a marker for ethical inquiry, specifically for what I have called an ethics of writing (González, *Journalism* 109–111). In literary works up to the nineteenth century, religious discourse was predominant whenever ethical issues were raised; in twentieth-century Latin American narrative, however, it is frequently the figure of the journalist who confronts moral questions and anguishes over them, and in a language that is predominantly secular and philosophical rather than religious. The reasons for this journalism-ethics linkage in Latin American literature are complex,[4] but in general they have to do with Latin American literature's constant return to its own discursive roots and to the historical importance of journalism as one of the founding discourses of Latin American writing. In "Press Clippings," furthermore, the artist characters are confronted through journalism with a transcription of reality unhampered by the norms of artistic and literary taste and decorum as Noemí and the sculptor understand them. The first clipping's performative use of language and the second's sensationalistic rhetoric enable both to name what the sculptures and Noemí's own text (as she foresees it at the story's beginning) repress or elide in the name of "good taste" or intellectual sophistication. By dealing openly with violence and crime, the press clippings expose literature's hypocritical denial of its links with evil.

Although this story's ethical inquiries are secular in nature, religious discourse still fulfills an auxiliary function in the text. Cortázar has seen fit to insert it obliquely through the allusion, in the protagonist's name, to the biblical story of Ruth. The allusion to the Book of Ruth in Noemí's name reinforces the theme of male-female relations in the story, but it also brings into play a figural allegorical framework derived from biblical exegesis.[5]

"Noemí" is the Spanish version of Naomi, who was Ruth's mother-in-law. Though not an unusual name in Spanish-speaking countries, where it is used by Christians as well as Jews, it nevertheless also suggests a figural link between the protagonist and the Argentine mother of the first clipping, who is Jewish.[6] The biblical Naomi, it should be recalled, was an Israelite woman who had gone with her husband and two sons to live abroad in the country of Moab. Her husband and sons die, and she is left alone with her Moabite daughters-in-law, Orpah and Ruth. When she decides to return to her native land, she tells her daughters-in-law to go back to their families, reminding them that they no longer have any obligation toward her; but Ruth is determined to remain with Naomi: "Where you lodge, I will lodge; your people shall be my people, and your God my God" (Ruth 1:16). This verse is a reminder that the story of Ruth, as Bible commentators have remarked, entails profound personal transformations:

In what amounts to a change of identity, from Moabite to Israelite (for there was as yet no formal procedure or even the theoretical possibility for religious conversion), Ruth adopts the people and God of Naomi. Religion was bound up with ethnicity in biblical times; each people had its land and its gods (cf. Mic. 4:5), so that to change religion meant to change nationality. (*Harper's Bible Commentary* 263)

The mutual loyalty between Ruth and Naomi throughout the story is seen in the rabbinical tradition as an example of *chesed*, "loyalty or faithfulness born of a sense of caring and commitment" (*Harper's Bible Commentary* 262). The story of Ruth also develops the theme of family continuity. The males in Naomi's family, who might be expected to perpetuate their family, disappear at the beginning of the story, and it falls to the women, an elderly widow and a non-Israelite, to achieve the continuity of the family through Ruth's marriage to Boaz (*Harper's Bible Commentary* 262).

Noemí and the Argentine mother from the press clipping stand in a figural allegorical relationship to the biblical Naomi. Like her, neither Noemí nor the Argentine mother has a husband (in Noemí's case because she is unmarried), and both seem to be women in their middle age or past it.[7] Like Naomi at the beginning of the Book of Ruth (1:20–21), Noemí clearly harbors a great bitterness (in her case, about her country's situation), and one may surmise that the Argentine mother harbors similar feelings, since her experience of losing her husband and her daughter parallels that of the biblical Naomi. Furthermore, like Naomi, both women display *chesed*—loyalty and solidarity—although Noemí does so in an unexpectedly evil fashion when she helps the tortured woman to turn the tables on her torturer. In contrast, the Argentine mother is closer to the instance of Naomi, since she petitions international organizations like the United Nations, the OAS, and Amnesty International for help in her plight; that is, she acts within a legal framework, as Naomi does to help her daugher-in-law Ruth at a time when Israel is under the rule of the judges (Ruth 1:1).

The figural allegory among Naomi, the Argentine mother, and Noemí clearly breaks down in the scene of violence in which Noemí is an active participant. This is the point when a chiasmatic reversal occurs in the narrative, a mirrorlike inversion of both the story of Naomi and the story of the Argentine mother. This section may be read as Noemí's dream or fantasy of wish fulfillment in which, by assuming the male's aggressive role, she ends up displaying the same dark impulses as the male power figures.[8] The question of gender comes shockingly to the fore in this section. Unlike the powerless women in the Book of Ruth and in the first press clipping, who must appeal to a higher—and masculine—authority for aid, Noemí takes violent action to defend the tortured woman and, in a gesture that connotes not only solidarity with the victim but a distrust of the male-dominated system of justice, helps her to get even using the same brutal methods a male might use.

Despite its graphic realism, the atmosphere in this section of the story is oneiric, suggesting a symbolic rather than a literal reading. Earlier, the narrator indicated a latent desire for wish fulfillment when she recalled a religious anecdote about the conversion of King Clovis:

I remembered something I'd read when I was a girl, in Augustin Thierry, perhaps, a story about how a saint, God knows what his name was, had converted Clovis and his nation to Christianity and was describing the scourging and crucifixion of Jesus, and the king rose up on his throne, shaking his spear and shouting: "Oh, if only I could have been there with my Franks!"—the miracle of an impossible wish, the same impotent rage of the sculptor, lost in his reading. (87)

As well as prefiguring the story's narrative strategy (the use of wish fulfillment), the anecdote foregrounds the ambiguous use of the representation of violence in religious and, by extension, narrative discourse. King Clovis's naïve reaction towards the story of Christ's crucifixion uncovers the violent subtext on which the narrative depends even as it symbolically suppresses it. Hearing the story, Clovis did not see the cross as a Christian symbol of redemption but as an instrument of torture on which Jesus was being unjustly punished.

Like Clovis, Noemí literalizes in the account of her experience elements from a symbolic system: in her case, it is the Freudian "primal scene." Evocative of Steedman's claim that the abused child is a modern symbol of the adult's "inner self" (3–5), the little girl's complaint ("My papa is doing things to my mama") rings with a psychosexual double entendre, suggesting a link with Noemí's unconscious but also with her literary work: earlier, Noemí tells the sculptor, "I've been writing a story where I talk, no less, about the psy-cho-log-i-cal problems of a girl at the moment of puberty" (87). It should be stressed that in the end, this process of literalization and wish fulfillment does not uncover so much

Noemí's unconscious as the hidden impulses behind the production of a literary text—in this case, the text to accompany the sculptures about violence. Cortázar's focus in this story, I would argue, is resolutely fixed on the gray no-man's-land (so to speak) between literature and psychoanalysis. Thus, the "primal scene" Noemí witnesses is not quite that of the sexual act between the father and the mother but yet another symbolization. Although sexual implications are still present in this scene (in the symbolic equation of sex with violence and death common to many cultures), in this instance the torture of the woman by the man may also stand for something else: writing. The connection with writing is carried out through a series of conventional symbolic equivalencies between the sexual act and the act of writing: the lighted cigarette is the penis/pen; the woman's body "burned from the stomach to the neck" (91–92) is the page; the "purple or red splotches that went up from the thigh and the sex to the breasts" (92) are a form of somatic writing.[9]

As a whole, the tableau that Noemí interrupts suggests an equation between sexuality, violence, and writing in a context of transgression—a view that has much in common with that of the French writer Georges Bataille in *La littérature et le mal* (Literature and evil, 1957). Bataille, who sees literature as the product of an unconscious human desire to exceed all boundaries (whether legal, religious, or cultural), offers a Nietzschean "hypermorality" as a position "above the fray," as it were, from which to judge literature ethically (8). Provocatively, to be sure, Bataille writes as if the question of evil in literature were already settled: "Literature is not innocent. It is guilty and should admit itself so" (8). Cortázar, on the other hand, seeks to go beyond Bataille's rather detached "hypermorality" towards a more personal and critical view of literature's links with evil. He wishes to show instead that there is no fixed, exterior place from which one can safely pass judgment. Just as the distinctions between male and female, inside and outside, reader and writer, torturer and victim are blurred in the story, so the possibility of rendering an objective moral judgment about events becomes more difficult, if not impossible, even as the need for such a judgment becomes more urgent.

In "Press Clippings," Cortázar creates a referential *mise en abyme* in which "literature" and "reality" (as both are symbolized in multiple ways in the story) continually reflect and interpenetrate each other at various levels, in a back-and-forth movement that ends in indifferentiation. We have already remarked how Noemí's story stands in a figural allegorical and chiasmatic relation with both Naomi's tale (in the Book of Ruth) and that of the Argentine mother; and how, by "gendering" (to use a fashionable verb) the narrator, by making his narrator female, Cortázar encourages an abysmatic reading of his authorial pronouncements in the story (how do we separate Noemí's utterances from those of Cortázar, or from Cortázar writing as Noemí, etc.?). Even when Noemí supposedly comes face-to-face with the grimmest reality in the second half of the story, literature creeps in. Noemí's actions, as noted above, are obvious wish fulfillments; but their improbable, conventionally fictional nature is further underscored by the narrator's reference to books and films in her description of the events:

What came afterward I could have seen in a movie or read in a book, I was there as if not being there, but I was there with an agility and an intent that in a very brief time—if it happened in time—led me to find a knife on the table, cut the bonds that held the woman. (92)

In another wish-fulfilling reversal, Noemí and the woman then tie the still-unconscious man to the bed and proceed to torture him as he had tortured the woman. The narrator refuses to offer the exact details of the man's torture, save by an indirect—and terrifying—reference to a story by Jack London ("Lost Face," 1910), suggesting that what the man suffers is different from what he had inflicted upon the woman (93).[10] Is this really so? The allusions to the Jack London story suggest a scene not of maenadic frenzy but of carefully deliberate dismemberment:

[N]ow that I have to remember it and have to write it, my cursed state and my harsh memory bring me something else indescribably lived but not seen, a passage from a story by Jack London where a trapper in the north struggles to win a clean death while beside him, turned into a bloody thing that still holds a glimmer of consciousness, his comrade in adventures howls and twists, tortured by women of the tribe who horribly prolong his life in spasms and shrieks, killing him without killing him, exquisitely refined in each new variant, never described but there, like us there, never described and doing what we must, what we had to do. (93)

The passage suggests that the man is subjected to a process of indifferentiation—he is turned, like London's character, "into a bloody thing"—which appears to be the opposite of what the woman suffered. I have already remarked that the cigarette burns on her body evoke a form of somatic writing, and as such they are connected to differentiation. It can be argued, however, that what we have here is another chiasmus, an "ABBA pattern of mirror inversion," and that in fact the fates of both the man and the woman are equivalent.

The way in which the narrator alludes to Jack London's story becomes in itself a clearer indication of what happened to the man. Unwilling to repeat in writing the horror in which she has participated, Noemí takes recourse to literature in order to avoid describing, while strongly suggesting, what took place. Not surprisingly, given the pervasive use of the *mise en abyme* in "Press Clippings," the referenced passage from London also performs the same act of elision by allusion. In "Lost Face," the narrator describes the torture thus:

So that thing before him was Big Ivan—Big Ivan the giant, the man without nerves, the man of iron, the Cossack turned freebooter of the seas, who was as phlegmatic as an ox, with a nervous system so low that what was pain to ordinary men was scarcely a tickle to him. Well, well, trust these Nulato Indians to find Big Ivan's nerves and trace them to the roots of his quivering soul. They were certainly doing it. It was inconceivable that a man could suffer so much and yet live. Big Ivan was paying for his low order of nerves. Already he had lasted twice as long as any of the others. (5)

As Noemí says, in London's tale the torture "by the women of the tribe" is "never described but there" ("Press Clippings" 93). In "Press Clippings," the allusion to London opens up a vertiginous *mise en abyme* of elisions, cuts, or "clippings." A paraphrase, the allusion itself is already a "clipping," a piece cut from London's text; furthermore, in its content, the passage avoids describing directly the way the trapper dies (another elision), although it strongly suggests that his death occurs through some variant of the proverbial "death of a thousand cuts," which is yet another grim metaphor for writing.

Commenting astutely on Cortázar's *Rayuela* (Hopscotch, 1963) in his essay "Del yin al yang (Sobre Sade, Bataille, Marmori, Cortázar y Elizondo)," the late Cuban novelist Severo Sarduy focuses on chapter 14 of the novel. In this episode, a marginal Chinese character named Wong shows the members of the Serpent's Club a portfolio of photographs of the Leng T'che, the "death of a thousand cuts," which he is using for a book on Chinese art because, as he explains, "In China one has a different concept of art" (*Rayuela* 70). Sarduy remarks that Wong symbolizes in the novel an alternative to the Western metaphysics of presence and to the yearning for totality that predominates in Cortázar's ideology in *Hopscotch*. Wong and his photographs emblematize the discontinuous, fragmentary nature of literary language and its links with death and emptiness. However, Sarduy points out, Cortázar's text does not fully

develop these implications, perhaps because they are too unsettling to the search for wholeness thematized in the novel (*Escrito sobre un cuerpo* 24–27). Both the man and the woman in "Press Clippings," therefore, attempt to destroy each other through a mutilation that is emblematic of writing. There is no symbolic death and resurrection here, no possibility of allegorically "healing" the break between the text and its meaning. A panorama of "cuts" or "clippings" extends as far as the eye can see.

"Press Clippings" proposes a view of writing as a cutting or mutilation that is very similar to Jacques Derrida's notion of "textual grafting":

One ought to explore systematically not only what appears to be a simple etymological coincidence uniting the graft and the graph (both from *graphion*: writing implement, stylus), but also the analogy between the forms of textual grafting and so-called vegetal grafting, or even, and more commonly today, animal grafting. It would not be enough to compose an encyclopedic catalogue of grafts . . . ; one must elaborate a systematic treatise on the textual graft. Among other things, this would help us understand the functioning of footnotes, for example, or epigraphs, and in what way, to the one who knows how to read, these are sometimes more important than the so-called principal or capital text. (*Dissemination* 202–203)

Could it be by chance that the scene of torture in the second press clipping, in which Noemí uncannily (vicariously?) participates, takes place in a shack next to "a vegetable patch with low wire fences that marked off planted sections, [where] there was enough light to see the skimpy mastic trees, the poles that supported climbing plants, rags to scare off the birds" (90) and with "a vague entrance full of old furniture and garden tools" (91)? This vegetable/textual space may also be read as a degraded, more visibly abject version of Borges's garden of forking paths: that space where writing and ethics converge, and in which violent cuts or breaks help to produce a potentially endless proliferation.

Cortázar's use of chiasmus not only denies the possibility of any allegorical interpretation that would give his story a sense of wholeness and transcendent meaning, but also makes visible the story's dependence on cuts or elisions at every level: from writing (as a systematic spacing of signs as well as an operation involving textual grafts), to structure (the story's binary divisions), to theme (the sculptor's works and the instances of torture and mutilation described in the text). Noemí's disjointed thoughts, while self-reflexively harking back to the story's overall theme of cutting or dividing, show that she has witnessed a terrifying truth about herself, not only as a human being, but as a writer:

How could I know how long it lasted, how could I understand that I too, I too even though I thought I was on the right side, I too, how could I accept that I too there on the other side from the cut-off hands and the common graves, I too on the other side from the girls tortured and shot that same Christmas night . . . (93)

The psychoanalytic element in the story helps explain the delayed appearance of the second press clipping, the one from *France-Soir*, as an instance of *Nachträglichkeit*, or deferred action. As Jonathan Culler summarizes it, this is "a paradoxical situation that Freud frequently encounters in his case studies, in which the determining event in a neurosis never occurs as such, is never present as an event, but is constructed afterwards by what can only be described as a textual mechanism of the unconscious" (*On Deconstruction* 163). Arguably, the event that precipitates the deferred action is the encounter with the little girl, which causes Noemí to construct a fantasy in which she acts out her neuroses; what is uncanny about the fantasy is that it is built out of elements from another clipping, one which Noemí had not previously mentioned (although she never denies having seen it before). The story leaves open the possibility, however, that Noemí might have learned about the events in Marseille from the little girl herself, who was the (presumably runaway) daughter of the couple in *France-Soir*, and that what we have read is Noemí's conflation of the little girl's account with her own wish-fulfilling fantasy.

In the end, it matters little. Clearly, there are two opposite ways to read this story: a "fantastic" one, which discounts the story's political and documentary elements (the first clipping) by subsuming everything into fiction, and a "realist" or "symbolic" one, in which the whole second half of the story (after Noemí leaves the sculptor's home) is Noemí's fictional response to the first clipping, a narrative within the narrative, and thus subject to a "symbolic" rather than a literal interpretation. This reading, however, is based on assumptions that are not fully and unequivocally supported by the text (i.e., that the story as a whole, or a large part of it, is a fiction penned by Noemí and therefore attests only to her "state of mind"), and it essentially acts to suppress the "fantastic" reading. The two readings conflict with each other, and both do violence to the text. I have been pursuing the latter, more "symbolic" reading, mainly because it has allowed me to focus on the story's many self-reflexive aspects, including the question of the narrator's gender, but it clearly breaks down when I try to explain, in a non-"fantastic" way, the chain of events of the story's second half. The preliminary authorial statement that one of the clippings is real and the other imaginary (81) further muddies the waters by first strictly delimiting two domains—"reality" and "imagination"—and then suggesting that, save for the first clipping, which has been "grafted" onto it, the story as a whole belongs to the "imaginary" domain. Nevertheless, even this apparently authoritative statement is subject to fictionalization, and more ruthless readers who want to opt for the "fantastic" view might choose to consider the powerfully performative first clipping to be purely fictional as well—an option that goes to the heart of the ethical issues raised by the story, as we will see shortly.

The ethical questions in "Press Clippings," however, focus foremost not on the reader but on the figure of the author. In a curiously perverse (chiasmatic?) version of his old theory of the *"lector cómplice"* (*Rayuela* 453–454), Cortázar posits in this story a theory of an *"autor cómplice,"* an author-accomplice, not of the reader but of the torturers, the criminals, and any entity that uses violence as a means to control others. The writer's craft is a sublimated version of the mechanisms of aggression used by those in power and those who wish to have power. To write is to cut, to wound, to hack away at something that is (or seems to be) alive: language, words, texts. Even if texts are viewed as already "dead bodies" or "epitaphs," writing is still a macabre affair, a form of necromancy or necrophilia.

Considering that all of Cortázar's novels since *Hopscotch* have fragmented, collagelike structures in which "expendable chapters" that are often quotes taken from newspapers and magazines (as in *Hopscotch*) or outright press clippings (as in *A Manual for Manuel*) play a significant role, "Press Clippings" clearly implies a broad and anguished reappraisal by Cortázar of a large portion of his own oeuvre. Cortázar, unlike Bataille, seems to find no reassurance in a view of literature as a form of desire and transgression. "Press Clippings" marks a point of crisis in Cortázar's work, a crisis that had been haunting that work at least since chapter 14 of *Hopscotch*, when Wong displays the photographs of the Leng T'che. The source of those photographs, as Severo Sarduy points out, is Bataille's *Les Larmes d'Éros* (1961; *Escrito sobre un cuerpo* 16, 24–25); "Press Clippings" is thus merely the latest episode in a long-standing and tense "dialogue" between Cortázar and Bataille's texts. Sarduy also remarks on the narrative distance with which Cortázar approaches the subject of art and evil and on the *"perturbation"* (Sarduy's italics) that Wong's presence brings into *Hopscotch* (*Escrito sobre un cuerpo* 25, 27). Cortázar continued to tiptoe around the subject of literature and evil in texts such as "Suspect Relations" (in *La vuelta al día en ochenta mundos*, 1967, published in English as *Around the Day in Eighty Worlds*, 1986), which can be considered a tepid gloss on De Quincey's *On Murder Considered as One of the Fine Arts*, and in *A Manual for Manuel* and "Apocalypse in Solentiname," which, in their searches for ideological solutions, are still merely rough drafts of "Press Clippings." Of course, Cortázar's stories have often featured characters who confront evil and perversity or who are themselves monstrous;[11] but in "Press Clippings," the terms of the equation (writing, politics, violence) are fully present and clearly laid out, the ethical questioning is deeper, and the sense of crisis is unequivocal.

The discomfort this story generates in both author and readers is directly traceable to the grafting of the first press clipping, that of the Argentine mother. This powerful text unsettles the story and critical readings of it, making them seem superfluous, if not downright immoral. Bringing legal discourse into play and evoking notions of justice and morality at their most fundamental level, the first press clipping uses ethical discourse as a shield and as a weapon to further its cause.

The clipping's ultimate effect is to make the critical reader feel like an accomplice to the crimes it denounces. It achieves this initially through its testimonial nature, which asserts the text's absolute truthfulness and almost literally rubricates it in blood. In general, testimonial narratives are profoundly ethical in that their stories are built around moral imperatives; one such imperative is "Thou shalt not lie." (From the reader's standpoint, this particular imperative translates as "Thou shalt not doubt.") Despite such narratives' frequent claims of objectivity, moralism is pervasive in testimonials, since, like melodrama (to which many of these texts recur), they always deal with fundamental polar oppositions: truth versus falsehood, justice versus injustice, society versus the individual (Brooks, *The Melodramatic Imagination* 4).

The clipping's second strategy for drawing the reader in as an accomplice is the use of the performative, which shifts the clipping's textual dimension to the level of an act. A text like the first clipping addresses itself to the readers, asking, almost demanding, that they do something. But what? Certainly, art, or literature, is not what first springs to mind. For the artists—Noemí, the sculptor, or Cortázar himself—the clipping poses an almost existentialist dilemma of how to react without betraying their personal identity, of which literature (in Noemí's and Cortázar's cases) forms an inseparable part. Cortázar's life and work, in particular, despite his ludic inclinations, were always characterized by his desire to be true to his vocation as a writer, as his sometimes strained but always close relationship with the Cuban Revolution attests. To the demands of the Marxist and *fidelista* hard-liners that he deal with subjects such as revolution and oppression in Latin America and elsewhere, Cortázar replied that he would do so, but "in my own way" ("Policrítica" 128). In interviews, Cortázar insisted on "the horror I feel with regard to anyone who is an 'engaged writer' and nothing else. In general, I've never known a good writer who was engaged to the point that everything he wrote was subsumed in his engagement, without freedom to write other things. [. . .] I could never accept engagement as obedience to an exclusive duty to deal with ideological matters" (Prego 131–132). At the same time, however, Cortázar's continuing involvement with Cuba, with the Allende government in Chile, and later with the Nicaraguan revolution, as well as his participation in human rights forums such as the Russell Tribunal, continued to remind him of the urgent need for action. The Russell Tribunal, which met in Rome in 1974, was an inquiry into human rights in Latin America led by a panel of intellectuals and writers from Europe and Latin America in which Cortázar and Gabriel García Márquez were the major figures (Goloboff 233–235). Although Cortázar had already begun to speak out about human rights in *A Manual for Manuel* in 1973, his work on the Russell Tribunal, hearing testimonies and sworn depositions from hundreds of witnesses of human rights violations throughout the continent, clearly had an enormous impact on him, which is evidenced in "Press Clippings."

Speaking about *A Manual for Manuel*, Cortázar states that in that novel he tried to "achieve a convergence of contemporary history . . . with pure literature. . . . That extremely difficult balance between an ideological and a literary content . . . is for me one of the most passionately interesting problems in contemporary literature" (Prego 133). The Argentine mother's clipping in "Press Clippings," however, does not allow for any such "balance." It is an imperative text, which demands that the reader give an ethically unambiguous reply to its appeal. Is a literary reply ethical? In his story, Cortázar addresses the question of how to react ethically *as a writer* to acts of violence and evil, only to discover that literature is itself violent. Like the torturers and their dictatorial masters, literature is impassive and heartless, not given (in Noemí's phrase) to "sentimental exaggeration." In the end, Cortázar appears to agree with Bataille's dictum, "Literature is not innocent." However, he does so grudgingly and with profound anguish, since this notion runs counter to Cortázar's publicly stated view of literature as playful, child-like, and therefore innocent.[12] At the story's end, in a last twist of figural-ism and chiasmus, the orphaned little girl (who, as we know from our study of Nájera's story, is an avatar of Goethe's Mignon, an emblem of writing) becomes a figure for the Argentine mother and for Noemí her-self. A witness to the horrors of the second clipping, the little girl, her innocence lost, is to be picked up by a social worker ("Press Clippings" 96), transferred to society. The best literature can do, it seems, is to "graft" the Argentine mother's clipping onto its own textual body and pass it on to the reader, along with the ethical dilemma it poses.

Perhaps one of the most frightening and polemical aspects of Cortázar's story is its graphophobic equation of the symbolic violence of writing with the physical violence committed by some individuals or groups against others. One could object that Cortázar unfairly lumps together a series of very different actions as if they were all the same. A reply to that objection would be that Cortázar's stance towards writing and vio-lence in "Press Clippings" is profoundly ethical and principled. Violence is violence, he implies, and any attempt to distinguish between "accept-able" and "unacceptable" degrees of it would be tantamount to sanc-tioning all violent acts. Another reply might be that Cortázar's gesture is not unusual, either in a literary or in a philosophical context. Myriad other examples can be adduced, besides the ones analyzed in this book, of Spanish American writers who associate writing with violence. The same is true of philosophy: Derrida's reading of Rousseau and Lévi-Strauss in *Of Grammatology* points to a powerful philosophical tradition dating back to Plato, in which writing is considered to be inherently violent and corrupting. The main difference between Derrida and Cortázar may lie in Derrida's acceptance of writing's violence as a methodological given, in contrast to Cortázar's emotional reaction of horror and disgust.[13]

In the course of this book I have explored how Spanish American writers since the late nineteenth century have viewed writing's relation to vio-lence and their own relationships to writing. In the process, I have pro-posed a theory about the origins and development of an ethics of writing in Spanish America. Although the ethics of writing is by no means a phenomenon unique to Spanish America, the study of how the ethics of writing developed within this particular literary tradition may shed light on similar processes that have taken place elsewhere. Specifically, my readings of Gabriel García Márquez (in the introduction), Manuel Gutiérrez Nájera, Manuel Zeno Gandía, Teresa de la Parra, Jorge Luis Borges, Alejo Carpentier, and Julio Cortázar have led me to posit the existence of two stages in the development of the Spanish American ethics of writing: the stage of "abuse" and the stage of "admonition." In the first, which encompasses texts from the late nineteenth and early twentieth centuries, there is an incipient awareness of the ethical implications of writing. This awareness, converging with the ancient but poorly recognized tradition of graphophobia, led Spanish American authors to suspect that writing, despite its positive sociocultural effects, is fundamentally "abusive," linked to violence and evil. However, perhaps because of their continued desire to use writing as an instrument of social change, writers of the nineteenth and the early twentieth centuries resisted that suspicion.

The second stage, which began around the time of World War II and is still in progress, involves an increased sense of graphophobia on the part of Spanish American authors, a growing willingness to regard writing as inherently violent and to view literature as an ethically compromised form of art. Of course, their devotion to an activity regarded by ethics at the very least with suspicion creates a dilemma for the contemporary Spanish American writers. In a violence-filled world, how can one justify dedicating one's life to writing, particularly when writing itself is complicitous with violence? In response, these authors have returned to a strategy first developed by Miguel de Cervantes in *Don Quixote* and other works during a similar period of cultural crisis, which consists of admonishing readers (as well as writers) about the dangers of the written word. This Cervantine strategy of admonition is meant to serve as an antidote or countermeasure to writing's perceived virulence, although it is still conveyed through writing. My own book inescapably falls under this latter category and also repeats the same contradictory gesture.

Not surprisingly, the fundamental ethical paradox found in Cortázar, as in all other writers who have given vent to their graphophobia, is the question of why, given a belief in writing's complicity with violence and evil, one should continue to write. As we have seen in our readings of Borges, Carpentier, and Cortázar, these authors' textual warnings about the dangers of writing and literature only serve to further complicate this paradox. One might also ask in an ethical vein what difference it makes to know that writing is violent or evil if no one will desist from writing, if we must still write. Would it not be easier to accept the notion that writing is on the whole a good thing, or at least a morally neutral entity, and thus avoid conflicting situations such as the ones studied in this book?

In my view, this alternative is untenable. Graphophobia is a real phenomenon that can be documented throughout literary history in a great many authors and is a significant aspect of the experience of writing. Despite all the attempts to suppress it, that mixture of respect, fear, and revulsion towards writing that is graphophobia always returns, like a Freudian repression. This is especially the case whenever writing is subjected to ethical scrutiny. As Borges's "The Garden of Forking Paths" teaches us, the radical otherness of writing and its tendency to proliferate indefinitely, although similar to the branching, discriminating structure of ethics, ensure that writing will remain dubious from a moral point of view.

For Spanish American literary criticism today, it is particularly urgent to take graphophobia and its effects into account. The predominant critical tradition in Spanish America at present is a variant of literary sociology that, despite its nationalist emphasis, has allowed itself to be colonized in recent years by the "postcolonial" and "cultural studies" modes from the United States and Europe. Displaying a profound fear of the letter, this critical tradition has tended to privilege orality over writing, favoring texts that mimic the immediacy and spontaneity of the spoken word, such as testimonial narratives, letters and diaries, legal and notarial documents, and so on. At the same time, it has sidelined or rejected the complexity and reflexivity of the written word and presented a rather simplistic view of literature as a solipsistic, alienated practice or, worse yet, as an instrument co-opted by the powers that control society. It is important to point out that this graphophobic style of criticism, unlike the admonitory texts we have read by Borges, Carpentier, and Cortázar, and unlike this book, is not engaged in an ethical critique of literature: it simply pays literature no heed. For the Spanish American "sociocritics," the apparent hermeticism and intransitivity of much of the fiction and poetry produced by what Angel Rama scornfully called "the lettered city" (*la ciudad letrada*) are scandalous, unsettling, even immoral traits. It is true, as we have seen, that literature is not altogether innocent of the accusations of elitism and violence leveled against it. However, orality is hardly blameless, as the etymology of the word "dictator" reminds us.[14] Feelings of guilt about being literate apparently underlie Spanish American literary sociocriticism, which seems to be ashamed of its links with literature and tries to forget them whenever possible. Instead, it aligns itself with the technocratic jargon of the social sciences, which it often does not fully understand, resulting in a type of criticism that is unconvincing either as literary analysis, as sociological research, or as interdisciplinary innovation.

It is my hope that these ethically focused readings of selected Spanish American narrative texts will serve to remind us that Spanish American literature, in its five centuries of struggle with issues of justice, power, and violence, has been able to produce through writing a profound and far-reaching critique of itself and its society, from which literary critics and theoreticians have much to learn. In all likelihood, the enigmas posed by the generally negative view ethics holds of writing will never be answered definitively. Nevertheless, pondering them may help all of us— readers as well as writers—to achieve a wiser relationship with the written word.

## Introduction

1. These two sayings are virtually untranslatable without losing a great deal of their violent imagery. The first literally translates as "The letter enters with blood." Its most common, and banal, meaning is "All learning takes effort." The second saying, literally translated, reads: "Letters don't dull the spear." This is a version of the Renaissance topic of "arms and letters," which held that soldiering and the practice of literature were not incompatible pursuits.

All translations in this book are mine, save where otherwise indicated. The English editions of some works listed in the bibliography are included for English-speaking readers' reference. Page numbers of citations refer to the Spanish editions on which I based my translations.

2. My layman's understanding of ethics is heavily indebted to a number of current books that attempt to link ethics with literature, some of which seek to expand on Derrida's rather cryptic statement in *Signéponge/Signsponge*: "the ethical instance is at work in the body of literature" (*L'instance éthique travaille la littérature au corps*; 52–53). Among those that I have found most useful— although they differ widely in approach— are J. Hillis Miller's *The Ethics of Reading: Kant, De Man, Eliot, Trollope, James, and Benjamin* (1987) and his *Versions of Pygmalion* (1990), and Geoffrey Galt Harpham's *Getting It Right: Language, Literature, and Ethics* (1992). Harpham, whose synthesis of the current problematics of ethics and literature I find persuasive, cautions that "ethics is not properly understood as an ultimately coherent set of concepts, rules, or principles—that it ought not even be considered a truly distinct discourse—but rather that it is best conceived as a factor of 'imperativity' immanent in, but not confined to, the practices of language, analysis, narrative, and creation" (5). Harpham nevertheless identifies certain recurrent traits in discourses dealing with ethics (such as works by contemporary thinkers as diverse as Cavell, Derrida, Foucault, and Levinas) or in works in which ethics plays a visible role (such as the narrative of Joseph Conrad). One fundamental theme is the concern with the Other, particularly with "an otherness that remains other, that resists assimilation" (6). In Harpham's view, "the appearance of the other marks an 'ethical moment' even in discourses not obviously concerned with ethics" (7).

3. These ideas, which have become commonplaces of poststructuralist or deconstructive criticism, are laid out by Derrida most explicitly in *Of Grammatology* and in *Dissemination*. A succinct and sympathetic introduction to the deconstructive view of writing may be found in Barbara Johnson's essay "Writing" in *Critical Terms for Literary Study*.

4. Walter J. Ong, whose insistence on the uniqueness of orality vis-à-vis writing is in itself rooted in Plato, usefully compares the Platonic antipathy to writing to the more recent critiques of computer technology (78–83). Although he does not develop this point further, it could be argued that graphophobia is indeed closely related to a more generalized distrust of technology. Such a distrust

usually comes to the fore in moments of intense or extensive technological change and has variously been directed at such technological developments as optical devices (the telescope and the microscope) during the baroque, steam engines in the nineteenth century, and electricity, nuclear power, and computers in the twentieth.

5. See Roberto González Echevarría's pertinent comments in this regard in "Latin American and Comparative Literatures" (51–53).

6. Among the most recent and advanced works on the conflict between indigenous and European modes of representation during the conquest and the colonial period are Mignolo's *The Darker Side of the Renaissance* (1995) and Adorno's *Guaman Poma: Writing and Resistance in Colonial Peru* (1986). Both of these texts can also be read as more nuanced and scholarly responses by specialists on Spanish America's colonial period to Tzvetan Todorov's bold attempt at a semiotic interpretation of the conquest in *La Conquête de l'Amérique* (1982).

7. The phrase "violence of the letter" was coined by Derrida in *Of Grammatology* in the title of a chapter in which Derrida critiques Lévi-Strauss's views on writing and compares them with those of Jean-Jacques Rousseau. Towards the end of that chapter, Derrida makes some highly suggestive, if densely packed, statements on the relations between speech, writing, and ethics:

The ethic of the living word would be perfectly respectable, completely utopian and a-topic as it is (unconnected to *spacing* and to différance as writing), it would be as respectable as respect itself if it did not live on a delusion and a nonrespect for its own condition of origin, if it did not dream in speech of a presence denied to writing, denied by writing. The ethic of speech is the *delusion* of a presence mastered. . . . There is no ethics without the presence *of the other* but also, and consequently, without absence, dissimulation, detour, différance, writing. The arche-writing is the origin of morality as of immorality. The nonethical opening of ethics. A violent opening. (139–140)

8. See González Echevarría, *Myth and Archive* 43–92. Many of his ideas are in turn inspired by Foucault in *Discipline and Punish: The Birth of the Prison*.

9. On Guamán Poma, see Adorno, *Guaman Poma: Writing and Resistance in Colonial Peru* and López-Baralt, *Icono y conquista: Guamán Poma de Ayala*. On Rodríguez Freyle, see González Echevarría, *Myth and Archive* 87–92; Pupo-Walker, *La vocación literaria del pensamiento histórico en América* 123–155; Johnson, *Satire in Colonial Spanish America* 50–63. On Caviedes, see Reedy, *The Poetic Art of Juan del Valle y Caviedes*; Luciani, "Juan del Valle y Caviedes"; and Johnson, *Satire in Colonial Spanish America* 86–106. On Carrió de la Vandera, see Stolley, *El lazarillo de ciegos caminantes: Un itinerario crítico* and Johnson, *Satire in Colonial Spanish America* 107–124. On Fernández de Lizardi, see González, *Journalism and the Development of Spanish American Narrative* 21–41; and Vogeley, "Defining the 'Colonial Reader': *El Periquillo Sarniento*." With regard to the Spanish peninsular literature of the same era, an insightful graphophobic reading (although he does not use the term) of Cervantes's *Don Quixote* and *Colloquy of the Dogs* is found in Alban Forcione's *Cervantes and the Mystery of Lawlessness*, particularly in chapter 6, "Language: Divine or Diabolical Gift?" See also Viviana Díaz Balsera's excellent article, "*El Jardín de Falerina* de Calderón y la escritura de Lucifer," in which she examines Pedro

Calderón de la Barca's allegorical portrayal of the Devil as a playwright and his suggestion that theatrical writing is potentially sinful.

10. My understanding of "abjection" in the context of writing and literature owes much to Julia Kristeva's *Powers of Horror: An Essay on Abjection.*

11. Margarita Ucelay Da Cal's *Los españoles pintados por sí mismos (1843–1844): Estudio de un género costumbrista* offers useful insights into the figure of the *diablo cojuelo* as an emblem of literary satire; see 49–52, 85–93.

12. For a detailed analysis of the writing-as-agony topic in a major poem by the modernist Rubén Darío, "El coloquio de los centauros" (The colloquy of the centaurs), see Echavarría, "Estructura y sentido poético del 'Coloquio de los centauros.'"

13. The recent controversy about the truthfulness of *I, Rigoberta Menchú* is illustrative in this regard. For a useful critical overview of the polemic, see Canby.

14. The most complete and up-to-date discussion of lovesickness and its "cures" in the Spanish Middle Ages is found in Michael Solomon's *The Literature of Misogyny in Medieval Spain.*

15. See Freud's 1937 essay "Analysis Terminable and Interminable." Peter Brooks further observes that

all of Freud's writings on the transference portray it as a realm and process of contest, over the lifting of repression and the mastery of resistances. In the case of 'Dora,' the analyst appears to gain his costly 'victory' by too much imposing his construction of the text; while Dora makes the ultimate riposte available to the storyteller, that of refusing to tell further, breaking off before the end. 'Constructions in Analysis,' along with 'Analysis Terminable and Interminable,' suggests that the analyst must learn to eschew such imposed solutions, that the collaboration and competition of the transference ultimately must put into question the privilege of the analyst. As with reader and text, there is no clear mastery, no position of privilege, no assurance, indeed, that the analyst and the analysand won't trade places, at least provisionally, and perhaps frequently. (*Psychoanalysis and Storytelling* 57–58)

16. From various internal allusions in the novel, Gene Bell-Villada calculates that "the action covers approximately sixty years, from circa 1875 to circa 1935" (192).

17. The January 1999 special issue of *PMLA* devoted to "Ethics and Literary Study" attests to the growing recognition of the study of the literature-ethics interaction as an emerging modality, if not an altogether new field, of literary criticism and theory. In the issue's introduction, "In Pursuit of Ethics," Lawrence Buell offers a useful overview of the various directions in which critical study of ethics and literature has developed. Buell identifies and comments on six branches in particular: the first is the more traditional approach, which dwells on the "moral thematics and underlying value commitments of literary texts and their implied authors" (7); the second is the "ethically oriented theory and criticism focused on the rhetoric of genre" (8); the third is the "reciprocal turn of certain philosophers," such as Martha Nussbaum and Richard Rorty, towards literature (8); the fourth is the ethical turn of deconstruction following the scandal produced by Paul de Man's wartime journalism and also resulting from the decades-long debate between Jacques Derrida and Emmanuel Levinas (8–9); the fifth is the return towards notions of selfhood and the exploration of the ethics-

politics relation in the later work of Michel Foucault and his followers (9–10); and the sixth is the "increased self-consciousness about professional ethics" (10–11). Mary Beth Tierney-Tello's very fine essay entitled "Testimony, Ethics, and the Aesthetic in Diamela Eltit," in this same issue of *PMLA*, expresses ethical concerns about the Latin American testimonial narrative with which I am largely in agreement, although I place greater stress than she does on the feelings of guilt about being literate that are encouraged by this narrative.

18. The latest installment in that dialogue (although probably not the last) is Derrida's moving eulogy on the occasion of Levinas's death in 1995, *Adieu à Emmanuel Lévinas*.

### Chapter One

1. The literary movement known as *modernismo* (modernism) began in Spanish America during the 1880s and lasted until the mid-1920s. Not to be confused with Brazilian *modernismo* (which is aesthetically and ideologically linked to the avant-gardes of the 1920s and '30s), it is usually regarded as the first literary movement to have originated in Spanish America, whence it later spread to Spain. Because most of the major modernists were poets of a stature not seen in Spanish-language literature since Spain's *Siglo de Oro*, estimations of modernism's importance were restricted by most critics to the realm of poetry. Recently, however, critical studies focusing on the vast amount of prose writing by the modernists—particularly their journalistic *crónicas* (chronicles)—have underscored the seminal importance of modernism to the subsequent history of Spanish American literature (see González, *La crónica modernista hispanoamericana*; Kirkpatrick; Rama, *Rubén Darío y el modernismo* and *Las máscaras democráticas del modernismo*; Ramos; Rotker; Schulman). Modernism, furthermore, was more than just the Spanish American version of French symbolism; to use Octavio Paz's well-known phrase, it was a "literature of foundation," an all-encompassing revolution in Spanish American literary and intellectual life without which the current achievements of Spanish American narrative would have been impossible. In this sense, it is a Spanish American version of the broad turn-of-the-century current of literary and cultural change in Europe and North America also known as modernism.

2. Referring to the Díaz regime, Octavio Paz writes: "He is the most enlightened of the Spanish American dictators, and his regime is sometimes reminiscent of the belle époque years in France" (*El laberinto de la soledad* 117). For a detailed account of the social and political tensions underlying the apparent peace of the *Porfiriato* (as the Díaz dictatorship was called), which would erupt into the Mexican Revolution of 1910, see Meyer and Sherman, *The Course of Mexican History* chaps. 26–29.

3. See the comments by Nájera's daughter, Margarita Gutiérrez Nájera, in *Reflejo: Biografía anecdótica de Manuel Gutiérrez Nájera* 37–39.

4. The crónica was a journalistic genre developed during the 1870s by the modernists on the basis of a similar genre, the *chronique*, invented by French periodicals such as *Le Figaro* and *La Chronique Parisienne* during the 1850s. Indeed, Manuel Gutiérrez Nájera is usually credited with being one of the first

to adapt the chronique into the Spanish language, along with the Cuban poet and patriot José Martí. Both men published their first crónicas in the late 1870s. In many instances, chronicles account for more than two-thirds of the modernists' published writings, as can be seen in the collected works of such major modernists as Martí, Nájera, Darío, Amado Nervo, and Enrique Gómez Carrillo. The crónicas were brief newspaper articles on virtually any subject, written in a self-consciously literary style. These articles were meant to be entertaining as well as informative. In fact, however, the modernists made of them much more than their content indicated. The chronicles became literary laboratories in which the modernists tried out new styles and ideas and made these known to other writers. From their beginnings in French journalism of the nineteenth century, the chronicles stood at the intersection of three textual institutions: philology, literature, and journalism. As a journalistic genre, the chronicle had to convey news of current events and be subject to the laws of supply and demand, since from a purely economic standpoint, the chronicle was simply merchandise. As a literary genre, the chronicle had to be entertaining and creative while also possessing the solid, well-crafted nature of a work written with the philological awareness of the historicity of language. Modernist chroniclers also often used the genre to reflect in essay form on the nature of time and history and on the question of modernity. See González, *La crónica modernista* 73–83 and *Journalism and the Development of Spanish American Narrative* 83–100.

5. Nájera's book was the first volume in a collection titled, significantly, "Biblioteca Honrada" (Honest library, *Cuentos completos* 49).

6. Ned J. Davison offers a compendium of different views of Spanish American modernism up to 1966 in *The Concept of Modernism in Hispanic Criticism*. Most of these coincide in emphasizing modernism's aestheticism, though they also recognize a "spiritual" dimension in the movement, manifested in many modernists' passionate curiosity about religion and the occult. A thorough and up-to-date study of modernist religiosity and occultism is found in Cathy L. Jrade's *Rubén Darío and the Romantic Search for Unity*; see also her recent Modernismo, *Modernity and the Development of Spanish American Literature*. Recent scholarship has continued to stress Spanish American modernism's cult of artifice, linking it to social conditions—such as the growing Spanish American middle classes' taste for imported manufactured luxury goods after the 1880s (see, for example, Jitrik and Ramos)—as well as to intellectual factors, such as the complex interplay between literature, philology, and journalism in turn-of-the-century Spanish American culture (see González, *La crónica modernista* 5–59; also Aching, Rotker, and Ramos).

7. I am alluding, of course, to Renan's book of the same title, *La reforme intellectuelle et morale* (1871), with which most Spanish American modernists were familiar.

8. In the Spanish-speaking world, the rise of a more "objective" journalistic style coincides with the decline of a previously predominant model based on oratory, which was far more "literary" (by today's standards) and allowed for greater self-expression. See María Cruz Seoane, *Oratoria y periodismo* 12–18, 333–350.

9. To my knowledge, the most blatant and self-conscious example of this sort of "perversion" of prosopopeia in today's literature (in Spanish or in any other language) is found in the postmodern narratives of the late Cuban writer Severo

Sarduy, whose characters' behavior is governed not by psychological verisimilitude, but by the laws of language (see González Echevarría, *La ruta de Severo Sarduy* 99–100, 153–155, 167–173). Essentially, I read Nájera as I would read Sarduy, because I consider both writers to share a similarly high level of literary self-reflexiveness and theoretical awareness. As a group, the modernists were Spanish America's first outright literary theorists, although—as is the case with many Spanish American writers before and since—their theoretical insights were better displayed in their fictions than in their critical essays. Nájera's essay "El cruzamiento en la literatura" (Cross-breeding in literature, *Obras. Crítica literaria, I* 101–106) gives some idea of his sophisticated understanding of the dynamics of literary history.

10. In 1888, Nájera briefly held the post of *diputado* (congressman) for the district of Texcoco in the state of Veracruz —a favor from his friends in the Díaz government, without which the otherwise scrupulously ethical Nájera would not have been able to afford to marry (Margarita Gutiérrez Nájera 89).

11. See the comments about the symbolism of Proteus in Nájera's work in González, *La crónica modernista* 102, 105. A. Bartlett Giamatti also underscores the ambivalence of the figure of Proteus in the Greco-Roman tradition, as it was reinterpreted during the Renaissance: Proteus appeared then simultaneously as a founder of cities and giver of laws, and as an evil wizard, an enemy of order and concord (438, 455ff.).

12. The gendered, and specifically patriarchal, connotations of the association between the (male) writer and the concept of style are suggestively explored in Derrida's influential essay *Spurs: Nietzsche's Styles/Éperons: Les styles de Nietzsche*.

13. As noted earlier, for Levinas, the confrontation with the Other prompts in the self a remembrance of the self's own death, which in turn prompts a sense of responsibility for the Other (*The Levinas Reader* 83). In this sense, Levinas argues, the self is always "hostage" to the Other, beholden to him, in large part because the self owes its selfhood to the Other's differentiated existence (*The Levinas Reader* 106–107).

14. It would be nearly impossible to make sense of a great many modern texts written by men in which woman plays a central role, without taking into account the wide diffusion and the force of this masculine construct, however erroneous and questionable it may be. In fact, ethical discourse itself suffers from this deformation: one of the most severe critiques directed at ethical discourse relates to its patriarchal Judeo-Christian background, which tends to identify the Other, in a patently essentialist and ideological way, with the female (Harpham 13–16). Nevertheless, all attempts to show that ethics is a patriarchal construct end up applying the very procedures of the ethical discourse they wish to suppress, thus suggesting that ethics is not a mere instrument of the patriarchy (Harpham 16).

15. Nájera's evocation of this concept shows intriguing parallels to its description by Julia Kristeva in her well-known essay *The Powers of Horror: An Essay on Abjection* (1982): "Loathing an item of food, a piece of filth, waste, or dung. The spasms and vomiting that protect me. The repugnance, the retching that thrusts me to the side and turns me away from defilement, sewage, and muck. The shame of compromise, of being in the middle of treachery. The fascinated start that leads me toward and separates me from them" (2).

16. Heidegger is but one possible example; his well-known dictum "*Language speaks*" (190; Heidegger's italics) mobilizes first and foremost the resources of prosopopeia in its quest for the "speaking" of language.

17. Calderón was, along with Shakespeare and Moliére, one of Nájera's idols. Besides his frequent allusions to *La vida es sueño* (Life is a dream), one also finds in Nájera's collected theater crónicas allusions to other plays by the Spanish baroque master, such as *La devoción de la cruz* and *El médico de su honra*. In his article "El centenario de Calderón" (1881), Nájera complains bitterly about the lack of any commemoration of the tercentennial of Calderón's death in Mexico (*Obras IV* 114–115).

18. As Kristeva notes, "it is not thus lack of cleanliness or health that causes abjection but what disturbs identity, system, order. What does not respect borders, positions, rules. The in-between, the ambiguous, the composite. The traitor, the liar, the criminal with a good conscience, the shameless rapist, the killer who claims he is a savior. . . . Abjection . . . is immoral, sinister, scheming, and shady: a terror that dissembles, a hatred that smiles, a passion that uses the body for barter instead of inflaming it, a debtor who sells you up, a friend who stabs you . . ." (4).

19. On the Spanish American modernist novel's history and characteristics, see my book *La novela modernista hispanoamericana* (1987).

## Chapter Two

1. Later in this chapter, I briefly discuss the two very different ways in which the title of this novel can be rendered in English. Although he was a physician, scholar, journalist, and poet, Manuel Zeno Gandía is known above all as Puerto Rico's preeminent nineteenth-century novelist and one of the founders of Puerto Rico's modern novelistic tradition. Long revered as a master of Puerto Rican letters, his reputation has grown lately throughout the Hispanic world as new editions and translations of his masterpiece, *La charca*, have been published in Cuba, New York, Spain, and Venezuela, and as critics have once again focused on the turn-of-the-century vogue of naturalist fiction, as seen in works by the Argentine Eugenio Cambaceres, the Cuban Miguel del Carrión, the Peruvian Clorinda Matto de Turner, and the Mexican Federico Gamboa. Zeno himself was not unknown outside Puerto Rico during his lifetime; he was a well-traveled, cosmopolitan person who had many important friends and acquaintances throughout Spain, Spanish America, and the United States. One of his friends who deserves mention here was the Cuban founder of Spanish American modernism, José Martí (see Gardón Franceschi, *Manuel Zeno Gandía: Vida y poesía* 16–17 and Alvarez, *Manuel Zeno Gandía: Estética y sociedad* 100–108). Zeno's oeuvre undoubtedly marks one of the high points in the "increase in quantity and importance" that Max Henríquez Ureña notes in the Spanish American novel of the 1880s and '90s (58). For additional biographical and bibliographical information on Zeno and on *La charca*, see Alvarez 61–113, 243–244; Gardón Franceschi 46 n (on *La charca*); González, "Manuel Zeno Gandía (1855–1930)" 321–326; and Rivera de Alvarez 2:1637–1638.

2. It was a project never to be fully realized: Zeno wrote four novels, of which

only two—*La charca* and *El negocio* (The business, 1922)—are interconnected in the manner of Zola's *romans-fleuve*.

3. In his well-known essay "The Experimental Novel" (1880), Zola proclaims:

This dream of the physiologist and the experimental doctor of medicine is also that of the novelist who applies the experimental method to the natural and social study of man. Our goal is theirs; we wish, too, to be masters of the phenomena of intellectual and personal elements in order to direct them. We are, in short, experimental moralists showing by experiment in what fashion a passion behaves in a social milieu. . . . To be master of good and evil, to regulate life, to regulate society, in the long run to solve all the problems of socialism, above all to bring a solid foundation to justice by experimentally resolving questions of criminality, is that not to do the most useful and moral human work? (Becker 177)

Theodore Dreiser ("the American Zola," as George J. Becker calls him) echoes Zola's views even more trenchantly in "True Art Speaks Plainly" (1903): "The sum and substance of literary as well as social morality may be expressed in three words—tell the truth. . . . Truth is what is; and the seeing of what is, the realization of truth. To express what we see honestly and without subterfuge: this is morality as well as art" (Becker 155).

4. Paul de Man, "The Dead-End of Formalist Criticism" 242–244. As Jonathan Culler synthesizes it, this poetics "imagines redemption or fusion of contradictions through poetic imagination" (*Framing the Sign* 110).

5. I have translated into English Zeno's Spanish version of the quotation. The original, from which Zeno elided three words, reads as follows: "Tout dire, ah! oui, pour tout connaître et tout guérir!" (To say all, ah yes!, in order to know everything and to heal everything!) The words are uttered by the freethinking doctor Pascal in the context of an impassioned discussion in chapter 4 with his mistress, Clotilde, who tries to persuade him to return to the church. One possible reason for the deletion of this epigraph from subsequent editions of *La charca* may be its contradiction to what is said in *La charca* about attaining knowledge, which would make the epigraph's relation to the novel highly ironic. *La charca* clearly is not an attempt by Zeno to analyze the totality of Puerto Rican life and society in his time. In fact, *La charca* takes for granted the impossibility of knowing everything, of attaining the positivist ideal of absolute knowledge. This belief can be seen, for instance, in the clumsiness of the scientists and pathologists who investigate Deblás's murder (chapter 8 of *La charca*), or in the assertion of ignorance with which the novel ends: "a pain without balm . . . that nobody knows!" (*un dolor sin bálsamo...¡que nadie conoce!*). In this regard, Zeno's novel also shows a debt to Lucretius, who speaks in book 6 of his poem about the difficulties of finding the causes of phenomena, in a passage reminiscent of the police investigation in *La charca*:

There are phenomena for which it is not sufficient
To state one cause, though only one will be true.
For example, if from a considerable distance
You see a corpse on the ground, it is by running over
The possible causes of death you will find the true one.
You cannot say whether the man has died by the sword,

Through the cold, by sickness or perhaps by poison;
What we do know is that he must have died by one of them. (195–196)

For a discussion of how Lucretius's and the Epicureans' epistemological approach contrasts with the Stoics' opposing penchant for positing a causal connection for everything, see Serres, *La naissance de la physique dans le texte de Lucrèce: Fleuves et turbulences* 230–233. My debt to Serres's ideas and methodology is evident throughout this chapter.

6. See the comments on Zeno's aesthetics and its relation to Spanish American modernism by Alvarez (87–100). Alvarez's book is by far the best overall study of the work of Zeno, and I am greatly indebted to its many insightful observations.

7. See, for example, the essays by Laguerre, Cabrera, and Quiñones.

8. Lack of access to Zeno's abundant journalistic writings, as well as to his personal diaries (which still remain unpublished), has prevented me from searching for direct allusions to Lucretius in the rest of Zeno's oeuvre. Zeno does allude in *La charca* to Epicureanism, which he includes as one of the philosophical attitudes among which Juan del Salto wavers (25). In any case, circumstantial evidence concerning Zeno's knowledge of Lucretius's poem is overwhelming. Like all physicians in his day, Zeno had studied Latin, and *De rerum natura* was a common reading for advanced students of that language (I thank my former colleague at the University of Texas at Austin, the late Juan López-Morillas, for this information). Scientific thought in the nineteenth century tended overall to vindicate the intellectual worth of Lucretius's poem, and scholars displayed a renewed interest in the philosophy of Epicurus, along with that of the pre-Socratics. For instance, Karl Marx's doctoral thesis in philosophy (written around 1840) dealt with the relation between Epicurus and Democritus (see Francine Markovits, *Marx dans le Jardin d'Epicure*). In 1869, the French philologist Constant Martha published a substantial study titled *Le poëme de Lucrèce: Morale, religion, science*. In 1884, the French vitalist philosopher Henri Bergson published an edition of *De rerum natura*, along with a detailed study, which was translated into English as *The Philosophy of Poetry: The Genius of Lucretius*. In the Puerto Rican context, already in 1860 an illustrious compatriot of Zeno, Ramón Emeterio Betances, who was also a physician, alluded to Lucretius in a letter to his friend José Francisco Basora: "I would like to devote myself ever more to materialist doctrines in order to convince myself more every day of the futility, of the emptiness and nothingness of things, and be able to end up like the great Lucretius" (cited by Bonafoux 394). Eugenio Astol, another Puerto Rican and a colleague of Zeno in journalism, published around 1890 an article titled "De Rerum Natura" in the island's most important newspaper, *El Clamor del País* (Pedreira 258). The only full translation of *De rerum natura* into Spanish is an eighteenth-century version by the abbot Marchena, and it was almost unavailable in Zeno's day. It appeared in an extremely limited edition of 250 copies made by Marcelino Menéndez Pelayo as part of the *Obras literarias de D. José Marchena* (1892).

9. See the critiques by J. Colón, Laguerre, Quiñones, Cabrera ("Manuel Zeno Gandía: Poeta del novelar isleño"), Lluch Mora, and, most recently, Barradas.

10. See the comments by George Depue Hadzsits in *Lucretius and His Influence* (332–367). Also see Michel Serres, *La naissance de la physique* 233ff.

11. It is worth pointing out that until recently it was common in studies of Lucretius to consider the clinamen Lucretius's sole concession to metaphysics, or at least to psychology, since according to the principles of mechanics, it seemed highly improbable that among many particles falling in a straight line through the void, one of them would suddenly "swerve," however slightly, to collide with others and thus form turbulences. The clinamen was thus frequently interpreted as an allegory of free will (Latham 12). Although this interpretation is not totally incorrect, since the polysemy of the term "clinamen" certainly allows for a psychological reading, Michel Serres has observed that the idea of the clinamen, which seems inconceivable in the physics of solid bodies, is perfectly acceptable in the context of hydraulics, the physics of liquids. It is a generally observable physical fact that within any liquid flow, no matter how smooth the surface on which it occurs, turbulences and whirlpools always arise. Those turbulences happen by chance, in a haphazard fashion, but their emergence becomes more likely when higher numbers of particles are involved. Hydraulic physics is, in fact, a science of probabilities, not of fixed determinations, and its mathematical expression requires the use of differential calculus. The clinamen is also, as Serres points out, a metaphor for difference (*La naissance de la physique* 9–15, 11, 26).

12. Because liquids are made up of loosely bound particles that do not react uniformly when force is applied to them, the science of hydraulics—unlike that of mechanics, which deals with the movements of solids—requires an analysis based on probability and differential calculus. It is thus a branch of physics that is more open to the operation of chance and less likely to fall into a gross determinism (Serres, *Feux et signaux de brume* 29–57; also Serres, *La naissance de la physique* 121ff.).

13. Some examples taken at random demonstrate the abundance of water metaphors: Juan del Salto, we are told, "wherever he saw evil being done, was moved to protest; wherever he discovered error, he needed to erase it, like the drowning man who has to take his head out of the water to breathe the ambient air" (17). Later, Zeno alludes to "the immense pool of stagnant water that was society in decay" (*la inmensa charca de la podredumbre social*; 25). In the description of the peasants' dance at Vegaplana, the narrator observes that "the great mob danced happily. The hall boiled like a murky liquid over coals" (87). Finally, in chapter 6, Juan del Salto's son Jacobo writes to his father from Europe: "You tell me of your joy because of my intense love for my homeland, but also that I shouldn't forget that along with the great beauties of its creation there are tidal waves that flood its beaches and swollen rivers that raze its fields . . ." (102).

14. Two salient examples are the following: just as *De rerum natura* begins with an invocation to Venus, *La charca* begins with Silvina's quite literal "invocation" of Leandra (whom the novel's text explicitly associates with Venus); and just as Lucretius's poem ends with the scene of the funeral pyres in which the victims of the plague of Athens are burned (book 6), *La charca* closes with the death and burial of Silvina.

15. Up to a point, the antithesis proposed by Francisco Manrique Cabrera between the terms *charca* and *charco* is valid: "*charca*, in the speech of the countryside, implies stagnation, watery deposit of stinking miasmas; it is the quiescence of waters that harbor decomposition and decay. It is not *charco*, a transient pool of clear running waters: the delight of peasant children" (*Historia de la literatura*

*puertorriqueña* 185). However, as I earlier pointed out, there is an inherent ambiguity in the metaphor of the "charca" that allows it to be read in a way that is more coherent with the novel's Lucretian postulates: in my view, what Zeno more likely had in mind with his use of the term "charca" was not the image of a natural pool or accumulation of rainwater, but that of a man-made pond or dam, by means of which the water of rivers and creeks is diverted from its natural course and used as an energy source. The text of *La charca* alludes prominently to the *hydraulic* machines used to shell coffee beans (165). (One such machine has been rebuilt and is currently in use at the Hacienda Buena Vista, a restored nineteenth-century coffee plantation and museum on the outskirts of the city of Ponce, on Puerto Rico's southern coast [see Baralt].) Zeno's "charca" is thus a reservoir of potential energy, always thirsty, always sucking new volumes of water as the reservoir is used up: it is a vortex, a slow but inexorable whirlpool.

16. This is particularly true if one accepts Jean-François Lyotard's rather atemporal definition of "the postmodern" in "Answering the Question: What Is Postmodernism?":

The postmodern would be that which, in the modern, puts forward the unpresentable in presentation itself; that which denies itself the solace of good forms, the consensus of taste which would make it possible to share collectively the nostalgia for the unattainable; that which searches for new presentations, not in order to enjoy them but in order to impart a stronger sense of the unpresentable. . . . The [postmodern] artist and the writer, then, are working without rules in order to formulate the rules of what *will have been done*. Hence the fact that work and text have the character of an *event*; hence, also, they always come too late for their author, or, what amounts to the same thing, their being put into work, their realization (*mise en oeuvre*) always begins too soon. *Post modern* would have to be understood according to the paradox of the future (*post*) anterior (*modo*). (81)

17. It is worth noting that Epicurean communities in antiquity "contrary to social convention, . . . admitted men and women, rich and poor, and even slaves on terms of equality" (*The Oxford Companion to Philosophy* 239–240). A tendency towards quietism is also evident in Epicureanism. Not surprisingly, among the few efforts Epicureanism encouraged its followers to pursue in order to reach equilibrium (*ataraxia*) was writing. Judging from Lucretius's example, writing was for the Epicureans a means to achieve ataraxia, but one that was strictly limited to the writer and a small group of readers, for what was most important was not to establish a norm or a generalized doctrine, but to provoke at most, through the slightest grazing of a text, through the least noticeable clinamen, an inclination on the part of readers toward their own independent reflection on reality. This explains why Lucretius addressed *De rerum natura* to one Memmius who perhaps would not be interested in the text; it also explains, I believe, why Zeno would write a social novel even when he voices in it the opinion that "this generation will not be saved" (*esta generación no se salva*; 252).

18. As I argue in chapter 1 of this book, the ethics of writing is based not only on a differential concept of writing but also on a notion of writing as a resistant Other. This last quality is in fact what makes the ethics of writing ethical, since, as Geoffrey Galt Harpham notes, "the appearance of the other marks an 'ethical moment' even in discourses not concerned with ethics" (7). Glossing the thought

of Emmanuel Levinas, Harpham points out that for the Franco-Lithuanian phi-losopher, "ethics . . . is not abstract, not a function of reason, not a matter for reflection, not even something to be understood. Rather, the ethical obligation issues directly from the encounter with the luminous and alien other in its hu-man density, and it both exceeds and precedes any cognitive grasp of duty" (7).

19. Among many instances that can be cited are the following: "Gaspar, who was fifty years old, with repulsive features and evil appearance, matted hair and a breath that smelled of alcohol, was not a meek husband" (10); "Gaspar, as if drain-ing a glass of liquor, drained Silvina, fogging her with his brutish breath" (11); "Marcelo, pulled by his emotions as well as by his illness, teetered without bal-ance: he was a bundle of nerves twisted by neurosis, pliant yeast that could just as easily surrender to good as to evil. A wandering soul, ready to move wherever the wind blew it" (32); "[Old Marta's] avarice was sordid, greedy, capable of commit-ting any crime. An egg abandoned by a chicken in the shadows of the forest— What good fortune! Rice or sugar fallen on the road from a ripped sack on the mule train—What a find! The bananas given away by neighbors—What an advan-tage! Hers was the anxious sickness of accumulation, the feverish madness of booty" (41). See also pages 55, 59, 90–91, 143, 160, 162–163, and 214.

20. A similar wavering between prosopopeia and objectivity can be seen in Zeno's descriptions of nature throughout the novel, in which, even as he insists on nature's disconnection from humanity, he consistently attributes humanlike qualities to nature, as in the following passages: "Throughout there sounded the voice of the forests: that wordless voice in which a hundred noises beat, indefinable murmurs boil up, and in which nature tells of its greatness under the wings of time. The forest appeared motionless, in a deceptive quietude invaded by currents of restless life, while the plants absorbed nourishment from their surroundings to power the magnificent labor of vegetable dynamics. And so, with all its strengths, the forest lay full of mysteries, surrounded by an almost sublime solitude, in the midst of a multitude of motionless beings" (72); "Only the river remained mur-muring in that deathly solitude, always movable, always restless, always sound-ing, as if it dragged along in its current the prolonged cry of a pain without balm, as if it carried, dissolved in its waters, caused by a great misfortune, tears that nobody dries, that nobody consoles, that nobody knows!" (214).

21. On abjection and hypocrisy, see Kristeva 4.

22. Zeno's contacts with Spanish American modernism were broad and deep, as attested by his lifelong friendship with José Martí. See Alvarez 87–113. How-ever, Alvarez points out Zeno's skeptical attitude towards all literary schools or modalities (108).

23. On Celestina and her literary "ancestors" and "descendants," see Roberto González Echevarría, Celestina's Brood. On Mignon's dissemination through-out nineteenth-century culture, see Steedman.

24. Steedman remarks on the "extraordinary plasticity of the terms 'child-hood' and 'child'" (7) throughout the nineteenth century. She further notes that

"Childhood" was a category of dependence, a term that defined certain relation-ships of powerlessness, submission and bodily inferiority or weakness, before it became descriptive of chronological age. The late nineteenth century fixed childhood, not just as a category of experience, but also as a time-span. The obvious place to look for the elision of childhood with chronological age is in the development of mass schooling, and its grouping of children together by age cohort. In the same period, the practices of child psychology, developmental linguistics and anthropometry also provided clearer pictures of what children were like, and how they should be expected to look at certain ages. (7)

25. As Elizabeth Bronfen notes in *Over Her Dead Body: Death, Femininity, and the Aesthetic* (1992), "the pictorial [and, I would add, narrative] representation of dead women became so prevalent in eighteenth and nineteenth century European culture that by the middle of the latter century this topos was dangerously hovering on the periphery of cliché" (3). Bronfen's psychoanalytically oriented book is the most thorough and insightful analysis of this topic.

26. That this question is not mere philosophical hairsplitting is evidenced by its reappearance in the contemporary social debate, in the U.S. and other Western countries, about the effects of violence in television and the movies on young viewers. See Wesseker, *Violence in the Media* and Kelly, *TV Violence: A Guide to the Literature*. The issue of the risks involved in the representation of evil dates in Western culture at least to the Middle Ages, as seen in such works as *The Book of Good Love* (1330) by the medieval Spanish author Juan Ruiz, who in his prologue declares (with no lack of irony, to be sure):

Wherefore, I with my small understanding and much great rudeness, perceiving how much wealth can cause the soul and the body to be lost, and the many evils that accompany it and bring to pass the foolish love of the sins of the world, choosing and loving with good intentions salvation and the glory of paradise for my soul, I made this little writing for the glorification of the good and I prepared this new book in which are written some of the manners and masteries and deceitful subtleties of the foolish love of the world which some persons follow in order to sin. [. . .] However, inasmuch as it is a human thing to commit sin, if there be any who desire (albeit I advise it not) to sample this foolish, worldly love, they will here discover certain directions to that end. . . . And I beseech and advise whomsoever sees and hears it to guard well the three things of the soul; the first that he may well understand and judge of my intentions wherewith I wrote it and of the meaning of my words because according to all rights words are subordinate to meaning and not meaning to words. God knows that my intention was not to compose it in order to provide directions for sinning nor to utter wickedness, but it was to convert all persons to the chaste remembrance of doing good and to set a good example of upright conduct together with exhortations to the way of salvation, and also in order that all persons may be warned and may the better ward themselves from such habits as those are prone to who follow after worldly love. (5–6)

Similar disclaimers may also be found, of course, in other famously ribald works of medieval literature, such as Boccacio's *Il decamerone* (1352) and Chaucer's *Canterbury Tales* (1387–1400), and during the Renaissance and baroque periods in works such as Rojas's *Celestina* (1502) and the novels of the picaresque genre. In modern times, the question of the representation of evil was foregrounded most strikingly by the work of the Marquis de Sade, but it did not become an explicit subject of reflection until the romantic period, in essays as diverse as De Quincey's chillingly ironic *On Murder Considered as One of the Fine Arts* (1827)

and Hegel's *Lectures on the Philosophy of World History* (1830–1832), in which the German philosopher remarks on historiography's perverse dependence on the "panorama of sin and suffering" that history presents to us (22).

### Chapter Three

1. De la Parra's work has been "rediscovered" outside her native Venezuela, to a large extent, only in the past two decades. Criticism has centered on her novels, *Ifigenia* and *Las memorias de Mamá Blanca*. The former, in particular, has generally been regarded as de la Parra's most avowedly "feminist" work, while the latter has been read largely as a reaffirmation of de la Parra's conservative values. *Ifigenia* has also generally been read in a tragic vein, or at least as a tragicomedy, in which María Eugenia's marriage to César Leal is seen as the tragic finale of the story. Edna Aizenberg's characterization of *Ifigenia* as a "failed *Bildungsroman*" is typical of the reaction of current-day readers to this novel (Aizenberg 549–546). Salient recent criticism on de la Parra includes Aizenberg's article, Elizabeth Garrels's book *Las grietas de la ternura: Nueva lectura de Teresa de la Parra* (1987), and the articles collected in Velia Bosch's critical edition of *Las memorias de Mamá Blanca* (1992) in the UNESCO-sponsored "Colección Archivos."

2. While the rise of a "female poetry" in Spanish America during the 1920s and '30s is a widely recognized phenomenon—with names such as Delmira Agustini, Juana de Ibarborou, Gabriela Mistral, and Alfonsina Storni—only de la Parra and the Chilean María Luisa Bombal are cited by literary historians as women novelists during this period (see, for example, Bellini 346–351, 497, 565–566). More recently, other female novelists of the 1920s and '30s, such as the Mexican Nelly Campobello (author of *Cartucho*, 1931, and *Las manos de Mamá*, 1938), have been recovered, and their works are being increasingly studied.

3. In the first of her lectures in the series *La influencia de las mujeres en la formación del alma americana* (The influence of women in the formation of the American soul), de la Parra remarks that "many are the moralists already who, with pleasant equanimity in many cases or with violent condemnations in a few cases, have attacked María Eugenia Alonso's diary, calling it Voltairian, perfidious, and extremely dangerous to the contemporary young women who may get their hands on it. . . . María Eugenia Alonso's diary is not a book of revolutionary propaganda, as some ultramontane moralists have tried to label it; no, to the contrary, it is an exposition of a typical case of our contemporary illness, that of Spanish American Bovaryism. It is an illness caused by an acute dissatisfaction resulting from a sudden change in the emotional temperature, and also from an environment that lacks fresh air" (*Obras completas* 684; see also 686).

4. Like many Greek names, "Iphigenia" can be spelled in more than one way; in my text I have chosen to use the more commonly accepted spelling, rather than the one favored by the classical scholars I cite.

5. See chapter 1 of this book for a detailed description of Semiramis as a literary character and as a symbol of a negative view of both writing and woman.

6. See, for example, María Eugenia's comments on this subject and her depictions of fragments of one of César Leal's speeches on pages 440–442.

## Chapter Four

1. Among the most salient recent readings of this story are those by Balderston in *Out of Context*, Echavarría in "Espacio textual y el arte de la jardinería china en Borges: 'El jardín de senderos que se bifurcan,'" Irwin in *The Mystery to a Solution*, and Weissert in "Representation and Bifurcation: Borges's Garden of Chaos Dynamics." Unless otherwise noted, all page number references to Borges's works in this chapter refer to *Obras completas*.

2. Borges alluded, often obliquely but sometimes directly, to historical events that were taking place as he was writing his stories; in certain cases, this is partly related to his use of journalistic discourse, since some of the stories in *Ficciones*—such as "El acercamiento a Almotásim" (The approach to Al-Mu'tasim), "Pierre Menard, autor del Quijote" (Pierre Menard, author of the Quixote), "Examen de la obra de Herbert Quain" (An examination of the work of Herbert Quain), and "Tres versiones de Judas" (Three versions of Judas)—masquerade as book reviews. On other occasions, the historical references, such as those to World War II and the struggle against the Axis powers, are political, although their precise intent must often be decoded. The importance of taking into account the historical allusiveness of Borges's writings has been underscored recently by Daniel Balderston in *Out of Context: Historical Reference and the Representation of Reality in Borges*.

3. There are very few direct allusions to ethics in Borges's oeuvre, but ethics and ethical problems are implicit in many of his most celebrated stories besides "The Garden of Forking Paths"—from "The Approach to Al-Mu'tasim" and "El sur" (The south) in *Ficciones*, to "Historia del guerrero y la cautiva" (Story of the warrior and the captive), "Deutsches Requiem," and "Emma Zunz" in *El Aleph* (1949), to "La intrusa" (The intruder) and "El informe de Brodie" (Doctor Brodie's report) in *Doctor Brodie's Report* (1970), among others. In all of these stories ethical reflection is prominent, and the relation among ethics, language, and writing is addressed. The essay "La supersticiosa ética del lector" (The superstitious ethics of the reader), collected in *Discusión* (1932), despite its title, deals primarily with the question of style in writing. In the prologue to his fifth book of poems, *Elogio de la sombra* (In praise of darkness, 1969), Borges misleadingly announces to his readers that he has included "two new topics: old age and ethics" (*Obra poética* 308), and then proceeds to contrast "Protestant nations" to those of "the Catholic tradition" in terms of the former's greater concern with ethics (308).

4. Sylvia Molloy's lucid observations on the "fear of names" in Borges are also perfectly applicable to Borges's attitude towards writing in general:

For Borges, names—names aspiring to account for a totality, and not the fragments, or allusions, his text offers—are clearly dangerous. For Borges, to name means to fix a segment of the text and proclaim it unique, disregarding the unsettling possibility that it may be simple repetition, a simple tautology. For Borges, to name with such faith (or with such superstition) is to disregard William of Occam's economical principle, which he frequently cites: *Entia non sunt multiplicanda praeter necessitatem*, entities should not be multiplied in vain. [. . .] Any sign, even when disguised, even when obliquely inscribed, as it is in Borges, always runs the risk of being *one more thing*, a superfluous accretion. Every sign accrues and multiplies. (*Signs of Borges* 79–80)

Molloy also notes Borges's affinity with the "puritanical" ethic of Stevenson and Hawthorne (81); the latter, in particular, according to Borges, never "ceased to feel that the task of the writer was frivolous or, what is worse, even sinful" (Borges, *Obras completas* 680).

5. "Tlön, Uqbar, Orbis Tertius" tells of the gradual takeover of reality by an apocryphal encyclopedia, while "The Circular Ruins" tells the tale of a magician who realizes that he, too, is an illusion.

6. Although Harpham seemingly does not develop this implied reading of Borges's story, in a sense he does. Without alluding to Borges or to the story directly, Harpham uses a number of the themes explored in "The Garden of Forking Paths" repeatedly, like leitmotifs, throughout his theoretical essay: espionage (Harpham concludes with a reading of Conrad's *The Secret Agent*), duplicity or doubleness (in his discussion of the split in the ethical subject between "I" and "one," 38–43), and paranoia (in his discussion of the notion of writerly "creation," 188–195), among many others. Arguably, despite the fact that it is not explicitly discussed, Borges's story is more central to Harpham's exposition than is Conrad's novel, or even some of the philosophers and theorists to whom Harpham alludes. For this very reason, any attempt on my part to "develop" or to "flesh out" Harpham's implicit reading of "The Garden of Forking Paths" would be largely redundant, since Borges's story is already at work in Harpham's book, helping to shape its arguments and providing some of its main themes. The absence of overt allusions to Borges in Harpham's essay (save for the phrase "garden of forking paths") itself seems to mimic the dynamics of the riddle, and the act of riddling, as it is explored in Borges's story: "Finally Stephen Albert said: 'In a guessing game to which the answer is chess, which word is the only one prohibited?' I thought for a moment and then replied: 'The word is *chess*.'" (479). Latin Americanists have by now grown used to this sort of dissemination and elision to which sources in Latin American literature are frequently subjected by U.S. and European theorists (as well as to their outright ignorance of these sources in many cases; see the comments by González Echevarría in "Latin American and Comparative Literatures"). One could even make the perverse argument that, were it not for that sometimes purposeful avoidance, important and useful theoretical studies such as Harpham's might never have been written, or more likely still, their focus would have been entirely different.

7. See Derrida's pertinent comments on "textual grafting" in *Dissemination* (202–203).

8. I allude here to Todorov's well-known essay "Narrative-Men" in *The Poetics of Prose*.

9. There are no female characters of any significance in *Ficciones*. Among the few female protagonists in Borges's two other early books of short stories are the Widow Ching in *A Universal History of Infamy* and Emma Zunz, Teodelina Villar, and Beatriz Viterbo in *El aleph*. Female characters are much more in evidence in several of the stories in *Doctor Brodie's Report*, although mostly in stereotypical roles, or as victims of male violence, as in "The Intruder" and "La señora mayor" (The elderly lady).

10. See Echavarría's comments on the toponymic and multilingual wordplay implicit in the joining of the name "Albert" to the phrase "on the Ancre," which leads to the name of the French city that is to be bombed: Albert-sur-Ancre (Echavarría, "Espacio textual" 100, 100 n).

11. An already canonical text on writing's doubleness and duplicity is Derrida's essay "The Double Session" (1970) in *Dissemination* (173–285). Derrida explores many of the issues raised in Borges's story and in the foregoing discussion of it: the interdependency between writing and reading; the question of activity versus passivity, necessity versus chance, in reading and writing; and the issue of the author's control over writing. In this early text, however, the ethical implications are left unexamined. Borges's interest in the whole question of lying and falsehood is evident from the very title of his book of stories, *Ficciones*, and is, of course, a leitmotif in his writings, at least since *A Universal History of Infamy*.

12. Borges offers five of these names in a humorous comment to John T. Irwin in 1983: "I have always had this fear that some day I would be found out, that people would see that everything in my work is borrowed from someone else, from Poe or Kafka, from Chesterton, Stevenson, or Wells" (Irwin xxii). As a concrete instance of his elision of authors, Borges cites and comments extensively on Nietzsche throughout the 1920s and '30s, but, perhaps because of Nietzsche's misappropriation by the Nazis, Borges later ceases to allude to him, or does so only in his typically oblique way, by alluding to Schopenhauer. Two other canonical names of modernity with whom Nietzsche is usually joined, Marx and Freud, are almost never mentioned by Borges. In the realm of fiction, Joyce is another case in point. Borges was the first Hispanic reviewer of *Ulysses* (from which he also translated a portion of Molly Bloom's final monologue into Spanish) in 1925 (Barnatán 439), but references to Joyce become more negative and less frequent in his texts after the forties. Also illustrative are Borges's varying attitudes towards the Spanish writers Miguel de Unamuno and José Ortega y Gasset; see González Echevarría, "Borges, Carpentier, y Ortega: Dos textos olvidados."

## Chapter Five

1. Among the many studies focusing on *The Harp and the Shadow* from an autobiographical perspective, the most salient are those by Barrientos, Bockus-Aponte, Chase, González Echevarría ("The Pilgrim's Last Journeys" and "Colón, Carpentier y los orígenes de la ficción latinoamericana"), and Valero-Covarrubias. A recent essay by Karen Stolley ("Death by Attrition: The Confessions of Christopher Columbus in Carpentier's *El arpa y la sombra*") gives the autobiographical reading of this novel a metaliterary twist by analyzing the text in terms of the ritual discourse of confession. I have been unable to find any study dealing explicitly with theatricality or the theater in *The Harp and the Shadow*. There are, however, essays by Bost and by Collard that focus on the theatrical elements in *Concierto barroco* (Baroque concert) and *Los pasos perdidos* (The lost steps), respectively. An insightful overview of the function of "performance" in Carpentier's work is found in Vicky Unruh's "The Performing Spectator in Alejo Carpentier's Fictional World." On the question of theatricality and self-reflexiveness, I have

benefited from the observations of Priscilla Meléndez in her book *La dramaturgia hispanoamericana contemporánea: Teatralidad y autoconciencia.*

2. On Cervantes and Carpentier, see also De Armas.

3. An indication of this is the frequent concern with theatrical authors, ranging from Sophocles to Shakespeare, among theoreticians of the relationship between law and literature. See Ward, and also Weisberg.

4. On "spatial form" and the novel, see Kestner.

5. That paragraph describes the papal procession as it winds its way deep into the inner chambers of the Vatican (11–12). Another indication of the novel's "Russian dolls" structure is the passage in which the character of Columbus remembers a mummy he had seen on the island of Chios: "it was like a box in human shape, within which there was a second box, similar to the first, which in turn enclosed a body for which the Egyptians, by means of the embalming arts, had preserved the appearance of life" (52–53).

6. For a similar, though more detailed, reading in this same vein, see González Echevarría, "Colón, Carpentier y los orígenes de la ficción latinoamericana."

7. See González Echevarría's comments on Carpentier's theatrically inspired use of allegory in *El siglo de las luces* (Explosion in a cathedral) in "Historia y alegoría en Alejo Carpentier" in *Isla a su vuelo fugitiva.* Also see Bost and Collard.

8. It is true, however, as Bermel emphasizes (27–32), that farce often uses otherness in a differential fashion in order to objectify persons and personify things, thus rendering ethical judgment moot; but it is its very explicit "othering" quality that gives farce its eminent theatricality, and its ethical potential.

9. The most thorough and advanced discussion of America-as-difference is that of Alonso in *The Spanish American Regional Novel: Modernity and Autochthony* (1–37). The concept of America as a region characterized by violence has by now become a cliché, so that it hardly requires documentation. Among the many studies of violence in Latin American literature, three in particular stand out: Raquel Chang-Rodríguez's *Violencia y subversión en la prosa colonial hispanoamericana, siglos XVI y XVII* (1982), Ariel Dorfman's *Imaginación y violencia en América* (1970), and David William Foster's *Violence in Argentine Literature: Cultural Responses to Tyranny* (1995).

10. See González Echevarría's analysis of Carpentier's use of numerological symbolism in *The Kingdom of This World* (*Alejo Carpentier: The Pilgrim at Home* 129–147). "Carpentier's hand," González Echevarría argues, "has already been shown in the act of violating that assumed harmony between history and nature in order to force history into the design of its own text, into the itinerary of his own writing. In the case of Henri Christophe's death, for instance, which did not occur on Sunday, August 22; or Mackandal's death, which occurred not on a Monday in January, but on a Friday" (*Alejo Carpentier: The Pilgrim at Home* 146).

### Chapter Six

1. For comments on ethics in works by García Márquez (other than *Love in the Time of Cholera,* which is discussed in the introduction to this book), Vargas

Llosa, and Poniatowska, see my book *Journalism and the Development of Spanish American Narrative*.

2. Other recent essays that comment on "Press Clippings" are Susana Reisz de Rivarola's "Política y ficción fantástica" and Maurice Hemingway's and Frank McQuade's "The Writer and Politics in Four Stories by Julio Cortázar." Unlike Boldy and Peavler, these critics view "Press Clippings" as a story that attempts to reconcile the fantastic with the political.

3. The quandary is similar to that raised in Borges's short story "La busca de Averroes" (Averroes's search), when, in the final paragraph, the narrator notes: "I felt that Averroes, wanting to imagine what drama is without ever knowing what a theater is, was no less absurd than I, wanting to imagine Averroes with nothing but a few drams of Renan, Lane, and Asín Palacios. On the last page, I felt that my narrative was a symbol of the man I was while I was writing it, and that in order to write that narrative I had to be that man, and that to be that man I had to have written that narrative, and so until infinity" (*El aleph* 101).

4. For a more detailed explanation, see González, *Journalism* 109–111.

5. The most complete treatment of figural allegory is still Erich Auerbach's classic essay "Figura," in which he defines figural allegory as "the interpretation of one worldly event through another; the first signifies the second, the second fulfills the first. Both remain historical events; yet both, looked at in this way, have something provisional and incomplete about them; they point to one another and both point to something in the future, something still to come, which will be the actual, real, and definitive event" (58). In my essay "Revolución y alegoría en 'Reunión' de Julio Cortázar," I comment more extensively on Cortázar's penchant for figural allegory, which is also evident in his novelistic masterpiece, *Rayuela* (Hopscotch).

6. Her maiden name, Laura Beatriz Bonaparte, suggests that (like the biblical Ruth) she is not of Jewish origin, but she is married to Santiago Bruchstein, who is insulted by the military as "a Jew bastard" ("Press Clippings" 86).

7. Noemí's acquaintance with the sculptor dates back twenty years ("Press Clippings" 81).

8. Inquiring about the origin of the wishes that incite dream-wishes, Freud remarks (in a passage that is highly suggestive with regard to "Press Clippings"):

I readily admit that a wishful impulse originating in the conscious will *contribute* to the instigation of a dream, but it will probably not do more than that. The dream would not materialize if the preconscious wish did not succeed in finding reinforcement from elsewhere. From the unconscious, in fact. *My supposition is that a conscious wish can only become a dream-instigator if it succeeds in awakening an unconscious wish with the same tenor and in obtaining reinforcement from it.* . . . These wishes in our unconscious, ever on the alert and, so to say, immortal, remind one of the legendary Titans, weighed down since primaeval ages by the massive bulk of the mountains which were once hurled upon them by the victorious gods and which are still shaken from time to time by the convulsion of their limbs. But these wishes, held under repression, are themselves of infantile origin, as we are taught by the psychological research into the neuroses. I would propose, therefore, to set aside the assertion . . . that the place of origin of dream-wishes is a matter of indifference and replace it by another one to the following effect: *a wish which is*

*represented in a dream must be an infantile one.* (*The Interpretation of Dreams* 591–592; Freud's italics)

9. See Susan Gubar's overview of sexual/textual metaphors and women's writing in "'The Blank Page' and the Issues of Female Creativity" (292–313).

10. In London's "Lost Face," an exiled Polish patriot, Subienkow, who had joined Russian fur trappers in Alaska in the early nineteenth century, faces certain death by torture at the hands of an Indian tribe. As he hears and watches his comrade, Big Ivan, being tortured by the women of the tribe (in the passage alluded to in Cortázar's story), he devises a way to achieve a quick, clean death at the hand of his enemies. Subienkow, who regards himself as "a dreamer, a poet, and an artist" ("Lost Face" 4), uses his wits to trick the chief into beheading him, thus depriving the tribe of the pleasure of torturing him. The narrator makes it clear that Subienkow is no pure, unsullied hero. Despite Subienkow's cultivated background and his noble dream of an independent Poland, he too has killed innocent people: the traveler in Siberia whose papers he stole (7, 8) and, of course, numerous Indians (7). "It had been nothing but savagery" (7) is a phrase that recurs like a leitmotif throughout "Lost Face." Interestingly, this is a story that also caught Jorge Luis Borges's attention. Borges translated it into Spanish and included it in an anthology he edited of short stories by London, *Las muertes concéntricas* (The concentric deaths, 1979). It is likely, however, that Cortázar read the story in the original English long before Borges's translation.

11. As Roberto González Echevarría remarks about the myth of the Minotaur in Cortázar's early play *Los reyes* (The kings, 1949):

The confrontation of the monster and the hero constitutes the primal scene in Cortázar's mythology of writing: a hegemonic struggle for the center, which resolves itself in a mutual cancellation and in the superimposition of beginnings and ends. [. . .] This primal scene appears with remarkable consistency in Cortázar's writing. I do not mean simply that there are monsters, labyrinths, and heroes, but rather that the scene in which a monster and a hero kill each other, cancel each other's claim to the center of the labyrinth, occurs with great frequency, particularly in texts where the nature of writing seems to be more obviously in question. (*The Voice of the Masters* 102–103)

12. "Ever since I began writing," Cortázar has said, "the notion of the ludic was profoundly meshed, confused, with the notion of literature. For me, a literature without ludic elements is boring, the kind of literature I don't read, a dull literature, like socialist realism, for example" (Prego 136–137). See also González Bermejo 103–112 and Picón Garfield's comments on games and the "man-child" in Cortázar's works in ¿*Es Julio Cortázar un surrealista?* (189–199).

13. Derrida's position later became more ethically oriented. See Harpham, "Ethics" 390–392.

14. Latin *dictare*, "to repeat verbally, to dictate" (*Diccionario manual latino-español/español-latino Sopena*, s.v. "*dictare*").

Abbagnano, Nicola. *Diccionario de filosofía*. Mexico City: Fondo de Cultura Económica, 1989.

Aching, Gerard. *The Politics of Spanish American* Modernismo: *By Exquisite Design*. Cambridge: Cambridge UP, 1997.

Adorno, Rolena. *Guaman Poma: Writing and Resistance in Colonial Peru*. Austin: U of Texas P, 1986.

Adorno, Theodor W. *Negative Dialectics*. New York: The Seabury Press, 1973.

Aeschylus. *Agamemnon*. In *The Oresteia*, trans. David Grene and Wendy Doniger O'Flaherty. Chicago: U of Chicago P, 1989. 35–94.

Aizenberg, Edna. "El *Bildungsroman* fracasado en Latinoamérica: El caso de *Ifigenia*." *Revista Iberoamericana* 132–133 (1985): 539–546.

Alonso, Carlos J. "*Rama y sus retoños*: Figuring the Nineteenth Century in Spanish America." *Revista de Estudios Hispánicos* 2 (1994): 283–292.

———. *The Spanish American Regional Novel: Modernity and Autochthony*. Cambridge: Cambridge UP, 1990.

Alvarez, Ernesto. *Manuel Zeno Gandía: Estética y sociedad*. Río Piedras: Editorial de la Universidad de Puerto Rico, 1987.

Auerbach, Erich. "Figura." In *Scenes From the Drama of European Literature*. Minneapolis: U of Minnesota P, 1984. 11–78.

Auerbach, Nina. *Woman and the Demon: The Life of a Victorian Myth*. Cambridge: Harvard UP, 1982.

Balderston, Daniel. *Out of Context: Historical Reference and the Representation of Reality in Borges*. Durham, N.C.: Duke UP, 1993.

Baralt, Guillermo A. *La Buena Vista, 1833–1904: Estancia de frutos menores, fábrica de harinas y hacienda cafetalera*. San Juan: Fideicomiso de Conservación de Puerto Rico, 1988.

Barnatán, Marcos Ricardo. *Borges: Biografía total*. Madrid: Ediciones Temas de Hoy, 1995.

Barradas, Efraín. "La naturaleza en *La charca*: Tema y estilo." *Sin Nombre* 1 (1974): 34–42.

Barrientos, Juan J. "Colón, personaje novelesco." *Cuadernos Hispanoamericanos* 437 (1986): 45–62.

Barthes, Roland. *Critical Essays*. Evanston: Northwestern UP, 1972.

———. *Le plaisir du texte*. Paris: Seuil, 1973.

Bataille, Georges. *La littérature et le mal*. Paris: Gallimard, 1957.

Bauman, Zygmunt. *Postmodern Ethics*. Oxford: Blackwell, 1993.

Becker, George J., ed. *Documents of Modern Literary Realism*. Princeton: Princeton UP, 1963.

Bellini, Giuseppe. *Historia de la literatura hispanoamericana*. Madrid: Editorial Castalia, 1985.

Bell-Villada, Gene H. *García Márquez: The Man and His Work*. Chapel Hill: U of North Carolina P, 1990.

Bentley, Eric. *The Life of the Drama*. New York: Applause Theatre Books, 1991.

Bermel, Albert. *Farce: A History from Aristophanes to Woody Allen.* Carbondale: Southern Illinois UP, 1990.

Bernard, John. "Theatricality and Textuality: The Example of *Othello.*" *New Literary History* 26 (1995): 931–949.

Bockus-Aponte, Barbara. "*El arpa y la sombra*: The Novel as Portrait." *Hispanic Journal* 1 (1981): 93–105.

Boldy, Steven. "Julio Cortázar (26 August 1914 - 12 February 1984)." In *Dictionary of Literary Biography.* Vol. 113, *Modern Latin American Fiction Writers: First Series.* Detroit: Bruccoli Clark Layman, 1992. 119–133.

Bonafoux, Luis. *Betances.* San Juan, Puerto Rico: Instituto de Cultura Puertorriqueña, 1970.

Booth, Wayne. *The Company We Keep: An Ethics of Fiction.* Chicago: U of Chicago P, 1988.

Borges, Jorge Luis. *El aleph.* Buenos Aires: Emecé, 1972.

———. "The Garden of Forking Paths" ["El jardín de senderos que se bifurcan" (1956)]. In *Ficciones*, ed. Anthony Kerrigan, with various translators. New York: Grove Press, 1962.

———. *Obras completas, 1923–1972.* Buenos Aires: Emecé, 1974.

———. *Obra poética.* Madrid: Alianza/Emecé, 1975.

Bost, David H. "The Operatic World of *Concierto Barroco.*" *Cincinnati Romance Review* 7 (1988): 113–124.

Bronfen, Elizabeth. *Over Her Dead Body: Death, Femininity, and the Aesthetic.* London: Routledge, 1992.

Brooks, Peter. *The Melodramatic Imagination: Balzac, Henry James, Melodrama, and the Mode of Excess.* New York: Columbia UP, 1984.

———. *Psychoanalysis and Storytelling.* Cambridge, Mass.: Blackwell, 1994.

Buell, Lawrence. "Introduction: In Pursuit of Ethics." In *Ethics and Literary Study*, ed. Lawrence Buell. Spec. issue of *PMLA* 114 (1999): 7–19.

Burns, Elizabeth. *Theatricality: A Study of Convention in the Theatre and in Social Life.* New York: Harper & Row, 1972.

Cabrera, Francisco Manrique. *Historia de la literatura puertorriqueña.* New York: Las Américas Publishing Co., 1956.

———. "Manuel Zeno Gandía: Poeta del novelar isleño." *Asomante* 4 (1955): 19–47.

Calderón de la Barca, Pedro. *La hija del aire.* Ed. Gwynne Edwards. London: Tamesis Books, 1970.

Canby, Peter. "The Truth About Rigoberta Menchú." Review of *Me llamo Rigoberta Menchú y así me nació la conciencia*, by Rigoberta Menchú. *New York Review of Books*, 8 April 1999, 28–33.

Carpentier, Alejo. "De lo real maravilloso americano." In *Tientos y diferencias.* Montevideo: Arca, 1967. 102–120.

———. *El arpa y la sombra.* Mexico City: Siglo XXI, 1979.

———. *El reino de este mundo.* Barcelona: Seix-Barral, 1972.

———. *The Harp and the Shadow: A Novel.* Trans. Thomas Christensen and Carol Christensen. San Francisco: Mercury House, 1990.

———. *Guerra del tiempo.* Barcelona: Barral, 1971.

Cervantes, Miguel de. *El ingenioso hidalgo Don Quijote de la Mancha.* Madrid: Espasa-Calpe, 1973.

———. *Entremeses.* Ed. Eugenio Asencio. Madrid: Castalia, 1970.

Chang-Rodríguez, Raquel. *Violencia y subversión en la prosa colonial hispano-americana, siglos XVI y XVII*. Madrid: José Porrúa Turanzas, 1982.

Chase, Victoria. "Rediscovering the New World: Columbus and Carpentier." *Comparative Civilizations Review* 12 (1985): 28–43.

Collard, Patrick. "La máscara, el traje y lo teatral en *Los pasos perdidos* de Alejo Carpentier." In *Actas del IX Congreso de la Asociación Internacional de Hispanistas*. Vol. 2. Frankfurt: Vervuert Verlag, 1989. 507–514.

Colón, Cristóbal. *Textos y documentos completos. Nuevas cartas*. Ed. Consuelo Varela and Juan Gil. Madrid: Alianza Universidad, 1997.

Colón, José M. "La naturaleza en *La charca*." *Asomante* 9 (1949): 50–59.

Conrad, Joseph. "The Secret Sharer." In *The Portable Conrad*, ed. Morton Dawen Zabel. New York: Viking Press, 1968. 648–699.

Cortázar, Julio. *Around the Day in Eighty Worlds [La vuelta al día en ochenta mundos (1967)]*. Trans. Thomas Christensen. San Francisco: North Point Press, 1986.

———. *A Manual for Manuel [Libro de Manuel (1973)]*. Trans. Gregory Rabassa. New York: Pantheon Books, 1978.

———. "Policrítica a la hora de los chacales." In "Documentos. El caso Padilla," ed. Carlos Fuentes. *Libre* 1 (1971): 126–130.

———. "Press Clippings." In *We Love Glenda So Much and Other Tales*, trans. Gregory Rabassa. New York: Knopf, 1983. 81–96.

———. *Rayuela*. Buenos Aires: Sudamericana, 1972.

———. "Recortes de prensa." In *Queremos tanto a Glenda y otros relatos*. Madrid: Alfaguara, 1981. 65–82.

———. *Todos los fuegos el fuego*. Buenos Aires: Sudamericana, 1972.

Cruz Seoane, María. *Historia del periodismo en España*. Vol. 2, *El siglo XIX*. Madrid: Alianza Editorial, 1983.

———. *Oratoria y periodismo en la España del siglo XIX*. Madrid: Fundación Juan March y Editorial Castalia, 1977.

Culler, Jonathan. *Framing the Sign: Criticism and Its Institutions*. Norman: U of Oklahoma P, 1988.

———. *On Deconstruction: Theory and Criticism after Structuralism*. Ithaca, N.Y.: Cornell UP, 1982.

Curtius, Ernst Robert. *European Literature and the Latin Middle Ages*. Princeton, N.J.: Princeton UP, 1973.

Darío, Rubén. *Poesías completas*. Madrid: Aguilar, 1967.

Davison, Ned J. *The Concept of Modernism in Hispanic Criticism*. Boulder, Colo.: Pruett Press, 1966.

De Armas, Frederick A. "Metamorphosis as Revolt: Cervantes's *Persiles y Sigismunda* and Carpentier's *El reino de este mundo*." *Hispanic Review* 49 (1981): 297–316.

de la Parra, Teresa. *Ifigenia*. Ed. Sonia Mattalía. Barcelona: Anaya & Mario Muchnik, 1992.

———. *Iphigenia*. Trans. Bertie Acker. Austin: U of Texas P, 1993.

———. *Las memorias de Mamá Blanca*. Ed. Velia Bosch. Madrid: Colección Archivos-UNESCO, 1992.

———. *Obra escogida*. Vol. 1. Mexico City: Monte Avila Editores & Fondo de Cultura Económica, 1992.

——. *Obras completas*. Caracas: Editorial Arte, 1965.

de Man, Paul. *Allegories of Reading*. New Haven, Conn.: Yale UP, 1979.

——. "The Dead-End of Formalist Criticism." In *Blindness and Insight: Essays in the Rhetoric of Contemporary Criticism*. 2nd. ed. Revised. Minneapolis: U of Minnesota P, 1983. 229–245.

Derrida, Jacques. *Adieu à Emmanuel Lévinas*. Paris: Editions Galilée, 1997.

——. *Dissemination*. Trans. Barbara Johnson. Chicago: U of Chicago P, 1981.

——. *Of Grammatology*. Trans. Gayatri Chakravorty Spivak. Baltimore: Johns Hopkins UP, 1976.

——. *Signéponge/Signsponge*. Trans. Richard Rand. New York: Columbia UP, 1984.

——. *Spurs: Nietzsche's Styles/Éperons: Les Styles de Nietzsche*. Trans. Barbara Harlow. Chicago: U of Chicago P, 1979.

Díaz Balsera, Viviana. "*El Jardín de Falerina* de Calderón y la escritura de Lucifer." *Revista de Estudios Hispánicos* 2 (1994): 141–162.

*Diccionario manual latino-español/español-latino Sopena*. Barcelona: Editorial Ramón Sopena, S.A., 1973.

Donato, Eugenio. "The Museum's Furnace: Notes Toward a Contextual Reading of *Bouvard and Pécuchet*." In *Textual Strategies: Perspectives in Post-Structuralist Criticism*, ed. Josué V. Harari. Ithaca, N.Y.: Cornell UP, 1979. 213–238.

Dorfman, Ariel. *Imaginación y violencia en América*. Santiago, Chile: Editorial Universitaria, 1972.

Eaglestone, Robert. *Ethical Criticism: Reading After Levinas*. Edinburgh: Edinburgh UP, 1997.

Echavarría, Arturo. "Espacio textual y el arte de la jardinería china en Borges: 'El jardín de senderos que se bifurcan.'" In *Jorge Luis Borges: pensamiento y saber en el siglo XX*, ed. Alfonso de Toro and Fernando de Toro. Frankfurt: Vervuert Verlag, 1999. 71–103.

——. "Estructura y sentido poético del 'Coloquio de los centauros.'" *La Torre* 65 (1969): 95–130.

Euripides. *Iphigeneia at Aulis*. Trans. W. S. Merwin and George E. Dimock Jr. New York: Oxford UP, 1978.

——. *Iphigeneia in Tauris*. Trans. Richmond Lattimore. New York: Oxford UP, 1973.

Forcione, Alban. *Cervantes and the Mystery of Lawlessness: A Study of El casamiento engañoso y El coloquio de los perros*. Princeton, N.J.: Princeton UP, 1984.

Foster, David William. *Violence in Argentine Literature: Cultural Responses to Tyranny*. Columbia: U of Missouri P, 1995.

Foucault, Michel. *Discipline and Punish: The Birth of the Prison*. Trans. Alan Sheridan. New York: Vintage Books, 1979.

Freud, Sigmund. "Analysis Terminable and Interminable." In *The Standard Edition of the Complete Psychological Works of Sigmund Freud*. Vol. 23. London: Hogarth Press, 1964. 216–253.

——. *The Interpretation of Dreams*. Trans. James Strackey. New York: Avon Books, 1965.

García Márquez, Gabriel. *El amor en los tiempos del cólera*. Barcelona: Bruguera, 1985.

————. *Love in the Time of Cholera*. Trans. Edith Grossman. New York: Alfred A. Knopf, 1988.

————. *One Hundred Years of Solitude* [*Cien años de soledad* (1967)]. Trans. Gregory Rabassa. New York: Harper & Row, 1970.

Gardón Franceschi, Margarita. *Manuel Zeno Gandía: Vida y poesía*. San Juan, Puerto Rico: Editorial Coquí, 1969.

Garrels, Elizabeth. *Las grietas de la ternura: Nueva lectura de Teresa de la Parra*. Caracas: Monte Avila, 1986.

Giamatti, A. Bartlett. "Proteus Unbound: Some Versions of the Sea-God in the Renaissance." In *The Disciplines of Criticism*. New Haven, Conn.: Yale UP, 1968. 437–476.

Goethe, Johann Wolfgang von. *Wilhelm Meister's Years of Apprenticeship*. Trans. H. M. Waidson. 6 vols. London: Calder, 1977.

Goloboff, Mario. *Julio Cortázar: La biografía*. Buenos Aires: Seix Barral, 1998.

González, Aníbal. "Ética y teatralidad: *El Retablo de las Maravillas* de Cervantes y *El arpa y la sombra* de Alejo Carpentier." *La Torre (Nueva Época). Revista de la Universidad de Puerto Rico* 27–28 (1993): 485–502.

————. *Journalism and the Development of Spanish American Narrative*. Cambridge: Cambridge UP, 1993.

————. *La crónica modernista hispanoamericana*. Madrid: José Porrúa Turanzas, 1983.

————. *La novela modernista hispanoamericana*. Madrid: Gredos, 1987.

————. "Manuel Zeno Gandía (1855–1930)." In *Latin American Writers*, ed. Carlos A. Solé. Vol. 3. New York: Charles Scribner's Sons, 1989. 321–326.

————. "Revolución y alegoría en 'Reunión' de Julio Cortázar." In *Los ochenta mundos de Cortázar: Ensayos*, ed. Fernando Burgos. Madrid: Edi-6, 1987. 93–109.

González Bermejo, Ernesto. *Revelaciones de un cronopio: Conversaciones con Cortázar*. Montevideo: Ediciones de la Banda Oriental, 1986.

González Boixó, Carlos. "Feminismo e ideología conservadora." In *Las memorias de la Mamá Blanca*, by Teresa de la Parra, ed. Velia Bosch. Madrid: Colección Archivos-UNESCO, 1992. 223–236.

González Echevarría, Roberto. "Borges, Carpentier, y Ortega: Dos textos olvidados." In *Isla a su vuelo fugitiva: Ensayos de literatura hispanoamericana*. Madrid: Porrúa Turanzas, 1983. 217–225.

————. *Celestina's Brood: Continuities of the Baroque in Spanish and Latin American Literature*. Durham, N.C.: Duke UP, 1993.

————. "Colón, Carpentier y los orígenes de la ficción latinoamericana." *La Torre (Nueva Epoca). Revista de la Universidad de Puerto Rico* 7 (1988): 439–452.

————. "Historia y alegoría en la narrativa de Carpentier." In *Isla a su vuelo fugitiva: Ensayos de literatura hispanoamericana*. Madrid: Porrúa Turanzas, 1983. 43–68.

————. *La ruta de Severo Sarduy*. Hanover, N.H.: Ediciones del Norte, 1987.

————. "Latin American and Comparative Literatures." In *Poetics of the Americas: Race, Founding, and Textuality*, ed. Bainard Cowan and Jefferson Humphries. Baton Rouge: Louisiana State UP, 1994. 47–62.

————. *Myth and Archive: A Theory of Latin American Narrative*. Cambridge: Cambridge UP, 1990.

———. "The Pilgrim's Last Journeys." In *Alejo Carpentier: The Pilgrim at Home*. Austin: U of Texas P, 1990. 275–297.

———. *The Voice of the Masters: Writing and Authority in Modern Latin American Literature*. Austin: U of Texas P, 1985.

Graves, Robert. *The Greek Myths: 1*. London: Penguin Books, 1973.

Gubar, Susan. "'The Blank Page' and the Issues of Female Creativity." In *The New Feminist Criticism: Essays on Women, Literature, and Theory*, ed. Elaine Showalter. New York: Pantheon Books, 1985. 292–313.

Hadzsits, George Depue. *Lucretius and His Influence*. New York: Longmans & Green & Co., 1935.

*Harper's Bible Commentary*. General ed. James L. Mays. San Francisco: Harper & Row, 1988.

Harpham, Geoffrey Galt. "Ethics." In *Critical Terms for Literary Study*, ed. Frank Lentricchia and Thomas McLaughlin. 2nd. ed. Chicago: U of Chicago P, 1995. 387–405.

———. *Getting It Right: Language, Literature, and Ethics*. Chicago: U of Chicago P, 1992.

Hegel, G. W. F. *The Philosophy of History [Lectures on the Philosophy of World History]*. Trans. J. Sibree. New York: Dover Publications, 1956.

Heidegger, Martin. "Language." In *Poetry, Language, Thought*. New York: Harper & Row, 1971. 189–210.

Hemingway, Maurice, and Frank McQuade. "The Writer and Politics in Four Stories by Julio Cortázar." *Revista Canadiense de Estudios Hispánicos* 13 (fall 1988): 49–65.

Henríquez Ureña, Max. *El retorno de los galeones*. Madrid: Editorial Renacimiento, 1930.

Irwin, John T. *The Mystery to a Solution: Poe, Borges, and the Analytic Detective Story*. Baltimore: Johns Hopkins UP, 1994.

Jakobson, Roman. "Shifters, Verbal Categories, and the Russian Verb." In *Selected Writings*. Vol. 2. The Hague: Mouton, 1962. 130–132.

Jiménez, José Olivio, ed. *Antología crítica de la poesía modernista hispanoamericana*. Madrid: Hiperión, 1985.

Jitrik, Noé. *Las contradicciones del modernismo*. Mexico City: El Colegio de Mexico, 1978.

Johnson, Barbara. "Writing." In *Critical Terms for Literary Study*, ed. Frank Lentricchia and Thomas McLaughlin. 2nd. ed. Chicago: U of Chicago P, 1995. 39–49.

Johnson, Julie Greer. *Satire in Colonial Spanish America: Turning the New World Upside Down*. Austin: U of Texas P, 1993.

Jrade, Cathy L. Modernismo, *Modernity and the Development of Spanish American Literature*. Austin: U of Texas P, 1998.

———. *Rubén Darío and the Romantic Search for Unity: The Modernist Recourse to the Esoteric Tradition*. Austin: U of Texas P, 1983.

Kelly, P. T. *TV Violence: A Guide to the Literature*. Commack, N.Y.: Nova Science Publishers, 1996.

Kestner, Joseph. "Secondary Illusion: The Novel and the Spatial Arts." In *Spatial Form in Narrative*, ed. Jeffrey R. Smitten and Ann Daghistany. Ithaca, N.Y.: Cornell UP, 1981. 100–128.

Kirkpatrick, Gwen. *The Dissonant Legacy of* Modernismo*: Lugones, Herrera y Reissig, and the Voices of Modern Spanish American Poetry.* Berkeley and Los Angeles: U of California P, 1989.

Kristeva, Julia. *Powers of Horror: An Essay on Abjection.* New York: Columbia UP, 1982.

Lacan, Jacques. Écrits: *A Selection.* New York: W. W. Norton & Co., 1977.

Laguerre, Enrique. "El arte de novelar de Zeno Gandía." *Asomante* 4 (1955): 48–53.

Lanham, Richard A. *A Handlist of Rhetorical Terms.* 2nd ed. Berkeley and Los Angeles: U of California P, 1991.

Latham, R. E. Introduction to *The Nature of the Universe,* by Titus Lucretius Carus, trans. R. E. Latham. Baltimore: Penguin Classics, 1951.

Lattimore, Richmond. Introduction to *Iphigeneia in Tauris,* by Euripides, trans. Richmond Lattimore. New York: Oxford UP, 1973.

Levinas, Emmanuel. *Le Temps et l'autre.* Paris: Presses Universitaires de France, 1991.

———. *The Levinas Reader.* Ed. Seán Hand. Oxford: Blackwell, 1993.

Lindstrom, Naomi. Introduction to *Iphigenia,* by Teresa de la Parra, trans. Bertie Acker. Austin: U of Texas P, 1993.

Lluch Mora, Francisco. *La naturaleza en* La charca *de Manuel Zeno Gandía.* San Juan, Puerto Rico: Folletos Puertorriqueños del Club de la Prensa, 1960.

London, Jack. *Las muertes concéntricas.* Ed. and trans. Jorge Luis Borges and Nora Dottori. Buenos Aires: Ediciones Librería de la Ciudad/Franco María Ricci Editore, 1979.

———. "Lost Face." In *Lost Face.* New York: Macmillan, 1910. 1–12.

López-Baralt, Mercedes. *Icono y conquista: Guamán Poma de Ayala.* Madrid: Hiperión, 1988.

Luciani, Frederick. "Juan del Valle y Caviedes: El amor médico." *Bulletin of Hispanic Studies* 64 (1987): 337–348.

Lucretius Carus, Titus. *De rerum natura: The Poem on Nature.* Trans. C. H. Sisson. London: Carcanet New Press, 1976.

Lyotard, Jean-François. "Answering the Question: What Is Postmodernism?" In *The Postmodern Condition: A Report on Knowledge.* Minneapolis: U of Minnesota P, 1984. 71–82.

Marinello, Juan. "Americanismo y cubanismo literarios." In *Ensayos.* Havana: Editorial Arte y Literatura, 1977. 47–60.

Markovits, Francine. *Marx dans le Jardin d'Epicure.* Paris: Minuit, 1974.

Martí, José. *Versos libres.* In *Obras completas.* Vol. 6. Havana: Editorial Nacional de Cuba, 1964.

Martin, Henri Jean. *The History and Power of Writing.* Trans. Lydia G. Cochrane. Chicago: U of Chicago P, 1994.

Meléndez, Priscilla. *La dramaturgia hispanoamericana contemporánea: Teatralidad y autoconciencia.* Madrid: Pliegos, 1990.

Menéndez Pelayo, Marcelino. *Obras literarias de D. José Marchena.* Seville: Imprenta de E. Rasco, 1892.

Meyer, Michael C., and William L. Sherman. *The Course of Mexican History.* 4th ed. New York: Oxford UP, 1991.

Mignolo, Walter. *The Darker Side of the Renaissance: Literacy, Territoriality, and Colonization.* Ann Arbor: U of Michigan P, 1995.

Miller, J. Hillis. *The Ethics of Reading: Kant, De Man, Eliot, Trollope, James, and Benjamin*. New York: Columbia UP, 1987.

———. *Versions of Pygmalion*. Cambridge: Harvard UP, 1990.

Molho, Maurice. *Cervantes: Raíces folklóricas*. Madrid: Gredos, 1976.

Molloy, Sylvia. "La política de la pose." In *Las culturas de fin de siglo en América Latina*, ed. Josefina Ludmer. Rosario, Argentina: Beatriz Viterbo Editora, 1994. 128–138.

———. *Signs of Borges*. Durham, N.C.: Duke UP, 1990.

Nájera, Manuel Gutiérrez. *Cuentos completos y otras narraciones*. Ed. E. K. Mapes. Mexico City: Fondo de Cultura Económica, 1958.

———. *Divagaciones y fantasías: Crónicas de Manuel Gutiérrez Nájera*. Mexico City: SepSetentas, 1974.

———. *Escritos inéditos de sabor satírico: "Plato del día."* Columbia: U of Missouri P, 1972.

———. *Obras. Crítica literaria, I*. Mexico City: Centro de Estudios Literarios, UNAM, 1959.

———. *Obras IV. Crónicas y artículos sobre teatro, II (1881–1882)*. Ed. Yolanda Bache Cortés and Ana Elena Díaz Alejo. Mexico City: UNAM, 1984.

———. *Obras XI. Narrativa I: Por donde se sube al cielo (1882)*. Ed. Ana Elena Díaz Alejo and Belem Clark de Lara. Mexico City: UNAM, 1994.

Nájera, Margarita Gutiérrez. *Reflejo: Biografía anecdótica de Manuel Gutiérrez Nájera*. Mexico City: Instituto Nacional de Bellas Artes, 1960.

*New Oxford Annotated Bible, The*. Ed. Bruce M. Metzger and Roland E. Murphy. New York: Oxford UP, 1991.

Newton, Adam Zachary. *Narrative Ethics*. Cambridge: Harvard UP, 1995.

Ong, Walter J. *Orality and Literacy: The Technologizing of the Word*. London: Routledge, 1982.

*Oxford Companion to Philosophy, The*. Ed. Ted Honderich. Oxford: Oxford UP, 1995.

Palma, Ricardo. *Tradiciones peruanas completas*. Madrid: Aguilar, 1953.

Parker, David. *Ethics, Theory, and the Novel*. Cambridge: Cambridge UP, 1994.

Patout, Paulette. "Teresa de la Parra, París, y *Las memorias de Mamá Blanca*." In *Las memorias de Mamá Blanca*, ed. Velia Bosch. Madrid: Colección Archivos-UNESCO, 1992. 151–174.

Paz, Octavio. *El laberinto de la soledad*. Mexico City: Fondo de Cultura Económica, 1980.

Peavler, Terry J. *Julio Cortázar*. Twayne World Authors Series, no. 816. Boston: Twayne Publishers, 1990.

Pedreira, Antonio S. *El periodismo en Puerto Rico*. Río Piedras, Puerto Rico: Editorial Edil, 1969.

Perkins, David. *Is Literary History Possible?* Baltimore: Johns Hopkins UP, 1992.

Petrey, Sandy. "1877, Emile Zola Publishes His First Working-Class Novel, *L'assommoir*: Nature, Society, and the Discourse of Class." In *A New History of French Literature*, ed. Dennis Hollier. Cambridge: Harvard UP, 1994. 774–780.

Picó, Fernando. *Historia general de Puerto Rico*. Río Piedras, Puerto Rico: Ediciones Huracán-Academia, 1986.

Picón Garfield, Evelyn. *¿Es Julio Cortázar un surrealista?* Madrid: Gredos, 1975.

Plato. *The Works of Plato*. Trans. B. Jowett. New York: Dial Press, 1936.

Prego, Omar. *La fascinación de las palabras: Conversaciones con Julio Cortázar*. Barcelona: Muchnik Editores, 1985.

Pupo-Walker, Enrique. *La vocación literaria del pensamiento histórico en América: Desarrollo de la prosa de ficción, Siglos XVI, XVII, XVIII y XIX*. Madrid: Gredos, 1982.

Quiñones, Samuel R. "Nuestro novelista de la tierra, Manuel Zeno Gandía." *Indice* 12 (1930): 183.

Rama, Angel. *La ciudad letrada*. Hanover, N.H.: Ediciones del Norte, 1984.

———. *Las máscaras democráticas del modernismo*. Montevideo: Fundación Angel Rama, 1985.

———. *Rubén Darío y el modernismo*. Caracas: Biblioteca de la Universidad Central de Venezuela, 1970.

Ramos, Julio. *Desencuentros de la modernidad en América Latina*. Mexico City: Fondo de Cultura Económica, 1989.

Reedy, Daniel D. *The Poetic Art of Juan del Valle y Caviedes*. Chapel Hill: U of North Carolina P, 1964.

Reisz de Rivarola, Susana. "Política y ficción fantástica." *Inti: Revista de Literatura Hispánica* 22–23 (1985–1986): 217–230.

Rivera de Alvarez, Josefina. "Manuel Zeno Gandía." In *Diccionario de literatura puertorriqueña*. Vol. 2. San Juan, Puerto Rico: Instituto de Cultura Puertorriqueña, 1974. 1631–1638.

Rojas, Fernando de. *La Celestina*. Ed. Mario Bruno Damiani. Madrid: Castalia, 1978.

Rotker, Susana. *Fundación de una escritura: Las crónicas de José Martí*. Havana: Casa de las Américas, 1992.

Ruiz, Ariel. "Reparos a la bondad de las crónicas periodísticas de don Manuel Gutiérrez Nájera." *Revista Iberoamericana* 137 (1986): 931–936.

Ruiz, Juan. *The Book of Good Love*. Ed. John E. Keller and trans. Elisha Kent Kane. Chapel Hill: U of North Carolina P, 1968.

Said, Edward. *Orientalism*. New York: Vintage Books, 1979.

Sarduy, Severo. *Escrito sobre un cuerpo*. Buenos Aires: Sudamericana, 1969.

Scarano, Francisco. *Puerto Rico: Cinco siglos de historia*. Bogotá: McGraw-Hill Interamericana, 1993.

Schulman, Ivan. *Génesis del modernismo: Martí, Nájera, Silva, Casal*. Mexico City: El Colegio de México, 1966.

Schwab, Raymond. *The Oriental Renaissance*. New York: Columbia UP, 1984.

Serres, Michel. *Feux et signaux de brume: Zola*. Paris: Grasset, 1975.

———. *La naissance de la physique dans le texte de Lucréce: Fleuves et turbulences*. Paris: Minuit, 1977.

Shattuck, Roger. *The Banquet Years: The Origins of the Avant-Garde in France, 1885 to World War I*. New York: Vintage Books, 1968.

Singleton, Charles. *Commentary to* The Divine Comedy: Inferno. Princeton, N.J.: Princeton UP, 1970.

Solomon, Michael. *The Literature of Misogyny in Medieval Spain: The* Arcipreste de Talavera *and the* Spill. Cambridge: Cambridge UP, 1997.

Steedman, Carolyn. *Strange Dislocations: Childhood and the Idea of Human Interiority, 1780–1930*. London: Virago Press, 1995.

Stolley, Karen. "Death by Attrition: The Confessions of Christopher Columbus in Carpentier's *El arpa y la sombra*." *Revista de Estudios Hispánicos* 3 (1997): 505–532.

———. *El lazarillo de ciegos caminantes: Un itinerario crítico*. Hanover, N.H.: Ediciones del Norte, 1992.

Tierney-Tello, Mary Beth. "Testimony, Ethics, and the Aesthetic in Diamela Eltit." In *Ethics and Literary Study*, ed. Lawrence Buell. Spec. issue of *PMLA* 114 (1999): 78–96.

Todorov, Tzvetan. *La Conquête de l'Amérique*. Paris: Editions du Seuil, 1982.

———. "Narrative-Men." In *The Poetics of Prose*. Ithaca, N.Y.: Cornell UP, 1977. 66–79.

Tyler, Stephen A. "On Being Out of Words." In *Rereading Cultural Anthropology*, ed. George Marcus. Durham, N.C.: Duke UP, 1992. 1–7.

Ucelay Da Cal, Margarita. *Los españoles pintados por sí mismos (1843–1844): Estudio de un género costumbrista*. Mexico City: Colegio de México, 1951.

Unruh, Vicky. "The Performing Spectator in Alejo Carpentier's Fictional World." *Hispanic Review* 66 (1998): 57–77.

Uslar-Pietri, Arturo. "El testimonio de Teresa de la Parra." In *Letras y hombres de Venezuela*. Caracas: Ediciones EDIME, 1958. 270–279.

Valero-Covarrubias, Alicia. "*El arpa y la sombra* de Alejo Carpentier: Una confesión a tres voces." *Cuadernos Americanos* 14 (1989): 140–144.

Vallejo, César. *Obras completas*. Vol. 8, *Poemas humanos: España, aparta de mí este cáliz*. Barcelona: Editorial Laia, 1977.

Vargas Llosa, Mario. "La literatura es fuego." In *Contra viento y marea (1962–1982)*. Barcelona: Seix Barral, 1983. 132–137.

Vientós-Gastón, Nilita. *El mundo de la infancia*. Río Piedras, Puerto Rico: Editorial Cultural, 1984.

Vogeley, Nancy. "Defining the 'Colonial Reader': *El Periquillo Sarniento*." *PMLA* 5 (1987): 784–800.

Ward, Ian. *Law and Literature: Possibilities and Perspectives*. Cambridge: Cambridge UP, 1995.

Weisberg, Richard. *Poethics and Other Strategies of Law and Literature*. New York: Columbia UP, 1992.

Weissert, Thomas P. "Representation and Bifurcation: Borges's Garden of Chaos Dynamics." In *Chaos and Order: Complex Dynamics in Literature and Science*, ed. N. Katherine Hayles. Chicago: U of Chicago P, 1991. 223–243.

Wesseker, Carol, ed. *Violence in the Media*. San Diego: Greenhaven Press, 1995.

Wittgenstein, Ludwig. *Notebooks, 1914–1916*. New York: Harper Torchbooks, 1969.

———. *Tractatus Logico-Philosophicus*. London: Routledge & Kegan Paul, 1974.

Zeno Gandía, Manuel. *La charca (Crónicas de un mundo enfermo)*. Río Piedras, Puerto Rico: Editorial Edil, 1978.

Zola, Emile. *Le docteur Pascal*. In *Oeuvres complètes*. Vol. 6. Paris: Fasquelle, 1967. 1156–1401.